FOUR GUINEAS

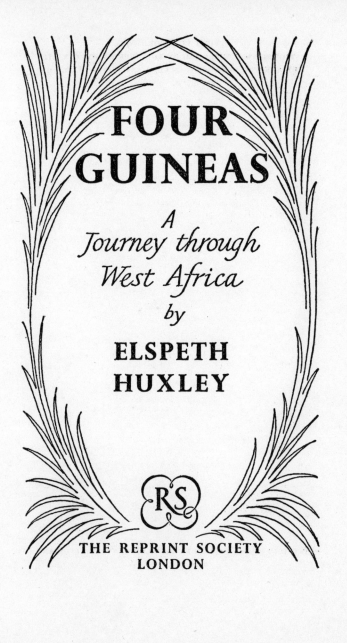

FOUR GUINEAS

A
Journey through
West Africa
by

ELSPETH HUXLEY

THE REPRINT SOCIETY
LONDON

FIRST PUBLISHED 1954
THIS EDITION PUBLISHED BY THE REPRINT SOCIETY LTD.
BY ARRANGEMENT WITH CHATTO AND WINDUS LTD. 1955

PRINTED IN GREAT BRITAIN BY RICHARD CLAY AND COMPANY LTD.
BUNGAY, SUFFOLK

CONTENTS

Maps in Text

5

LIST OF PLATES

ALL PHOTOS BY THE AUTHOR UNLESS OTHERWISE STATED

An Ashanti girl
Ashanti schoolgirls display one of the old-time dances
A village in the Northern Territories
Celebrating the enstoolment of a chief in an Ashanti village
The banana department of the market near Odumasi,
  by the Volta river
Elmina: a corner of the old Dutch castle
Fishermen hauling in their nets

Between pages 224 and 225

School on stilts in a creek village near Lagos
Street of tinsmiths in Ibadan
Ibadan: a market stall
The herbalists' and magicians' department
Benin: the bronze workers' street
Yoruba market-woman
Bida: the homestead of a well-to-do guildsman
Glass bangle-making in progress
The Wamba head, belonging to the prehistoric Nok
  culture, found in Northern Nigeria in 1944
    Photo: Mr. Bernard Fagg
Bronze plaque, representing an Oba with attendants,
  from Benin.   *Photo: British Museum*
An Ife bronze head, probably a past Oni
    Photo: British Museum
Kano: street scenes

Between pages 256 and 257

An Emir of Northern Nigeria
A District Head on his rounds north of Kano
A Fulani woman in her home of corn-stalks north of Kano
A Birom girl outside her home near Jos
Transport in the Eastern Provinces: goods go by cycle
Palm oil puncheons float down to the sea
A "second burial" party among the Ibos: guests firing
  off Dane guns
"Community development" near Enugu: building a road
A fertility image on land ready for new yams in Iboland
Roadside memorial of a clerk from Calabar: juju shrine
  on the left
An Ibibio masquerade.   *Photo: A. Aloba*
Dr. Azikiwe talks to Mr. Mbadiwe in the House of
  Assembly.   *Photo: Public Relations Department*

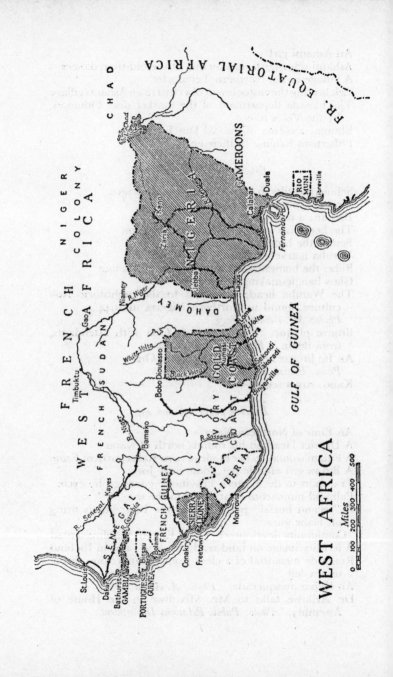

WEST AFRICA

GAMBIA

A NOTE ON
GAMBIA

POPULATION: 277,457 in 1952, excluding about 15,000 "strange farmers". Roughly 40 per cent are Mandingos.

CAPITAL: Bathurst, population about 20,000, of whom half are Wolof. British number 222.

AREA: 4,132 square miles, divided into the Colony (Kombo St. Mary and St. Mary and Macarthy Islands) and the Protectorate, a ten-mile strip on each bank of the River Gambia extending about 300 miles up-stream. The river is navigable to Kuntuar, 150 miles from Bathurst.

TRADE: Groundnuts are the only major export. In 1953, £2,563,603 worth were shipped overseas by the statutory Gambia Oilseeds Marketing Board, whose profits go to a Farmers' Fund to benefit producers. Small quantities of palm kernels are also exported. Imports, valued at £2,219,203, consisted mainly of cotton piece goods, hardware, kola nuts, apparel, foodstuffs and tobacco.

HISTORY: The Gambia River was discovered by the Portuguese in 1455. British trade began in 1587, when two English vessels returned with cargoes of hides and ivory, but was stifled by the "Portugalls". The English explorer George Thompson got some way up-river in 1618, and Richard Jobson described the region (optimistically) in *The Golden Trade* in 1623. Portuguese, Dutch, French and British Chartered Companies struggled for control of the trade for about three centuries, the fort on James Island, occupied intermittently from 1661 to 1779 by the British, being captured five times by the French. In 1816 a British settlement on St. Mary's Island laid the foundations of Bathurst, and treaties negotiated with various chiefs, the last in 1907, consolidated the British connection. In 1888 the Gambia was detached from Sierra Leone and in the following year its boundaries were settled with the French. In 1902 it was placed under a Protectorate.

GOVERNMENT: In 1947 a rudimentary Legislative Council was enlarged to include one elected member and six unofficial members nominated by the Governor. In 1951 the number of elected members was increased to three, giving the Council an unofficial majority, and a Gambian Vice-Chairman appointed. Further changes in 1953 introduced a Speaker in place of the Vice-President, reduced official membership of the Legislative Council to five and increased unofficial membership to sixteen, fourteen of them elected. These also provided for a majority of non-officials on the Executive Council, of whom two were appointed Ministers and charged with responsibility for certain Government activities. Committees to advise these Ministers form part of the new constitution. In Bathurst, a Town Council set up in 1946 has an elected majority. In country districts, the Native Authorities, which consist of the traditional chiefs of each district, are being "democratized" by the introduction of elected councils. "Africanization" of the Civil Service has proceeded some way, and several heads of Government departments are Gambians.

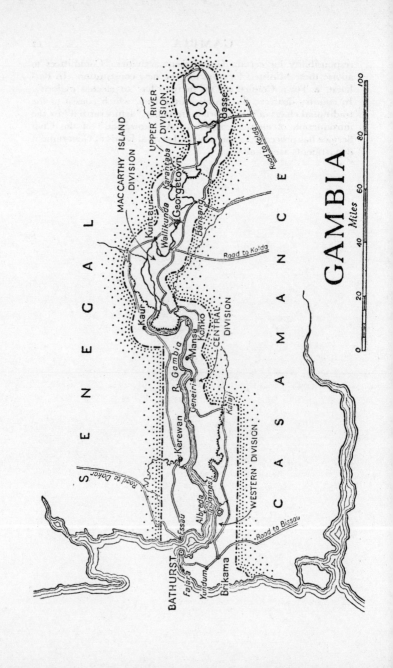

GAMBIA

THREE Moors stood in voluble debate outside a Syrian shop in Bathurst. Thin, bearded, hollow-cheeked, with black diamond eyes, they waved bony hands in argument like Hebrew prophets discussing the authenticity of Moses' tablets. The passions of Othello ran, perhaps, in the blood of these fanatical men, with their great frizz of matted hair imprisoned under turbans, their fine bones and dirty robes—for dirty they were, beyond doubt; hair greased with rancid butter injected a sickly smell into the hot afternoon air. Into their belts were thrust crooked silver-handled daggers like the *jembia* worn by dhow-captains of the Persian Gulf. As the dispute thickened, their fingers seemed to flutter round the hilts like dragon-flies. The object of the argument was a white cardboard box, about the size of a brick, clasped by one of the Moors in claw-like hands. At their backs, framed in a dark cavernous doorway, a pale-faced Syrian girl watched impassively with features regular, sensuous and biblical, her head swathed in a crimson scarf, as if Rebecca herself had paused from drawing water at the well.

One of the Moors, with a quick lunge, snatched at the cardboard brick and plucked from it a bottle of Seven Seas cod-liver oil. And all at once the dispute collapsed. The bottle slid back, its owner walked away and his two opponents turned and sauntered down the street hand in hand, their beards wagging. I watched them out of sight, still holding hands like schoolgirls, until the smell of rancid butter slowly faded and, like galleons under full sail, a group of Wolof women billowed by.

That evening, on a *patio* overlooking a hard brown lawn, I heard a story about one of the Chief Secretaries of the Gambia. A Chief Secretary is a very eminent official, the next man to the Governor, himself perhaps a Governor-to-be. He rules the Secretariat; he orders promotion; he is the biggest frog in the pond.

This Chief Secretary, a man of middle age soon due for pensioned retirement, had served since his cadetship in Africa. There lived in Bathurst at this time a notorious rogue, the trader Ali, and Ali suggested that if the Chief Secretary would give him some money to bury in the Muslim cemetery, the sum would double overnight. The Chief Secretary ventured five pounds and got back ten. Then a hundred, and two hundred returned.

Now this money-doubling is one of the oldest games in Africa, and I daresay elsewhere. From east to west, the money-doublers net a steady harvest from a baseless sea of gullibility. Every policeman and magistrate has heard the laments of the cheated. One might have assumed that the Chief Secretary was playing a cat-and-mouse game with Ali, for it is possible to best a money-doubler if you stop at the right moment. But when the Chief Secretary extracted some £2,000 from the colony's exchequer, it was impossible to assume anything except that the poor man had gone soft in the head. Ali and the money vanished and the Chief Secretary ended a broken career in jail.

I have mentioned these two incidents to illustrate what seems to me the most African of Africa's characteristics. To some, this is a continent of sinister mystery; to others, a backward area, or yet again a racial testing-ground. Above all, I think it is a haunt of the ludicrous, the incongruous, the illogical, a playground of events that own no pedigree and will breed the unforeseen. The gods of Africa are numerous, malicious and unpredictable; it is the habitation of Pan, of Silenus, of the spirit of the *opéra bouffe*. These deities have excavated, before their thrones, *oubliettes* into which have tumbled all the hopes, ideals and good intentions that have approached them during the last few thousand years: pits covered with innocent-seeming grass, green after rain; deep as the sea and silent, save for the echo of a gust of ribald laughter as some confident new victim drops quietly out of sight.

◌ 2 ◌

I have seen nothing like the Wolof women elsewhere in Africa. They are tall and dress to enhance their height, wearing head-ties of brilliant stripes and patterns fastened with bows and loose knots of gay *insouciance*. As they glide along dusty streets in sandals, they look like flowers on the move. Their carriage is imperial, their features Asiatic, scarcely at all Negroid; their fine eyes are rimmed with antimony and their long, satiny gowns glow boldly on mahogany skins: gowns of cerise and apple green, gold and magenta, electric blue, iris purple and claret red, cut in the Empire style, with square necks and many flounces down the wide sleeves. Over their dresses most women wear white muslin slips, absolutely clean and creaseless, through which the colours glint and shine. This Empire style was brought by the French to St. Louis, then the capital of Senegal. During the last century Frenchwomen have followed many fashions, but this one alone, fusing with an African love of finery and flounces, as it were jelled, and became a Wolof necessity.

Ears and arms are hung with golden ornaments made in little shops off poky back streets, some in filigree but more in the shape of solid bangles, rings and pendants, and of whorled, shell-like encrustations for the ears. As the women walk, the gold glistens against their firm, peach-like skins. They look healthy, provocative, wanton and proud.

And they wear wigs. These are made either of hair mixed with black four-ply wool and wound into buns standing out from the temples like horns, or of a soft, silky, very fine substance derived from the bark of the baobab tree, beaten into downy fibres that sell in the market for one and sixpence a skein.

These Wolofs, who range throughout Senegal, follow customs and habits quite different from those of the Negro peoples they live among but so little resemble and will not marry. The women's fine dress and proud deportment proclaim a feminine freedom most unusual, especially in Muslim lands. Not for them the bondage of the hoe, the water-pot and the mortar. It is said that the clothes on the back of any Wolof woman will have cost between £50 and £100 and that every married man is heavily burdened by his efforts to provide his wife with the dresses, the jewellery and the soap—what they must spend on soap!—she considers her due. Husbands are picked, enjoyed, exploited and exchanged with a most un-African laxity. Children go with the mother, who sometimes tires of them when she bears a new one, and these Wolof must be almost the only folk in Africa among whom unwanted children can be found.

It is the custom for the bride's elderly female relations to hide near the marriage bed and, after consummation, to carry out the bridal sheet for inspection by the waiting crowd. Loud applause greets the bloodstains always to be found upon it. As it seldom happens that a Wolof bride is actually a virgin, one of her aunts is ready to cut the throat of a chicken.

Of course not every Wolof leads this light-hearted existence. You could not, for example, find a more sober, respectable citizen than Mr. Garba-Jahumpa, local leader of the Muslim Congress and a member of the Legislature. A dignified, spectacled, portly man, rather pedantic in speech, he professes a quietly Rotarian sort of benevolence and has in his time attended conferences in Manchester. We met in a small parlour brightly decorated in green and white and crammed with photographs, the walls lined with chairs as if for some round game.

As I faced Mr. Jahumpa across the small, busy room, a Mrs. Jahumpa sailed in: tall, stately, bejewelled, her hair done into Wolof horns protruding under a gay scarf. Her dress was of green and cerise, with layers of yellow braid. We smiled mutely, and she deposited a small Jahumpa, dressed in frilly petticoats, to gambol on the floor, while she herself sat upright on one of the hard chairs lining the wall.

Her husband spoke of a pan-African fellowship of Muslims from French and British territories. A second Mrs. Jahumpa entered and sat down beside the first, whom, to a stranger's eye, she closely resembled in her thin, chiselled features, her calm, commanding look; and another little Jahumpa appeared, this one of a size to prefer refreshment at the breast. Its father spoke of the need for more Koranic education. In came a third Mrs. Jahumpa, no less a-glow and a-glitter, and no less fecund either: and presently the statutory four were ranged round the wall, all silent, self-possessed and proud.

The existence of several Mrs. Jahumpas, as of several wives to most non-Christian notables, sets a nice problem for colonial officials. Should the invitation be marked "Mr. and one Mrs. Jahumpa", or "Mr. and the Mrs. Jahumpa", or in what manner? The practice, as usual dictated by expediency, is to ask one Mrs. only, throwing back on to the husband the task of selection. How is this accomplished—by seniority, good conduct, drawing lots, caprice? I did not like to ask, but was interested, when I met Mr. Jahumpa later on at a chiefs' conference up-river, to observe the youngest and newest wife at his side.

A young Wolof wife

Scenes in Bathurst: a rest by the roadside

A difficult problem of fashion

" The bush is stronger than the cannon ":
ruined fort on James Island

Bringing in the rice harvest up the Gambia river

A "company" of farmers off to harvest rice up the Great Scarcies river

In the cool of the evening: women fishing near Kenema

Mr. Garba-Jahumpa's colleague in the Legislature is the Rev. John Faye, who would be the leader of the Opposition if there was one. Like everything Gambian, he is a very mild, innocuous version of the type, in this case the nationalist politician; but still a point of growth, a focus of change. (Curiously enough this Bathurst deacon of the Church of England, born and bred here in the Gambia, is the spit and image of his opposite number in Kenya, Mr. Eliud Mathu. Both have the same rather unusual bullet-shaped heads and high cheek-bones, the alert eyes, the small brush of a moustache and the gift of oratory.)

"While others talk, we do," said the Rev. John Faye, gratified that Gambians are filling many positions formerly held by Europeans. The Post Office, the Customs and the office of the Auditor-General have been "Africanized" all through, and run well. African doctors are in entire charge of the big Bathurst hospital. And certainly there is no sign of any colour-bar.

I saw in the Fayes' house several of those little paper houses, astonishingly intricate, made by Muslim children for their New Year festival. Fretted by balconies and speckled with windows, they look like miniature Victorian railway stations gone mad, and in them lighted candles are paraded through the streets at night. Round each lantern clusters a band of children clothed in white. Afterwards, the children give away these paper houses to their favourites. It is typical of Gambian tolerance that Muslim children should present them to a Christian deacon.

~ 3 ~

The Gambia's capital has the unpretentious, intimate air of an English market town. At one end lie the wharves, jetties and workshops that keep afloat the boats on which the whole Gambia depends; for this curious finger thrust into the great hulk of French Senegal consists merely of 300 miles of river frontage never more than ten miles deep. Here, on a narrow beach between street and water, are men shaping old timbers into cutters of a design introduced two centuries ago by the Portuguese and still unchanged. These cutters go up-river to bring down the groundnuts which are the beginning and end of Gambian trade.

Near the cutters' anchorage, a line of long, slender, fast-looking canoes reposes on a sandy foreshore. These are French, and oddly enough they look French in a way impossible to describe, just as a Paris hat looks more French than any British imitation. On their prows a cluster of paper charms keeps at bay a host of surely rather frivolous devils. The shells are gaily painted in pastel colours; the paddles are heart-shaped, Cambridge blue and decorated with silver stars. Nothing could be more feminine. What a contrast to the sound, rough, weather-worthy, workman-like cutters! In fact, their main occupation is smuggling.

"What," I asked of an official, "do they mainly smuggle?"

"Everything," he replied, looking at them with affection.

Small, cave-like Syrian shops; a police station with thick white Portuguese walls and arches (and what geniuses for building the Portuguese were!); a covered market, like all markets full of crawling infants, nameless litter, penny piles of red peppers and queer condiments, and a stench of high fish; unpaved, dusty, hot streets; crowds of people strolling, squatting, gossiping; then Macarthy Square, the town's heart, with schoolboys playing cricket on its brown turf, and the shade of casuarina trees.

I searched the streets one morning for Pa Jones, an auctioneer over eighty years old and said to remember yoked and chained slaves. He had an "upstairs" house, perhaps Portuguese, it was so old and flaking, with thick walls and wooden doors and shutters sloughing away from age. Pa Jones was out—all elderly men are addressed as Pa—and we traced him through many hot streets before losing the trail, finding ourselves obliged to ask as often in French as in English. On our way we called on a young woman who was feeding two small girls with spoonfuls of native porridge in a bedroom so miniscule that she could not stretch out her legs. Young, plump, round-limbed, she responded to our remarks in slow, lazy monosyllables, not unfriendly but not very interested either, all her attention on those two silent, pig-tailed little girls.

She did her cooking outside, in an open-fronted shelter knocked together out of old corrugated iron, on the fire between three stones and in the rounded black pot that caters to hunger from one side of Africa to the other; and in the pot simmered that stodgy, spiced, glutinous porridge that fills every belly from

the Nile to the Zambezi. A few paces off stood a separate building, the parlour, locked and unused, and through the window we
glimpsed a shining electric cooker, unsullied by employment,
flanked by ugly varnished furniture, a refrigerator, a brand-new
radio standing proudly on a table in the centre of the room. All
were wired for electricity, but there was no power laid on.
Everything was clean and dusted and bore no relation whatever
to the woman feeding her little girls in the tiny cubicle outside.
Her husband, a senior school-master, used this parlour only for
the entertainment of his friends.

∾ 4 ∾

Nothing seems, on the face of it, more ridiculous than that a
country with a population smaller than Leicester's should be
equipped with the full paraphernalia of colonial government:
Governor, Chief Secretary and his Secretariat, Financial Secretary, Attorney-General and all the rest of it, every department
with its Director, and all the pomp and ceremony, precedents
and files, committees and despatches considered needful to
administer countries the size of India. There is something Gil-
bertian about it all, for the whole Gambia would go into a single
district of Nigeria, with one District Commissioner and a couple
of assistants in charge. Confronted with this, Gambian officials
say despairingly: "Yes, but what can you *do*? The country must
have a Government." And so, to pay for this need, Gambians
suffer the heaviest taxation in British Africa.

The present Governor is a vigorous new broom from what is
called, with varying degrees of disapproval, The Other Side. He
came at the age of forty-three from one extreme of the Chief
Native Commissionership of Kenya, as stormy and exacting a job
as exists in Africa, to the other extreme of this quiet, good-tempered, well-mannered little benefice. But Sir Percy Wyn-Harris
is not the sort to paddle backwaters. He is a man who took leave
without pay while a District Officer in Kenya to assault Mt.
Everest with Shipton, Mallory and Irvine, and with them to
climb to Camp 6 at 26,000 feet, the highest ascent then recorded. With Shipton, who was a Kenya settler, he was the

first man to reach the summit of Mt. Kenya since Sir Halford Mackinder, thirty years earlier.

Tough, stocky, packed with Welsh pugnacity and vigour, loquacious, intolerant of slovenly standards, a glutton for work, Sir Percy Wyn-Harris has galvanized the sleepy Gambia. He belongs to the new school of men who have come up from the districts through hard work, sound judgment, ability and good fortune, who understand administration and like constructive change. There is nothing about him of the scholar, the diplomat or the dilettante. He is never likely to start a scandal, create a legend or neglect a duty. Being Welsh, he must love and hate with intensity. One can guess his hates—slovenly work, spivishness, idleness, dishonesty—and for love he follows danger with that curious, indestructible passion some men obey all their lives. Now that mountains are out of reach he sails small boats, whereever possible in stormy seas. His last leave was spent in solitary and hazardous discomfort in a four-ton yawl. In Bathurst, after tea, he takes a little dinghy with an outboard motor into an estuary swept by Atlantic rollers, full of sharks and rimmed with boiling surf and treacherous sandbars, to emerge at dusk soaked to the skin, his face reddened by wind, exhilarated and happy.

Out of the salty estuary lead innumerable creeks quite sheltered from the ocean's gales and breakers. Here the dinghy with the outboard motor chugged as smoothly as a rolling marble along a silky channel, leaving the water creased by gentle undulations. The sun was sinking behind a gauzy mist that turned it silver and the sky filled with a brittle aluminium light fading quickly into the blue-grey of rising wood-smoke or a dove's plumage. We chugged slowly forward into greyness. The blue-grey of the calm water merged into the blue-grey of the sky; and before us, as the light faded, a clear pale moon hung like that silver fruit by which the King of Spain's daughter was enchanted: at such moments, and in primeval places, there is always magic in the air. For how many centuries, or scores of centuries, had this creek been as we saw it then, unchanged by root or ripple? For how long had snow-white egrets clustered together on a mangrove island to limn with ivory those dark, twisted branches? A tern skimmed by low on the water and a grey heron trailing spidery legs flapped across, as the blue drained slowly from sky and water to leave a soft, fine-grained, uncrumpled satin greyness spread over all.

On either hand, mangroves thrust their long, twisted fingers deep into the mud. Their reflection was so perfect, without a flicker of motion, that we seemed to be gazing up a tunnel ringed by slim and fibrous arms: a Gothic nightmare in miniature, such as might have been found in the dank woodlands that encompassed the Castle of Otranto. They are queer things, these amphibious mangroves; inch by inch they advance, imperceptibly narrowing the channel until in time the creek may become wholly colonized. But at their back, some disaster is occurring— a flood perhaps—and the water overthrows them. Century after century, this silent battle has gone on between the irresistible power of moving water and the persistent, undefeated encroachment of the mangroves, which match against the river the very force of life itself. Slowly, invisibly, the maze of channels moves and shifts; like the battle of life and death, it never ends, and no one will record its changing fortunes. From the air, all these creeks entwined among the mangrove forests look like thick strands of mud-gold hair brushed back in wide sweeps across the forehead of the land. Man's work exists still on sufferance—a few clusters of pimples linked by thread-like paths among mangroves, mud and sand.

At last we chugged out of the creek and into the main stream. Life returned to the water; a breeze flecked its surface and moonlight danced over it like a swarm of fireflies. The lights of Bathurst came into view strung along the water-front, each one a steady eye on a pillar of flickering light reflected in the river. We passed the anchored cutters, and beached French canoes with family parties clustering round a small fire amidships. Pyramids of groundnuts loomed like ancient monuments against a sky still grey, but darker, adorned by the moon and all the host of stars.

~ 5 ~

Round Bathurst's airport, engagingly named Yundum, the bush which chokes every untilled acre has vanished. Yundum wears a desert look. This is man's doing, not Nature's. Yundum was the site of the egg scheme which wasted nearly a million pounds of British money.

Nearby, on the flat and now treeless plain, stand row upon row of close-packed houses built of concrete blocks and roofed with asbestos sheeting. Good quarters, I thought, for labour, if barrack-like and dreary as labour lines nearly always are. Why had the egg scheme, I asked, needed so many men?

"Labour lines?" was the reply. "But those are hen-houses!"

They stand empty and forlorn behind a falling-down sign-board. Grass is growing up to screen a whole row of abandoned seed-drills and disc harrows and two old tractors in a rusty shed. These cement-block houses once held over 300,000 head of poultry, and all save ninety birds died of fowl pest (Newcastle disease).

Beyond Yundum lies Brinkama, a district headquarters, equipped with a native treasury, a court-house and a Commissioner. The Gambia has only four Commissioners: a sturdy, resilient New Zealander; an ex-officer of the Pakistan Police with one eye put out by a *lathi*; and two good-looking, spruce young Englishmen fresh from the Army. Modern young Commissioners seem, as a rule, alert, enthusiastic, intelligent and possessed of charming manners of a rather formal kind; they open doors for passengers, they are punctilious about standing up for females and seniors and lighting other people's cigarettes, they call their elders "sir" and speak with deference. As a rule they drink little (there are exceptions to this, of course) and often only beer; they marry young and have babies, which destroys their single-mindedness but improves their health. They consider it their right to inhabit houses which by earlier standards are palatial in size and Lucullan in comfort; they travel in cars, not on foot or on cycles, and do not live as close to Africans as their predecessors did. In some ways they know more than did the men of an earlier generation, but when their time is up they will understand less, for they are more insulated from the people by family life and better living; and different motives bring them here. They come to make a sound, respectable and pensionable career, not to escape from England in search of danger and adventure. Oddly enough, one is most struck here in West Africa, with its legend of the white man going to seed, by a con-

ventional, correct, almost Sunday atmosphere that has died out
in most parts of Britain.

But if the Commissioner who drank a bottle of gin before
lunch and a bottle of whisky before dinner, who knew every
native footpath and (in the biblical sense) many native women,
who sweated out his malaria every month—if he is disappearing,
so is the type of African with whom he knew so well how to deal:
the old reprobate sighing in his heart for the return of the slave-
trade, the despotic chief, the beer-soaked and custom-steeped
elder, the young man with a spear. Warriors have turned into
school-teachers, respecting the formalities of committee-work as
deeply as their fathers revered the ceremonies of blessing crops.
Curiously enough, they too, like the Commissioners, are rather
proper, formal and polite.

◦◦ 6 ◦◦

Like all its Gambian fellows, Brinkama is a hot and dusty little
town, approached by a sandy road driven between thickets of
twisted trees and scattered oil palms. No one could call this
country beautiful. It is dead flat, ragged and, at this time of
year, uniformly brown. The trees lack height and dignity, the
grass is coarse, the sky not blue but almost burnt white, drained
of colour and unrelieved by cloud. Everything is parched, and
no rain can be expected for another five months. Harvests are
in. Not far ahead looms the "hungry season", an annual visita-
tion which since time immemorial has been accepted as the in-
escapable lot of every Gambian. The present Governor says that
he has set himself two aims. One is to achieve an inspired
administration; the other, to abolish the hungry season.

Naturally, something as ancient as this hungry season, as deep-
rooted in climate and geography, is the hardest thing in the
world to alter. People must grow more food, obviously. But
how? Their agriculture is exceedingly primitive. They live on
a mixture of millet and guinea corn called *coos* whose yield is piti-
fully low. Small wonder, for they cultivate soil that lacks all
humus and is virtually sand, and their tools consist simply of the
bent, short-handled hoe found all over West Africa. Cattle are
few, for this is tsetse country. Even legumes will not enrich the

soil with nitrogen as they do elsewhere because the bacteria which cluster in nodules on the roots and fix the nitrogen will not live in Gambian soils—why, no one knows. As the population rises, the soil's fertility falls, for its resting period is steadily encroached upon. Peasant families cannot cultivate a larger acreage partly because there is not enough land, partly because their women cannot cope with a bigger acreage than they handle already.

The men? They are lying on the *bantabà*. This is a platform of woven mats, about waist-high, erected in every village under the largest tree, generally one of the handsome, buttressed, thick-foliaged kapok or silk-cottons. On it the men recline like Romans in their full cotton robes, chewing kola nuts if they have them, playing the complicated form of draughts found all over Africa and subjecting to the closest imaginable analysis every event, situation and anticipation germane to the village and its inhabitants. Like the Carlton or the Travellers', it is a club for men only. The women are out on the sweltering farms hoeing or reaping, carrying firewood, pounding grain or spinning cotton.

A young Irishman who speaks Mandinka, the commonest language here, mentioned two points of interest about conversations on the *bantabà*, in which he often takes part. One is a universal fondness for mathematical riddles and a great speed in solving such problems as this: if a baboon has nine wives, and each wife has nine children, and each child eats nine nuts for nine days, how many nuts will be stolen from the farm? The other is that he has never, in all his *bantabà* sessions, heard a Mandingo tell a dirty story.

"Very different from the Arabs," he remarked. (Or the English, he might have added.) "They can tell one dirty story after another all day long."

He added: "These sessions on the *bantabà* falsify all the conclusions of the economists. Experts calculate that if you bring in mechanization, tractors say, you save x man-hours, and those hours can be spent on cultivating a larger acreage and producing more food. But they won't be. They'll be spent on the *bantabà*."

He is by no means the first observer to comment on the easy tempo of Gambian life. In 1623 Richard Jobson, author of *The Golden Trade*, remarked of the Mandingos:

The men for their parts do live a most idle kinde of life, imploying themselves (I mean the greater part) to no kinde of trade nor exercise, except it be onely some two months of the yeare, which is in tilling, and bringing home their countrey corne, and graine, wherein the preservation of their lives consists, and in that time their labour is sore. All other times of the yeare, they live wandering up and downe, from one to another, having little understanding, either to hunt in the woods, or fish in the waters; notwithstanding, both the one and the other, in their kindes, are infinitely replenished, that to their very doores wilde beasts doe resort, and about their houses in every corner, abanduance of *Ginny* hennes, and excellent partridges. In the heat of the day, the men will come forth, and sit themselves in companies, under the shady trees, to receive the fresh aire, and there passe the time in communication, having only one kind of game to recreate themselves withall, and that is in a peece of wood, certaine great holes cut, which they set upon the ground betwixt two of them, and with a number of some thirtie pebble stones, after a manner of counting, they take one from the other, untill one is possessed of all, whereat some of them are wondrous nimble.

Life among the Mandingos does not seem to have changed at all during the last three centuries.

As Jobson observed, there are periods of hard labour when the rains come and the land must be prepared. The villages are neatly kept, each compound surrounded by a fence of reeds or split bamboos. There are men to be seen weaving cloth on the little narrow native looms that came, they say, from Egypt across the Sudan; and the groundnut crop is mainly the men's business.

In fact the groundnut crop is one of the reasons for the hungry season. If people grew less to sell they could grow more to eat. But the price has soared, demand is great and cash needed. When your granary is truly bare, the Government will feed you. So it is better to grow the groundnuts and chance the hunger.

We stopped at a village to look into some of the little round granaries standing up on stilts. Each wife has her own. Its contents must first feed her own family, and the surplus she can sell. But there never is a surplus here. Just now, the harvest is newly in, and these little granaries are not half full. In them are heads of guinea corn and millet, a little rice, a few pumpkins; that is all.

"What will you do when this is gone?" asked the young Commissioner, pointing to the meagre store.

"Come to you, sir, to feed us." So answered patly the village *alkali:* a tall man in a long white robe and round cap embroidered in gold, puffing at a short pipe. His face was weather-beaten, pock-marked, clever and grave, his speech courteous; he wore the habit of command, and looked at us with a quizzical expression.

"The Government can't feed everyone," the Commissioner rather tartly replied. The *alkali* smiled. "What have you done with your groundnut money?"

That had gone on clothes. The Muslim faith, here considerably attenuated, imposes on men the need for long cotton robes and baggy trousers, and on women at least a cloth a year; and the price of cotton has quadrupled, or more.

"And the money your wife got for palm kernels?"

He shrugged his shoulders. "As it came, so it went." There was the house tax, and then the money-lender. . . .

A neighbour was more specific. He was a younger man with a sad, patient face and a brood of children of all ages in charge of a girl of twelve or thirteen. In a year's time she would be ready for marriage and the bride-price of £12 or £15, paid in instalments, would clear off a portion of her father's debts. This man had sold eight bags of groundnuts for £16, from which he had paid £4 in debts and his tax of £1. With the balance he must buy food and clothing for ten people for a year. There is little chance of paid work within reach of his home.

Nearby, some heads of guinea corn were stacked on a platform in the yard, and not in the granary. I asked:

"Won't the birds eat these?"

The man smiled—a sweet, patient smile.

"Yes, madam, they will."

"There you have the Gambia," said the Commissioner, without bitterness.

These people have, indeed, great charm. Their manners are delightful, their friendliness uncorroded by racial spite. It is pleasant to find oneself in an African country not choked by politics. Of course that is not to say that everyone is contented with things as they are; but the Gambia still lies outside the vortex of nationalism. Perhaps it will be sucked in, perhaps even a country of a quarter of a million people will embrace with bitter passion the notion of self-government. But now an afternoon aroma of peace pervades the air. There is everything to be said for backwaters when the main stream is in flood and running, so far as anyone can tell, through caverns perilous to man, down to a sunless sea.

∾ 7 ∾

The ruins of the fort occupy almost the whole of James Island, and one is appalled to think of a garrison of soldiers and several hundred slaves boxed up on this scrap of land—cramped, roasted, bored to death and rotten with sickness. Not even their graves remain, for the river is encroaching on the island; the chapel and the slave quarters have vanished altogether under the estuary. Nothing remains of the generations of young men who suffered here and died, not their names, nor their memories, nor any legend: only a few regimental buttons, some Georgian coins and broken bits of wine-flagons.

It has been said that Africa is the only continent without a history. Not because history has not been made here: because Africa devours its history as it goes along, eats up its monuments, destroys its artifacts and absorbs its invaders, like a boa-constrictor that swallows a kid. On this island, only baobabs survive: queer, ugly, pale, almost leafless trees, their thick, stubby trunks as grey and glistening as a sick man's face. Their elongated fruits hang down on pendants like the weight of a grandfather clock, and their roots undermine the old walls. In fact the whole fort is crumbling away. Africa is after it with sun and rain, tree-root and termite, and the fort is doomed. A pity, for it is the oldest British settlement in West Africa. The first man to be buried on the island was a Venetian sailor called Andrew, under the command of Alvise da Cadamosto, who, in the service of Henry the Navigator, discovered the mouth of the Gambia river in 1455.

The first fort to stand here was built some two centuries later by the Duke of Courland, head of a Baltic state and a godson of James I. He sent out families with a pastor and tried to set trade in motion, fired by stories of a mountain of solid gold standing at the headwaters of the Gambia river. It was the quest for gold, not slaves, that first drew white men to this coast. Indeed, in 1620 Richard Jobson, offered a coffle of slaves by a Gambian "king", rejected them with the words: "We are a people who do not deale in any such commodities, neither do we buy nor sell one another, or any that have our owne shapes."

The Dutch took the fort from the Courlanders, and then in 1661 the British took it from the Dutch and renamed it after Charles II's brother, the Duke of York. Thereafter this island had a switchback, bloody history which cannot be recounted here. The French set up a trading station at Albreda, within sight of the island on the river's north bank, and they captured James Island three times, on the last occasion demolishing the fort so thoroughly that it was never rebuilt.

Nothing is now left of old Albreda but a single building and a small hole in the ground, the socket of a flagpole. This is where the Union Jack used to mark the limits of the French territory, and any slave who touched it could claim his freedom. Can this be the origin of the children's game "French and English"? The French stayed in Albreda until 1857, when they ceded it to Britain. Now it is just a groundnut buying post, and the home of a formidable trader called Mrs. Cleopatra Dana. A short, stout party in a bright head-tie, with a close-clipped grey beard and heavy grey eyebrows, she greeted us with a gift of bananas, a cold stare and the assurance: "I love white people too much."

After the French finally demolished the fort in 1799 the island was not reoccupied, but at the end of the Napoleonic Wars Sir Charles Macarthy, then Governor of Senegal, asked for a garrison to control violators of the anti-slavery laws. Captain Alexander Grant of the 2nd West India Regiment was sent to look for a healthier site. He chose another island, which lies at the tip of a peninsula jutting into the estuary like a turkey's head, and bought it from the chief of Kombo for a yearly tribute of 103 bars of iron. He renamed it St. Mary's Island, and called his settlement after the Secretary of State.

From the first Bathurst thrived, although it proved no healthier than James Island. Out of a contingent of 199 soldiers who arrived in May, 1825, 160 were dead by Christmas. Next year a further 200 men were sent out and in a few months 101 were dead and thirty-three invalided. After this, at very long last, authority acknowledged the climate to be unhealthy for white troops, and West Indians, who did much better, were stationed there.

∾ 8 ∾

The whole crew of the *Mansa Kila Kuta* is African: quiet, blue-sweatered men who work with the smooth, easy calm of the altogether competent. They know the river as a herdsman his cattle, every bar and current of it, and the river is not easy to know. The banks are flat beyond belief, and for the first 150 miles or so, where salt tides run, lined with a dark belt of mangroves lacking totally in landmarks; yet the quartermaster can pick up a buoy at midnight correctly to within 100 yards of his reckoning.

These men are local aristocrats, elevated by wealth and the prestige of office. The quartermaster in command, a tall, grizzled sailor with an admiral's dignity, has served for nearly thirty years in the Gambia Marine and has acquired the solidity of an oak tree. Africans of this kind, who have accepted and discharge responsibility, arouse great confidence. They grow to full stature when pruned by discipline and fertilized by trust.

Despite a sparkle on the water, a clear sun-bleached sky, grey herons flying, this salty Gambia might prove a dull river were it not for all the little creeks that wind inland, their mouths hidden among the mangroves. In a native fishing-craft fitted with a motor, we wove our way first through mudbanks gripped by the mangroves' black talons, then through flat fields of paddy or of grass so long and thick-stemmed that the stalks all but met overhead. Posts mark the channel, which disappears under-water at the spring tides, and a-top each post sits one pied kingfisher. Squacca herons, reef herons and another small kind, buff not grey, fly ahead slowly; spur-wing geese circle at a distance; egrets encrust the foliage of bushes; ring-doves coo.

A bird-adorned, gentle, placid scene that reminded me of East Anglia; this might almost have been a giant Alde

> *that flows*
> *Quietly through green level lands,*
> *So quietly it knows*
> *Their shape, their greenness and their shadows well;*
> *And then undreamingly for miles it goes,*
> *And silently, beside the sea.*

Save for the crocodiles, of course, dozing on mudbanks, and rice, and the mosquitoes. . . . Foreign parts seem often to provoke in English people the most inappropriate comparisons. Driving through the rain-forest of Eastern Nigeria, on every side tangles of creepers, giant mahoganies and oil palms, passing an occasional mud village full of coal-black occupants, a man observed: "This reminds me so much of Warwickshire." And a Yorkshireman once remarked in the Celebes, gazing at Javanese in huge soup-plate hats driving water-buffaloes harnessed to wooden ploughs through liquid mud: "This is just like the country round Hull."

We came here and there to a narrow bund ending at the water's edge. The Government have chivvied the people into building these bunds, to enable them to penetrate more easily into the swamps to transplant rice, using money from the Farmers' Fund, derived from official profits on the groundnut crop.[1] Transplanting obliges people to wade all day in mud and water up to their knees, living bait for mosquitoes and leeches, bent double under the hot sun. This, needless to say, is women's work. If you see a man in the paddy-fields he is usually one of the "strange farmers" who come from French territory in their thousands to grow a season's crop on land provided by Gambians, in return for a rent consisting of about half the tenant's working time.

It is uphill work, getting people to help themselves. They would rather starve, not as a matter of choice, but because their

[1] This, following a pattern common to all the British West African territories, is purchased by the Government through the Gambia Oilseeds Marketing Board and sold in world markets, hitherto at a handsome profit, which is spent on improving the peasant's lot and developing natural resources.

wish for leisure is even stronger than their wish for food—just as we go on having wars not because anyone wants them, but because some men's wish for power is stronger than their wish for peace. Here in Gambia you do not die of hunger, or not often. Hang on, and the rains will come to put a little flesh back on your ribs. So you do no more work than your wife can manage.

Our boat chugged underneath a bund that spanned the narrow channel and we watched the women file across, yellow rice-ears piled on their heads in great golden cones like an oriental head-dress. They walked with a smooth, easy glide, their bodies gleaming, feet bare, a cotton cloth twisted round the waist, arms swinging loose. They were bringing in the rice to a village raised a few feet above the flooded flats, like all villages neatly encased in screens of *krinting*, a kind of reed. And like all villages, pullulating with children—flocks, droves, packs of little ones.

At Geneiri, some way up this creek, the Medical Research Council had an experimental village. They still have large laboratories outside Bathurst for work on human nutrition.

Fifty per cent at least of all Gambian children, their scientists estimate, die before they are ten. That is so all over Africa—in some places the figure is a good deal higher. (Curiously enough, the Gambia is relatively free from gut parasites like hookworm.) Under Dr. B. S. Platt, a Professor in the London School of Hygiene and Tropical Medicine, a team is experimenting on how to cut down this mortality and at the same time improve a grievously low standard of nutrition. A village called Keneba is being systematically cleared of malaria infection by repeated spraying with insecticides. Already infant mortality has tumbled in a spectacular fashion. At another village, Sekuta, every other new-born baby has received a dose of chloroquin (which kills the parasite) and not a single dosed baby has died of malaria. Moreover, the dosed infants look twice as well and plump as their undosed companions. One would of course expect malaria to keep a child back, but Dr. Platt and his colleagues are asking "why?" and, out of this question, new lines of enquiry are opening up. For instance, malaria parasites in the blood need nourishment. So do the antibodies which the blood makes to fight the parasites. All these organisms perhaps use valuable proteins which the body needs to build its tissues, and of which it is thus deprived. African diets are notoriously short of proteins, so short that probably few Europeans could live healthily on them. Has the African managed to adapt his body to extract more nitrogen from his diet and to make better use of it, just as he has adapted his body, through pigmentation, better to resist the sun?

All this laboratory work is deep and fascinating, and will add new facts to the sum of knowledge. But the consequences are as pregnant with threat and promise as the discovery of nuclear fission. Every baby inherits the necessity to fill its belly twice a day for sixty, seventy, eighty years to come. Consider this little black infant, mewling and puking, at Keneba or Geneiri: if all goes well, it will need before it dies at least twenty tons of rice, the flesh of several bullocks, two or three tons of fish, and vegetables, grain, fruit, spices besides. Say that in one small village twenty babies are born this year. Ten that would otherwise die are saved by doctors, and the next year ten more, and the year after that. In twenty years, that means 200 extra people: each year, 4,000 extra tons of rice, the flesh of a dozen bullocks, seven or eight tons of fish. By now the saved ones have in their turn started breeding, and soon the process gets out of hand, as threatening as a cancerous tumour. Where will all this rice come from, this corn, those fish and beasts? Who will grow them, on what land?

Already, perhaps nine Africans out of ten are under-nourished. How can under-nourishment be swept away at the same time as people multiply? Do the doctors not see that they are chasing simultaneously a fox running north and a hare running south? Doctors, bearers of mercy though they be, must yet be seen as the gravest threat to the future peace of Africa. They decline responsibility for the results of what they do. "That's for politicians and administrators to settle," they say. "*Our* job is to save life." How can the poor politicians find a solution when the doctors present them with something quite insoluble? With the needle that repels smallpox, bubonic plague and yaws they have upset the balance set up by Nature to match our human population to the resources which must support it. All over Africa, in hundreds of thousands of villages like Sekuta, babies that would formerly have died now stay alive. Here and there, new farms are won from bush and forest to feed them. But new land cannot be bred like people and Africa is running out of new land. In places it has run out already and famine has begun to come back. If malaria is conquered, the doom of millions by starvation will almost certainly be sealed.

Doctors worship exclusively the god of life, and to him make innumerable sacrifices. Indians know better, and render homage to Siva, the Destroyer, no less than to Vishnu, the Preserver, and Brahma, Creator of all.

◇ 9 ◇

Now and again you meet a man whose love for his work has a propellent quality that whirls forward not only himself but all in his path. Mr. O'Halloran, an Education Officer, is such a man. His dream is to see every Gambian child with book and pencil in its hand. To this end he has invented a way of instilling literacy, his own version of the Laubach system, which seems to work with astonishing speed on these round-eyed, thin-limbed little Mandingo guinea-pigs.

The school he took us to had only been open for a fortnight. All the pupils are boys; fathers still resist the notion of girls' education. (Girls with schooling might eschew toil in the fields.) At random, Mr. O'Halloran picked out three or four pupils and told each one to read a page of simple Mandinka words and phrases. All responded, although a fortnight earlier the written word had been as foreign to them as the movements of the stars.

These boys want to learn as passionately as O'Halloran wants to teach them. The reason lies in magic. Signs made on paper appear to these people cabbalistic. They are the pentagon, the swastika, a magical instruction to the unseen masters of the white man's world. And now here come men like O'Halloran offering to reveal the very secret of their fabrication, the heart of mystery—to make every man into a master, almost a god. Once possessed of the clue, what a future will lie open to succeeding generations! Command of the white man's power and riches will be theirs. Oddly enough, it is to children that the white man wishes to reveal these mysteries. This may seem strange to

B

elders, but they accept it and apprentice their children in confident expectation of benefits to come.

The teacher at this school, a quiet young man with good English, is an Aku from Bathurst who refused a good post there to come up-river and work among alien Mandingos. To do this is exceedingly rare. All down the West Coast, civilization is in the seaboard cities which the hem of Europe has brushed. Their citizens, however poor, give themselves the air of initiates. In Bathurst and Freetown they spring from homeless people—repatriated slaves—without social anchorage, and fear the lustier folk of the hinterland. So they affect to despise them, and would sooner half-starve in the capital than go inland to isolation, hard work and good pay. There are exceptions, and this teacher is one.

"There is more idealism in the Gambia than in the Gold Coast," Mr. O'Halloran generalized. "Less unrestrained self-interest. These Mandingos are the nicest Africans I know."

And he really does love them, you can see that. He delights in the dusty, sun-baked villages, the muddy, dozing creeks, the freakish baobabs and oil palms, so far and so very different from the soft green pastures of his native land. It is strange and rare, this true expatriation.

Before 1947, two schools served the whole country outside Bathurst, and less than 200 children attended. Now the number is rising as fast as teachers can be turned out, and the Training College up-river at Georgetown is expanding to meet this great demand. A piece of good fortune has just come its way. The college badly needs new and much larger buildings, but lacks the funds to put them up. And then a bright idea occurred to the Director of Education. No one was using the hen-houses at Yundum. . . .

"Knock out the perches and put on a coat of whitewash," he said, "and there you are—better dormitories than we could ever have hoped for."

So the future teachers are the heirs of the poultry scheme.

At another school, farther up-river, we found the same eagerness and brightness among the pupils but a less forcible technique. To display his English, an older boy read a description of the Maltese hospices of the Knights of St. John, which must

have conveyed very little meaning. We asked the young children
to sing. With gusto they chanted:

> *It was sad when the big ship went down,*
> *It was sad when the big ship went down,*
> *Husbands and wives,*
> *Little children lost their lives,*
> *It was sad when the big ship went down.*

It was strange to hear, so far in the heart of Africa, this ballad on
the calamity of the *Titanic*.

ঔ 10 ঔ

Dust. Dust billowing up in moving plumes behind the car to
settle softly in a red glaze over grass, trees, bush, people: dust
with a sharp, sweet, almost peppery taste in the mouth: that is
my chief recollection of the Colonial Development Corporation's
ambitious rice scheme near Wallikunda.

A year ago, sixty or seventy British ex-soldiers were at work
with big drag-lines, ripping out irrigation channels, building
their accompanying bunds and sluices and erecting a pumping
station. Most of them have gone now, leaving a signature
sprawled over the landscape in costly steel and concrete, in sheds
and bulldozed bush. Will it endure? Or will the bush once more
prove stronger than drag-line and bulldozer?

The object is to grow 3,400 acres of rice under irrigation.
Although nobody says so openly, it is clear that everyone knows
the scheme to be uneconomic and wasteful. At least a million
pounds will be spent and, for that, 3,000 tons or so of rice is a
very meagre return. Costs of production are likely to be so high
that the project will pay its way only if two crops a year can be
grown. No one knows yet whether they can be, and a distinct
note of anxiety creeps into the tones of those who explain why, by
all the rules, two crops a year ought to grow.

The first of the 3,400 acres are not yet even planted, but I saw
at Wallikunda big steel-framed implement sheds and expensive
machinery of all kinds, including a giant American combine-
harvester costing over £2,000 (in precious dollars) so heavy that

it must surely founder in the soft rice-fields, if it survives the battering in store for it on rough ground with inexperienced drivers. To treat in this manner more than a fragment of Africa would be impossible, and the scheme has no lessons in it for the peasantry save the one they always learn so quickly, that the white Government can conjure money from the air and scatter it like dust, and never lack for replenishment.[1]

By contrast, the little towns that cluster along the river know nothing of machines, of steel and concrete, of Western hustle. The *secco* standing on each water-front, a square enclosure now piled high with a pyramid of groundnuts, is, I suppose, almost the only innovation less than a century old. Cutters moored alongside are loading groundnuts for transport to Bathurst, where the nuts will wait in bigger *seccos* for steamers from Liverpool. These groundnuts are bagged and then unbagged again five times. Processions of men carry the bags to and from *seccos* and cutters, earning twopence a sack—good pay. All this is inefficient, but it spreads the money round.

All money, sooner or later, finds its way to the market, where all the colour of the country seems concentrated: the vivid Wolof dresses, kit-boxes gaily stippled all over with paint, heaps of oranges, penny piles of chillies red as pillar-boxes, above all the many-patterned cloths. And then the sandals—a tragic sight.

Every market has its sandal-makers, and a few years ago they would have been sewing dyed Moroccan leather into serviceable footwear. Now they turn out atrocities made of plastic in pastel shades, decorated with little plastic bows . . . the contribution of the West! Another is a perfume greatly favoured by chiefs and notables in place of frankincense and myrrh. It is called Bint-el-Sudan, and is manufactured in Hackney.

At every market, men are to be seen (always men—this is not women's work) outside every little shop treadling away in the shade at a sewing-machine, pausing now and again to gossip

---

[1] Since this was written, the scheme has been abandoned and £1,115,000 written off by the C.D.C. Only 200 acres of rice was planted and yielded only half a ton to the acre; no more than acreages planted by native methods. The C.D.C.'s terse conclusion was: "Continuation not a commercial risk." Besides the rice and poultry schemes, a fisheries project (over £500,000) involving a costly factory ship, the *African Queen*, also came to total grief in the Gambia.

with a passer-by. Machines hum and buzz from every veranda, like the drone of distant aircraft on a fine English day. At nearly £40 each, so many hundred machines must add up to a large capital investment. Somebody in the Gambia must be making money.

In the same veranda, very often, a man sits cross-legged on the floor embroidering, with great skill and care, one of the cotton robes worn by chiefs and rich men. He follows a traditional pattern of circles, whirls and other geometric designs, done with tiny stitches in beige thread on off-white material. The effect is dignified and pleasing, in sharp contrast to the plastic slippers. The art of embroidery is handed down from father to son. It is remarkable how often men's work entails a quiet sitdown in the shade with good money; the women's, hard unpaid labour in the hot sun.

❧ II ❧

On a dais sits a phalanx of officials in shining topees newly pipe-clayed, carrying swords and gloves and looking magisterial, scrubbed and constrained by high collars most unsuited to the tropics. Out in front, behind a red plush cushion and beneath a Union Jack, flanked by two policemen as erect as saplings, stands the Governor, addressing a gathering of chiefs spread before him in a billowy crescent of white and blue robes, grave and judicial black faces, and yellow leather slippers. (For best— the plastics are for every day.) As each chief rises and goes forward to take his oath of loyalty before the red cushion, he leaves his slippers by his chair and walks barefooted. The sun streams down over all.

A curiously old-fashioned, Sanders-of-the-River scene of British imperial power staging its little pageant beside this ancient, inimical waterway into the alien heart of Africa, and staging it well, with immaculate white men, loyal chiefs, orderly spectators; flags, bunting, bugles; the oath of loyalty, the Queen's message, the sense that this remote and uneventful little cluster of huts and bush is a part of a greater fellowship from which it can draw nobility and purpose, that its rulers are also servants of a greater power, as that power is the servant of God.

An out-of-date concept, having little to do with the ballot-box and the doctrine of equality. The forces of progress and liberation will soon obliterate such scenes even from the placid little Gambia, as they have done elsewhere.

While they last, they have a mystical significance which, however out of fashion in the West, appeals to some profound, enduring African emotion. The instinct to revere authority and the sacred element in chieftainship lies deep in the heart, and I doubt if any amount of imported democracy will obliterate it. The forms will change, certainly, and new symbols replace the old. But the essence will remain, the respect for ceremony not as a pleasing bit of pageantry but as an essential part of magic ritual.

Sir Percy Wyn-Harris has the disadvantage (at public functions) of being rather short and stocky, but a sense of authority flows from his energetic voice, his ruddy-complexioned face and his muscular frame. The quality of leadership is there. At such ceremonies a Governor wears his topee with a difference. It has a high crest of white feathers with red ones showing through. In West Africa almost every form of juju involves the use of cocks' feathers; indeed, anything to do with poultry, including eggshells, appears to have a magical use. White cockerels are especially significant, and are sacrificed in the most important ceremonies. A cockade of snow-white cocks' feathers, not to mention the red ones peeping through (a blood-red cockerel must seem to be indeed a rare, noble and potent bird), may impress the onlooker as a truly irresistible juju.

After the opening ceremony the chiefs were entertained in the Commissioner's parched garden, under the neme trees. These burly men in their full embroidered robes sat in silence round small tables set with small cakes and drank thickly sugared tea. Industriously the European ladies, hatted, gloved and nyloned, circulated among them, dispensing goodwill and small-talk of a peculiarly difficult kind, since it had for the most part to be conducted through interpreters. No chiefs' wives were present. As the ladies moved from table to table so graciously smiling, questioning, radiating racial equality, what was in the minds of these chiefs? These men who judge women by only two criteria: fecundity and muscles? For the weak and the infertile they have no more use than a farmer has for a barren cow. I feared that on these counts none of us could be earning good marks, and suspected, behind their polite façade, an indifferent contempt.

Every chief has brought a retinue of followers, and in the evenings the streets of Georgetown are lively and gay. Little groups parade everywhere: first a man carrying a huge red or gold or blue umbrella; then the white-robed chief walking majestically, followed by the bearer of his silver-headed staff; then a taggle of attendants, including several *griots* playing musical instruments. These *griots* form a caste of ex-slaves who hold a monopoly of music and entertainment and seem closely comparable with medieval jesters and troubadours. Their instruments include the ever-present drum, a kind of small violin from which a plangent, unmelodious keening is coaxed by means of a miniature bow, and the *kora*, made from a gourd, a sort of mandolin.

When the afternoon heat began to abate, a sound of drumming drew the crowd to a broad street where a kapok tree threw a cloak of shade over the hot, red, dusty ground. Here came the *kankarang* dancers, swathed all over with leaves and bark and looking like animated bundles of vegetation. Their faces were invisible behind a mask of bark-strips tied to a high head-dress, and their leafy covering extended to their feet. They leaped about with marionette-like agility, each man—there were three —waving a cutlass and making short rushes at the younger spectators, who drew back with screams of mock terror. To terrify is, indeed, the object of these dancers, whose real function is to conduct certain parts of the circumcision ceremony. *Kankarang* dancers must certainly present a very sinister appearance in the bush, on moonlit nights, to an audience of boys filled with tales of devils and tabus—sinister and typical, for is not the prime object of art in Africa, whether sculpture or dancing, to intimidate the spirit, rather than to enchant the eye?

Edging into a circle of spectators, I found myself next to a group of young women dressed in their finery. Their cotton prints were spotlessly clean, their hair done in a mass of stiff little plaits, golden ornaments clung to their ears and their smooth necks were adorned with bright red and blue beads. They had the shy, light-footed air of fawns, arrested by some half-heard sound, who gaze round all a-quiver, uncertain whether to bound off or to settle back to their browsing. At the same time their gentle cinnamon cheeks, their moth-like eyes, their full high breasts under taut bodices, their soft round arms, above all the instinctive provocation in their glances all proclaimed them to be like ripe plums against a warm wall, poised for the matrimonial plucking. When I spoke to them, they fell into paroxysms of shyness deeper than any schoolgirl's, yet there was about them an undertone of most unchildlike maturity. It was sad to think how soon the bloom on these satin-skinned, graceful young creatures would all be rubbed off and they would grow into farm and household drudges, with placid faces and ugly pendulous breasts. African girls can be lovely and the faces of old women as full of character as a weather-beaten tree, but in between lies a waste of mediocrity. Not that they look depressed or bad-tempered, like many Europeans; only that, as a rule, they lack grace.

∽ 12 ∽

The conference over, we proceeded a little farther up the narrowing river to Karantaba, another groundnut selling point, and, just beyond, to a plain stone memorial standing amid dry, prickly scrub to mark the point where one of the greatest of all explorers started both his expeditions to reach Timbuktu and unfold the mystery of the Niger. At that time Dr. Laidley, a trader, had a house on the spot, and he befriended the young Mungo Park, who learnt Mandinka there while waiting on the weather.

Even to reach his memorial from the river, a distance of some twenty paces, you must push through prickles and thorns, over sandy soil almost grassless and sprinkled with the burst dry fruit of baobabs. Visibility is only a few yards. And Mungo Park had hundreds of miles of this ahead of him, unmapped, unexplored, almost waterless and full of hostile, warring tribes.

Seldom can a humbler expedition have set forth into great dangers. Mungo Park, aged twenty-four, took with him one Negro servant and one slave lad, mounted on asses which carried also their meagre stock of beads, amber and tobacco. Park himself rode a pony and carried little more than his compass and sextant and two fowling-pieces. In a very short while everything was stolen and he was forced to barter a handkerchief, or a button off his coat, for a little soaked corn or a handful of ground-nuts. At last the Moors, who held him a contemptuously-treated captive, reduced him to begging scraps from slaves. Once, suffering agonies of thirst, he approached some Moors who were drawing water for their cattle and they, scorning the touch of Christian lips on their bucket, permitted him only to shoulder his way in among the cattle and kneel down at the filthy trough.

In spite of all these torments he escaped from the Moors alone, in darkness, without food or so much as a handful of cowries—a hunted man; he was befriended by Negroes; and at last, six months after his departure, he gazed upon the Niger, flowing east-wards, and so became the first European to prove with his eyes the unlikely course taken by this wayward river.

A modern reader of his *Travels* or his biography cannot but wonder what force it was that propelled him forward through this bog of misery. He did not covet fame. As for fortune, his exploits did not bring him even a competence. Sheer lowland Scots obstinacy was an element, but, much more, a profound belief that the dour but living God of the Calvinists had him under personal care. There is a touching passage in his Journal where, after he had been robbed by Fulanis even of the clothes off his back, he sat down and gave way to one of his rare moments of despair. Here he was,

in the midst of a vast wilderness in the depth of the rainy season, naked and alone; surrounded by savage animals, and men still more savage. I was five hundred miles from the nearest European settlement. All these circumstances crowded at once on my recollection; and I confess that my spirits began to fail me. . . . At this moment, painful as my reflections were, the extraordinary beauty of a small moss, in fructification, irresistibly caught my eye. I mention this to show from what trifling circumstances the mind will sometimes derive consola-tion; for, though the plant was not larger than the top of one of my fingers, I could not contemplate the delicate conforma-tion of its roots, leaves, and capsula, without admiration. Can that Being (I thought) who planted, watered and brought to perfection, in this obscure part of the world, a thing which appears of so small importance, look with unconcern upon the situation and sufferings of creatures formed after his own image?—surely not! Reflections like these would not allow me to despair.

And so, supported by that little fruiting moss, he went on, and in a few days his luck changed. Eighteen months after he set out, he returned safely to this spot on which we stood in all our comfort and security.

Park's first lonely journey, financed by the private subscriptions of a group of *savants* headed by Sir Joseph Banks, aroused such interest that nine years later he returned at the head of a large Government expedition. He took a Lieut. Martyn and over thirty English soldiers ("the most *dashing* men I ever saw"), six carpenters, two personal friends from the Border, tools to build boats on the Niger and plenty of merchandise. It must have been with high hopes that this caravan set off, once more from Karantaba, on a May morning in 1805.

A May morning—there is the key to their disaster. They had left the start too late. It was not Park's fault. The Colonial Office summoned him urgently to London in September. His plans were in the hands of the Secretary of State by October 5th. And then he encountered the perennial phenomenon of official delay, more fatal to him, as it turned out, than all Africa's fevers. For three months he was kept hanging on to await an official decision. Those three months were crucial. For, as Park well knew, only in the dry season could travellers move and white men survive. The rains start in June, and the season of sickness follows. Then Europeans are indeed cut down like flowers and have but a short while to live.

And so Park's second expedition started too late. When, after a four months' journey, they at last reached the Niger, only six soldiers survived out of thirty-four, and the Border friends were dead. They built a boat of sorts—their carpenters had perished —and only Park himself, Lieut. Martyn and three soldiers were left to launch their vessel. Weakened by illness, under constant attack, they navigated the river for nearly a thousand miles before they were drowned in the rapids at Bussa while fighting off an ambush. Of all the men who marched so hopefully from this point at Karantaba one and one only, the interpreter Isaaco, returned.

And so Park failed to trace the Niger to the sea. But when the story of his great journey was pieced together, geographers could have but little doubt that it flowed into the Atlantic, rather than into the Congo, the Nile, or some unknown inland lake or swamp. The mystery was three parts solved.

Not far from Karantaba, Park came across an object which gave the words "mumbo-jumbo" to the English language. This was a bark dress, much, I should imagine, like that of the *kankarang* dancers. When a man's wives quarrelled, according to Park, the mumbo-jumbo was sent for. Dressed in this bark disguise, he heralded his nocturnal approach by loud and dismal screams; on his entry to the village, everyone paraded and the women were obliged to dance and sing. About midnight the mumbo-jumbo picked out his victim, and she was stripped, bound to a tree and beaten, while her sisters gathered round to jeer and jibe with the self-righteousness of the reprieved. "Daylight," remarked Park primly, "put an end to this indecent and unmanly revel."

❧ 13 ❧

Above Karantaba, the river is navigable well into French waters, and we saw big French barges coming down loaded with groundnuts. They hooted as they passed and dipped their flags politely; pennants fluttered from their rigging, pied kingfishers and white egrets haunted the banks, all was bright and amiable. The fevers, the cruelty and despair revealed to Park and the early traders seemed all gone—but only, perhaps, into hiding. Even amid the sheltered comfort of a royal launch, on the last up-river trip the Governor's secretary caught sleeping-sickness from a roving tsetse. Not long ago this disease was painfully fatal. Now there is a drug, infallible if diagnosis is made in time. In this case it was, by an African doctor in Bathurst; and the secretary, flown to England for the cure, will soon be back at her task.

Our returning launch sped swiftly down-river, passing overnight from scrub and palm trees to the now familiar mangroves and, at one point, through a party of delightful hippos who poked their pink snouts through rippling water. Hippos are amongst the most endearing of wild animals to the traveller, but not to the farmer, for at night they pad about the rice-fields and do a great deal of harm. Already there is ominous talk of shooting them out. Their supporters are branded as sentimentalists, and of course no argument can save animals when men are short of food. Elephants do not wish to wipe out giraffes, nor cows set upon goats, because both compete for grazing; only man strives to confront all other species with a choice between subservience and extermination. And so probably these playful, pug-like river-horses are doomed.

But somehow one does not mind about baboons. They infest these river-banks, plundering groundnuts; or did, until a price of two shillings was put upon each tail. Over 35,000 baboon tails have since been brought in. All sorts of dodges were tried, like splitting tails in two. When, in another part of Africa, a price was put on rats' tails to assist in stamping out bubonic plague, several *entrepreneurs* started rat farms which did very well. Baboons would be harder to breed, and authority feels reasonably satisfied that about 35,000 have in fact been killed.

We watched a small flock going to roost in the palm trees. Up they climbed, up the straight and slender bole, mothers with babies clinging to their backs, to assemble in the crest of fronds. A tremendous chattering broke out, a scolding, screeching and yattering; branches tossed as the altercation grew. A thick-necked old man on the topmost branch intervened to curse and chastise his women; infuriated females jumped up and down; others hurried up the tree-trunk to join the party. The fronds danced wildly against a flat, pale-pink sunset sky. All else was peace: the quietly flowing river, the clustering egrets, a still air, a fish lazily leaping, the lost call of guinea-fowl from the dry, immobile bush. Only the monkeys erupted, for all the world like politicians bent on liberating their fellow-men.

As we chugged westwards, a Danish trader, Axel Johnsen, told me a little about the places we passed which thirty-seven years in the Gambia, at the closest of quarters, had taught him. There, for instance, he said, pointing at a low line of thatched roofs, was a village where he had drunk blue tea. Finding his early morning cup was off-colour in every sense, he discovered that several days before a traveller in a blue gown had fallen into the well. No one had bothered to fish him out; after all, he was dead, and nothing could bring him back to life again; as for the taste of the tea, no one except Axel Johnsen had noticed anything peculiar.

And so to Bathurst, with its lazy, gentle air, its hot dust, its casuarinas and bougainvilleas, its bright Wolof dresses, its wild-haired Moors; the encircling mangrove swamps, the dark Syrian caverns with their brilliant silks and cottons, the honey-coloured church in the square full of Christian women in straw hats and tight print dresses. And then, at dawn, to Yundum airport, past derelict hen-houses so soon to fill with earnest students, past flat, brown scrub and baobabs and patches of long, spindly cassava, sunlight flooding an empty sky with sudden might and glory. So to the little airport with its solitary windsock, its baked beds of petunias stuck in red sand and carefully watered by half-asleep attendants; and so into the big lumbering Wayfarer aircraft, and down the coast over Casamance and Portuguese Guinea to Sierra Leone.

SIERRA LEONE

SIERRA LEONE

POPULATION: Estimated in 1952 at 2,000,000, of whom some 95,000 lived in the Colony. About 30,000 of the latter are "Creoles", descendants of freed slaves, some of mixed blood. The Mende and Temne tribes each account for nearly one-third of the Protectorate's population. There were 964 Europeans and 2,074 Asiatics, mainly Syrians and Lebanese.

CAPITAL: Freetown, founded in 1787 by freed slaves sent out by Granville Sharp, the friend of Wilberforce. In 1799 it was made into a Corporation with Mayor and Aldermen.

AREA: 27,925 square miles, divided into the Colony (269 sq. m.), a peninsula about twenty-five miles long by ten to twelve miles wide, with mountains rising to 3,000 feet, and the Protectorate, bounded by French Guinea, Liberia and the Atlantic Ocean.

TRADE: Food-growing, with rice the staple, is the people's main activity. The major exports are palm kernels and iron ore, each of which accounted in 1953 for over £4 millions out of a total export trade worth £12,202,214. Ginger, cocoa, piassava and palm oil are also exported. The Sierra Leone Produce Marketing Board, set up in 1949, is the sole exporter of palm kernels, palm oil, benniseed, copra, coffee and cocoa, and made a profit, in 1951, of over £1,500,000. The Sierra Leone Selection Trust (an associate of de Beers) holds a sole concession for the mining of diamonds, of which 416,742 carats were exported in 1953. Chrome ore is also exported. Imports to the value of £11,095,161 consisted mainly of cotton piece goods, foodstuffs and drink, clothing, machinery and hardware.

HISTORY: Sierra Leone received its name in 1460 from Pedro da Cintra. The first Englishman to land there was probably Sir John Hawkins, on a slaving expedition in 1562. The settlement for freed slaves started in 1787 was raided constantly by tribesmen and in 1794 sacked by the French. In 1808 it was transferred from a Chartered Company to the Crown. After the abolition of slavery, a naval squadron was stationed at Freetown to intercept slave ships and thousands of the freed slaves remained on the peninsula, which was ceded by Temne chiefs. Trade developed, and treaties of friendship with inland chiefs established a British "sphere of influence" whose boundaries were defined in 1885 (with Liberia) and 1895 (with the French). A Protectorate over these areas was declared in 1896, but two years later an attempt to collect "house tax" precipitated a revolt, suppressed in 1899, since when the country has remained peaceful.

GOVERNMENT: A constitution introduced in 1951 and amended in 1953 enlarged the Legislative Council to include an elected Vice-President, twenty-one elected members, two nominated members and seven officials. Of the elected members, seven represent the seven districts of the Colony, twelve are elected by the District Councils in the Protectorate, and two are elected by the unofficial members of the Provincial Assembly. There is also an Executive Council consisting of the Governor, four officials and six Ministers drawn from among the elected members of the Legislative Council, all six being members of the Sierra Leone People's Party led by Dr. Margai, M.B.E. The rest of the Colony is administered under a three-tier system of local government, based on twenty-eight Village Area Committees, six Rural District Councils and a Rural Area Council for the whole peninsula. The Protectorate is, on the one hand, divided into eleven districts, each under a District Commissioner responsible to the Governor; and, on the other, into 161 chiefdoms, each under a Paramount Chief assisted by a council, the Tribal Authority. In 1946 partially elected District Councils came into being, and in 1951 these were given powers to spend grants from the central Government on local development. Each of these District Councils elects two members to the Protectorate Assembly, which, with a minority of official members, has a general watching brief over the interests of the Protectorate.

SIERRA
LEONE

SIERRA LEONE

A WHITE-HAIRED Negro wearing a black city coat and baggy pin-striped trousers, carrying a battered umbrella, stepped across a big open drain, bowed with great courtesy and shook hands. Heat rose like steam off the tarmac; beyond him, under a huge silk-cotton tree, half a dozen young men in tilted hats lounged in the shade; in a yard behind the hotel, schoolgirls in tight butcher-blue frocks and tight black pigtails danced in a circle round a teacher, singing an insipid song. Behind the silk-cotton tree rises the solid Victorian façade of the law-courts, embellished with heavy, curved rococo sculpture; most of the buildings are heavy too, and dark-red, the red of dried blood; the bay below is azure, speckled with white sails. All is sleepy, scorching and slow; people amble to and fro —not so long ago the well-to-do were carried down the street in hammocks—and hills rise straight up from the town to cut it off from the interior.

Freetown has won harsh opinions. Clusters of Nissen huts left over from the war are as drear as the prefabs on the outskirts of any English city; in the wet season, rain batters down, as if spite elementalized, on to iron roofs; then the torrid air streams, insects breed in millions and malaria rages. But I saw it in the dry weather, under a bright sky and against a splendid panorama of bush-clad, buttressed hills, and to me it had an air of permanence and solidity found in no other West African seaport. Especially in the villages round about with English names like York and Kent, Hastings and Wellington, you feel that you are not in Africa so much as in the Caribbean. These little cottages of unpainted boards weathered to every shade of chocolate, rust and burnt sienna are West Indian. So are the plump women in tight bodices and brilliant head-ties who flounce and waddle down the streets. Yet Creoles are outnumbered by folk from the interior by more than three to one, and over half the population is Muslim.

Creoles—the word is used here to mean a descendant of freed

slaves—are proud of their white blood, their Christian inherit-ance, their way of life, which reflects, at some distance, that of the European. The African tribes that surround and so greatly outnumber them (there are less than 30,000 true Creoles) they affect to despise—"our less favoured brethren"—but inevitably fear. They represent a lost cause, and like most lost causes have a charm denied to the saved and successful. Europeans find them soft, feckless, idle, good-mannered and often exasperating.

What they have achieved since 1787, when their Pilgrim Fathers (so to say) were set ashore—351 assorted Negroes freed by Lord Mansfield's famous anti-slavery decision and sixty shanghaied Plymouth prostitutes—is to build a complete society with its rich and poor, its masters and men, tinkers and tailors and doctors and thieves, heroes and scallywags, with customs, *patois*, manners and life all their own. They are not Africans. Wrenched free of tribalism, nearly all of mixed blood, they pos-sess no native ethos, no roots, above all no land. There is land for the asking in valleys close at hand, but they are an urban people and despise the soil. The successful do not pine for wives and cattle, they want to be called to the Bar.

What the Creoles have not done, so far as I know, in this cen-tury and a half, is to create anything. There is no serious Creole art, literature, drama or music. The sculpture and dancing of the native have gone with tribalism. Apparently you cannot destroy selectively, obliterating savagery and yet leaving intact the "good" things of native life, the forms of self-expression, for these arise out of the life that you destroy. Progress is like a bull-dozer, it flattens flowers as well as thorns.

◈ 2 ◈

Freetown has a class structure like our own before the age of equality. There are aristocratic families whose members fill the professions and whose weddings, funerals and "at homes" are recorded in the local newspapers: the Brights, the Taylors, the Cummings, the Wrights and others. Many go to England for their education; the money for this they draw mostly from their ownership of Freetown property.

I called on Dr. Taylor Cummings, the Mayor, who, with a wholly Creole staff, administers the city. He and his Council maintain one of the nicest small parks I have seen in Africa, with neat flower-beds and enormous frangipani trees covered now with pink, bell-shaped blossoms that look as if they had been modelled in wax. Dr. Taylor Cummings is a man of property and cultivated manners whose grandfather came off a captured slave-ship and was perhaps a Yoruba, though as to this he can only speculate. Like many eminent Creoles, he is deeply distressed at the turn events have taken since the Governor, Sir George Beresford-Stooke, started to pursue with energy, sincerity and good humour the task entrusted to him by his masters: that of pushing forward self-government in Sierra Leone.

But self-government does not mean the same thing to Sir George Beresford-Stooke as it does to Dr. Taylor Cummings. To the British it means the rule of the majority, which is something quite different from self-rule. Democratic government in Sierra Leone must imply the sovereignty of the tribes of the Protectorate, who lack tenderness towards Freetown Creoles. Dr. Taylor Cummings is like a Roman Briton who distrusts and fears barbarians beyond the Wall. Though they fight with votes instead of spears, though they learn table manners, they are still after the villas, the tax-rolls and the consulships, and they are not Roman citizens. Dr. Taylor Cummings is.

Now there has been a big victory for the men beyond the Wall. Under the new constitution, they return to the Legislative Council twice as many members as does the Colony, which is a small boot-shaped peninsula, with Freetown at its toe, harbouring nearly all the Creoles. So the Creoles can be permanently outvoted by Protectorate tribesmen who, in Creole eyes, though certainly not in their own, are wild men from the bush full of jujus, leopard societies and heathen gods.

At present a *bloc* of British colonial officials holds the balance, but these men will soon withdraw, stage by stage, leaving the field to Africans. It is only a matter of time, and not a very long time at that, before the Creoles will be at the mercy of Protectorate Africans. You cannot blame the older Creoles for resenting and dreading this. Some of the younger ones realize its inevitability and give the constitution their support.

In a city of 65,000 people there are no less than eight newspapers of a sort, although the circulation of the largest is not above 1,500. How they exist is a mystery. Their journalistic standards are deplorable, but they serve their purpose, which is the same as that of most British and American newspapers, not so much to enlighten as to entertain.

I called on the editor of one, climbing up a bare and dirty staircase to reach a dusty, cramped room where he sat in his shirt-sleeves, attended by a single listless messenger. No apparatus here of tape-machines and telephones, just the elemental basis of a newspaper—a man with a pen and an urge to convert others to his point of view.

"We stand for self-government," said this plump, sweaty and fluent editor, leaning back in his chair, "but this constitution is not self-government at all. It is dictatorship. The Protectorate members form a permanent majority. They will always outvote the Colony. How can this be democratic?"

"If they represent the majority——"

He swept this aside. "We in the Colony are British subjects. In the Protectorate they are not British subjects at all. They may come to Freetown and live here as they please, but if we go to the Protectorate we must pay a settler's fee. Is that democratic? Is it right they should permanently outvote us? We demand equal rights for all!"

At the same time one of the Creoles' spokesmen and leaders, Mr. Wallace Johnson, adheres to Communism. The office of his newspaper proudly displays an article of his, illustrated with his portrait, cut from a Prague contemporary. One thinks with some surprise of the Creoles, clingers to privilege, owners of property, enthusiastic church-goers, *bourgeois* to the marrow, as ardent Marxists. But I doubt if one of them has read a word of Marx.

I enquired how they squared their Communism with a strong belief in private property and with an *élite* supported mainly by the rents of slum houses.

"You are thinking of the European form of Communism. *We* believe in an African form."

"And that is . . .?"

"We have no objection to private property. But in an African household, anyone who comes can share the family meal."

The "African form" of Marxism seems to equal open hospitality. Marx would find Africa full of surprises.

❦ 3 ❦

There can be few colleges in the world in a lovelier setting than that of Fourah Bay. To reach it you drive up and up, curling away from the heat-bathed roofs of Freetown, past rivulets by whose pools washer-women whack their cottons on the rocks, up to the old naval fortifications which command the harbour. Below spreads the great blue bay: large enough, they say, to take the whole British fleet. Now it is speckled with the little white triangular sails of the Bullom boats, so called because they bring produce to Freetown from the Bullom shore.

The College is like a magpie's nest, perched high and flung together out of bits and pieces. Despite its fine tradition it struck me as a rather sad place, rather neglected, as if it lived on memories. Its history goes back for over a century. Founded by the Church Missionary Society, for many years it supplied the whole West Coast with educated men, clerks and the like; even today, one-third of its 300 resident students are Nigerians.

Now new suns are rising to eclipse it—the great new universities in Nigeria and the Gold Coast, to which most of the prestige and money are going. Fourah Bay's principal, Mr. Dain, has plans for expansion which would cost at least a million pounds. An architect has visited the site and nearly half this sum has been voted from the Colonial Development and Welfare Fund, but some of the money has to go on maintenance, and I had the feeling that no one really believed that the full plans and hopes would quite materialize. Nearly one-third of the students are women, incipient teachers mostly, though, with their brilliantly coloured dresses, their graceful movements, their self-assurance and air of gay *insouciance*, they do not, to an English eye, in the least have the air of schoolmarms. The trouble at present is not to get staff, who are nearly all white, conscientious and correctly qualified, but to get students well enough schooled to profit from the teaching. It is not a question of inherent intelligence, but of the small proportion of the children who go to school and the low quality of so much of their schooling. This is a perplexity common to all Africa, and one that can only be slowly remedied.

A sort of Victorian respectability lies like a crust over this tropical seaport whose Pilgrim Mothers were Plymouth prostitutes. Philanthropy founded it; Missions sustained it; now trade and government carry it on. On Sundays the Cathedral and the many churches are packed and gay but the offertory plates of the Cathedral, the harvest of three well-attended services, net only £5.

The house of Gordon Ash, the Public Relations Officer, stands in the city's heart, and sometimes he and his wife are kept awake by drumming, singing and screams of pain issuing from a patch of nearby waste land which is used by the Bundu, the society controlling the initiation of women, for their circumcision rites.

Christian morality struggles gamely against a tropical climate and a rootless population. The girls can be lovely, life is short and in the rains it is impractical to go out of doors. Even the Church must compromise sometimes. I was told of an epitaph (though I did not see it) on a tombstone in one of the villages along the coast. It commemorates a pastor who "for forty years was a martyr to his flock and gonorrhœa, from which he died".

∽ 4 ∾

There is a drive through the plum-coloured villages of Wellington and Hastings that is truly magnificent. On one side rise the jagged, lion-thundering mountains, silent now and wisped with cloud; below, a sea fringed with sandy bays so warm and gentle that you might have reached the shores of Cytherea. Villages lie among the palm trees, and a street-lamp rising from the promontory warns fishermen coming in after dark. By the shore I came upon an elderly man building a canoe. Very patiently he scraped away the timber with an adze to make a thin shell. This is the sort of task that looks crude and easy—only, after all, scooping out a log—but conceals great skill, for these canoes are so delicately balanced that the least stirring of a clumsy passenger will capsize them.

Inland, one is struck by the country's locked-up fertility. Here it lies, within easy reach of a great seaport, well-watered, much rained upon, tropical—and bearing scrub. Here and there a patch has been dug to make a little garden, a cassava field, a tiny citrus orchard. The slopes are too steep, say the people, for cultivation. It is true that if you merely cleared the bush and dug, the soil would wash away.

But think of Madeira: that steep mountain's every inch is terraced and tilled and each terrace walled with stone. Some are no broader than a table, but bear double crops, vegetables shaded by vines. Long stone *levados* carry irrigation water for miles to every plot. Think of the vineyards of Burgundy and Italy, or the flooded paddy-fields of Java reflecting sunlight in a long series of step-like mirrors. There—terracing, irrigation, toil, care, fertility; here—indifference and waste. The Grafton Valley could feed not only Freetown and its ships but many of the world's hungry as well, were you to turn loose in it a few thousand Italians or Portuguese. In a few years they would transform it from wilderness to garden. Politics prevents this, politics and racialism: for there are more racial penalties and embargoes against whites in Africa than there are against blacks in Europe.

About twenty miles out of Freetown we called on a Syrian who has rented 800 acres from a chief and started a banana plantation. Only thirty acres are as yet in bearing, but every three weeks Mr. Courban sends off a shipment of Lacatans, the best variety of banana. Between the rows he plants beans, and feeds them, together with any damaged bananas, to the pigs, and the pigs supply Freetown with bacon. All this is being done without any of the complex machinery and lavish expenditure always found in Government projects; and already, I feel sure, it pays. It *produces*. The soil is fertile, the rainfall ample, and there is plenty of unused land for which chiefs are glad to get a rent of two shillings an acre; others—Africans, perhaps?—could follow suit and enrich the country, but so far he is a lone pioneer.

Mr. Courban, one could see, really loves his pigs and bananas, and above all his roses, which he grows in large numbers of home-made pots, watering them all by hand. Sierra Leone is his home and he means to live and die here; like many of his compatriots, he will never return to the Levant. They live a queer life, these Syrians, turned in on themselves and belonging neither to the African nor the British world. No matter how successful, the British never accept them socially, as they now accept, with acclamation, top-level Africans.

Unlike Africans, Syrians do not flatter by imitation; in their own closed world they keep their customs and beliefs; they cling together, as indeed they must, for Africans resent their commercial skill and sharpness and the British distrust it, nursing a vague feeling that no Syrian is really honest; they out-smart Africans, they smuggle diamonds, they evade the immigration laws, there is something about them elusive, ancient, self-contained. The British official mind shies off the retail trade, still feeling it to be not quite serious, not quite honourable, to make your money out of selling things unless this is done on a big enough scale, and with titled directors.

Syrians have no titles, no political rights, no recognition; when they can, they doubtless evade such nuisances as income tax and customs duties; yet in remote and comfortless places they trade in peace, industriously; they carry out a necessary task the African is often too easy-going to bother with, the European too exacting. In their closed houses they breed large families which go to Mission schools with African children; they expect no leave with pay at stated intervals; they will travel 100 miles in crowded lorries to buy a sack or two of ginger and sell a bag of salt. A few grow rich, and charter aeroplanes to take their raven-haired, olive-skinned children and their fat, over-blown, silk-clad women back to Damascus and Aleppo, Antioch and Beirut.

On our way back we stopped at Newton, just inside the small Colony, where dwells, in some isolation, a young Agricultural Officer who introduces new crops and experiments in better methods of husbandry. He keeps a nursery of seedling oil-palms, bred by scientists, which yield four times as much oil as the local variety. These he gives away, free, to anyone energetic enough to dig holes to plant them in. (The holes have to be inspected first, otherwise the canny would not plant the seedlings at all, but sell them to the less canny.) He parts with pedigree pigs and cockerels at cost price to small-holders, he has dammed a stream to irrigate land and doubled the crops on it with the use of compost. People look at all this with mild interest, but scarcely anyone goes and does the same. Mr. Jones is not disheartened, any more than a good preacher is downcast because his flock does not grow Christian overnight. The word, he thinks, will spread slowly, once it can be seen that there is money in the new ways.

We drove back at evening through the Grafton Valley. Behind us lay the sea, a bed of gold stretching westwards to eternity; in front, the Lion Mountains rose in great folds that should have sheltered buffaloes and leopards, but held only solitude. Our road wound among bush-clad cliffs lit by a setting sun as if a mighty spotlight played across a cosmic stage. At this time of day all the bushes and trees look as if they had been cut out of cardboard. Edged with brilliance, they take on a new mysterious glory. Down the valley flood great rivers of golden light, the air is quiet and full of magic and every sound—the calling of a partridge, the cry of a child—comes with bell-like clarity, as if over water, to an ear seemingly more sensitive. Things take on a new meaning; even the bedraggled little houses with their rusty roofs look as if they hugged a secret and delightful life of their own.

And so into the trim suburbs of Freetown, the big, comfortable bungalows, the mown grass and bright gardens of Hill Station, where a little enclave of order and correctitude defies the casual sprawl of Africa; a tight, suburban island in a sea of timeless and callous unconcern.

<ов 5 сю>

We embarked on the Agricultural Department's launch at Rokupr, a miniature seaport full of bustle and shouting and men unloading boats—only small river launches, but still boats, bringing bananas, rice and groundnuts down from the interior to be transhipped to Freetown.

My companion, an Agricultural Officer, pointed out a warehouse by the river-side. It belongs to a Swiss.

"That man made this district," he said. "Until he came, there was no trade. He built a home-made launch and started to buy produce and take it down to Freetown. The idea caught on, and now some of the local people have their own launches. After he'd been here a year or so, he decided that the people needed, above all, two things—mosquito nets and tinned milk! So he sold them at cost price, or under. *They* caught on too. Now health and wealth are on the up-grade—thanks largely to that Swiss."

Our launch chugged smoothly down the Great Scarcies River. The landscape here is like Norfolk's, lush and open, with a few tall trees. Flights of whistling teal circle over and grey herons flap above the level fields. Here and there, a carmine bee-eater dips his black beak into the water. All is placidity and ease. On the banks are low stacks of rice and, farther inland, lines of harvesters, hooks in hand, bend over the short-strawed crop.

These Temne have worked out an excellent way of harvesting rice. The men go round in companies to each farm in turn. We passed several such companies going out in canoes. Each flew a house-flag at the stern and the men and boys sang as they paddled. Two or three women in their best cloths went along to cook. The scene was gay and cheerful, with the sun on the river, a flash of paddles and a chant of song. Each evening the owner of the rice provides a feast and home-brewed beer unlimited, and the reapers dance most of the night; an expensive business, but better fun, perhaps, than hiring a mechanic with a combine.

Mooring the launch, we walked along a bund that ran inland from the river, with flat rice-fields on either hand. The bund ended in a clump of mangroves; an old man embroidering slippers with beads guarded the entrance to the village. We made our way over dusty paths to the chief's bungalow, built of mud blocks, and iron-roofed—the house of a rich man.

All his household's life is on the veranda. Wives in printed cloths wander to and fro, babies crawl underfoot and men sit in deck-chairs talking of trade and local politics. The rice crop is coming in, and here it is always ample, and there are bananas, groundnuts (the women's crop) and citrus as well. No hungry season, but a comfortable surplus. What a difference that makes to the whole spirit of man!

Bai Farima Tass II is a youngish man with a bull neck, a tough, strong face and plenty of intelligence. He used to be an instructor in the Agricultural Department. Although a Muslim, in his youth he was too fond of alcohol; but one day, realizing that drink had all but undone him, he said: "I have drunk well

for twenty-one years, and now it is behind me." It has stayed
behind, and there are few better chiefs. He is also a member of
both Executive and Legislative Councils. While we sat and
talked, a messenger arrived on foot with a heavy packet of
official documents.

"Isn't it difficult," I asked, "to find time to read all that?"

"I read only at night, there is too much noise by day," he
said, smiling at the crowd of women, children and relatives in
which he was all but immersed. Even at night, all this family
life must be packed in somewhere. Each of the four official wives
has her own bedroom, and the lord of the household his austere,
earth-floored apartment with no more furniture than a camp
bed and a hurricane lantern set on a chair. Into this *ménage*
pours a flood of mimeographed literature and statistics framed in
officialese; nearly all of it, I should think, either unread or in-
comprehensible. I felt sorry for Bai Farima Tass, hereditary
lord of so many people yet condemned (if he is conscientious) to
perch uncomfortably on his camp bed and, night after night,
pore over these dreary documents while droves of fat flying
beetles noisily besiege the bush lamp.

∾ 6 ∾

All this fertile country must be developed, so great is the
general need for rice. The Tanganyika groundnut and the
Gambia rice and poultry fiascos have cast a wide shadow, and
much local effort is now given to avoiding the eye of Government corporations with teams of experts and bottomless purses,
which are all too apt to disrupt district economies and make
everyone believe that money grows on trees. Sierra Leone is
developing rice in a piecemeal, economical fashion so completely
in contrast to the way of the big battalions that it is perhaps
worth a brief description.

First of all, in this district on the lower Scarcies, a new rice-
mill, erected by the Department of Commerce and Industry and
managed by an up-and-coming Creole, hulls the rice and par-
boils it. Canoes and barges bring the harvest to the landing-
stage from this Corot-like country, and take the money back tied
up in handkerchiefs.

Production schemes are based on three notions: that if tractors do the ploughing, hand labour can do the rest; that schemes must be local; and that each scheme must aim at paying for itself. Wisely, the authorities carried out a pilot scheme for three years with a single tractor, and were thus able to ascertain, not to estimate, how much work a tractor can do and at what cost. Now twelve tractors have been ordered for this district, each of which can be expected to plough about 600 acres yearly; and by charging land-holders £2 an acre, the project will be self-supporting.

Other development proceeds in a belt of low-lying, creek-riven, inundated swamp-land called Bonthe, accessible only by sea. Here an Indo-Chinese rice is being tried which, so I was told by sober scientists, can add up to six inches a day to its stature in order to keep its head above the rising flood-water, and grows up to twenty feet in height. When the waters recede, this rice with its immense long straw subsides in a tangle to the ground, and you would think that to harvest it would be impossible. But Nature is more thoughtful, and from the top node the straw bends and shoots upwards so as to offer its neck to the sickle.

The native crop as grown at present consists of low-yielding, poor, genetically mixed varieties, and the scientist's first task is to test strains of rice from other parts of the world under local conditions. This they do at a new rice research station at Rokupr, serving all West Africa, where no less than 232 different varieties and strains are on test. On the face of it, yields could be trebled merely by planting some of the far more prolific varieties common in the East, but matters are not as simple as that. For reasons still obscure, many practices common in the East do not work in Sierra Leone. (Most things in Africa are upside down. For instance, the vegetation's winter falls at the hottest time of year; when driving long distances by car, you must at intervals let air out of the tyres instead of pumping it in; and wardrobes in the very hottest capitals are fitted with electric heaters.) As to rice, research is needed and more research, lasting many years.

Rokupr itself, well sited on a hill above the river, wears a melancholy air. All round are swamps, and a feeling of isolation and lethargy. Sandflies are multitudinous and hungry, with a result that dengue fever is common. Yet half a dozen pale-complexioned but lively white children were to be seen playing in the gardens after tea. That is something new in West Africa, the presence of white children in these remote spots not long ago considered to be quite lethal to women and children, and supportable to men only with the lavish help of whisky. Now beneficent drugs sustain the women and children, and few men with families can afford much whisky. Nor can they afford any longer to keep their families at home, or the expense of boarding-schools. How to educate their children is becoming a serious question for many of them.

Bachelors are the best off. The young Agricultural Officers especially struck me as happy men, for they have a job they believe in, unmixed with politics, and the training to understand their surroundings. Each of the three stationed at Rokupr has found a species of plant new to science which the Kew authorities have named after him: one an orchid, one a shrub and the third a small ditch plant. Perhaps it is not much to have one's name attached to a small ditch plant, but it marks a certain achievement and, indeed, a kind of immortality.

From Port Loko, for some abstruse reason known as Black Man London, we drove east towards the mountainous heart of the Protectorate, passing en route curious vegetation called Lophira bush. Its brilliant pale-green leaves have the leathery, bloodless look of seaweed and flop down in the same distraught and ragged fashion. I had the feeling that we were driving along under-water. This type of bush is said to be a sign of run-down, eroded land ravaged by frequent fires, several of which were crackling and spitting in the long, coarse grass as we passed, reducing young trees to charred sticks. The trees will shoot again, but each ordeal gravely weakens them. All over West Africa, fires are preventing bush regeneration and helping to waste away the land's fertility.

A flock of brown hawks had settled on the road in front of an advancing line of flames which drove a multitude of grasshoppers, mice, little snakes, insects and rodents of all kinds before it. So intent were these birds on the approaching holocaust that they ignored our car. We slowed down and hooted. Grudgingly, the hawks flapped out of the way at the last moment and closed in again behind us, scarcely turning their proud yellow eyes aside from the ribbon of fire and its helpless refugees.

It was typical of my companion, Gordon Ash, Sierra Leone's Public Relations Officer, that he should take trouble to avoid injuring a hawk. A diffident, self-effacing young man, at times so shy that his voice sinks into a mumble, you might at first doubt whether he could command the authority to fill one of the trickiest jobs in any country. But you soon find that his quietness conceals purpose, competence and enthusiasm, his shyness an ability to sum up trends and men. At heart a romantic, Sierra Leone is still for him a land of mystery and adventure, the people in it are all a little larger than life. Wherever we went, Africans came up to greet him with a spontaneous warmth which was remarkable. Gordon Ash is the kind of Englishman Africans like, because he likes them and gives himself no airs, and because he is kind, good-tempered and not in too much of a hurry. It is always foolish to make haste in Africa and especially, I should think, in Sierra Leone. Time's wingèd chariot is inaudible— Africans, as we are often reminded, never invented the wheel. Time carries his load of years, like everyone else, at walking pace, on his wife's back.

We drove now through the country of the Temne tribe. A sixteenth-century traveller wrote of their capital: "Neither in the houses nor streets was so much dust to be found as would fill an eggshell." Either he was a liar or things have changed. Temne villages look to me exceptionally clean, but have enough red dust in them to fill all the eggshells in Denmark. Every house is built to the same circular pattern, with one segment open to form a veranda. On every veranda hangs a hammock and in every hammock lies a man. These inert male forms, one limp arm perhaps sagging over the hammock's edge, are a sort of Sierra Leone trade-mark.

Outside some of the houses, platforms made of bamboo poles had been erected under a canopy of hand-woven, gaily-patterned cloths. One might have thought them hustings ready for an oratorical orgy. The village was en fête, with flags aloft on bamboo poles and people dressed in party clothes.

"The girls are returning from the Bundu bush"—such was the

explanation. Each girl was to mount the platform outside her home amid the acclamation of her relatives and, for a day, to be treated like the season's beauty queen.

The Bundu is the initiation society for girls corresponding to the Poro for boys, and you are not long in Sierra Leone before you hear a lot about both. When a boy reaches the age of fifteen or sixteen, a Poro "devil" is heard wailing in the bush and arrives at night, well disguised, to carry the lad off to the closely guarded Poro ground. For a woman to set eyes on a "devil" or an initiate is full of danger. Once a boy leaves his home he is dead to his family and must be re-introduced to them under a new name on his return. The boys live a Spartan life in the bush under the absolute authority of the Poro master. Sleeping on sticks and kept awake half the night by dancing, beaten sometimes to learn the mastery of pain, they must absorb the customs, dances and morals of their tribe.[1] The girls receive a similar, if less rigorous, treatment in the Bundu bush, and are taught practical accomplishments like spinning and cooking.

Circumcision often takes place at the start of the ceremonies, not as their climax. No boy must flinch, even slightly, when the operator gets to work with an old razor-blade. The female version is the excision of the clitoris, and must cause dreadful pain. Unlike the male operation, doctors condemn it because the resulting scar-tissue impedes childbirth; and it serves no beneficial purpose whatever. Yet this operation is performed all over the black belt of Africa, from west to east. Millions of girls must suffer from it every year and all the admonitions of missionaries and officials have had only an insignificant effect.

I have never heard a satisfactory explanation of the origin of this barbarous operation, or of its widespread diffusion. Its main effect is, of course, to deprive women of their chance of full sexual pleasure. Is this a masculine attempt to enforce fidelity by removing a part, at any rate, of the temptation to err? A sort of African chastity belt? If so, it seems to have met with little success. Or is it an example of the blind copying of masculine customs—like (in our society) women's uniforms, or joining clubs?

[1] An interesting first-hand account of Poro ceremonies among the Sherbro, near Freetown, is given in *Sierra Leone Story* by Pearce Jervis. For an anthropological summary, see *The Mende of Sierra Leone* by K. L. Little.

C

At the end of the boys' initiation period, which may vary from a few weeks to a year or more, the Poro "spirit" is driven away after a night of feasting and dancing. Next morning the only woman member, a sort of matron, binds the toes of the initiates with moss and thread so as to link them together in token of their lifelong comradeship. Sacrifices are made to ancestors, heads are shaved, vows of secrecy taken and the boys, their bodies smeared with palm-oil, return in procession to their villages as fully-fledged young men. The visible signs of their initiation are rows of little lumps in different patterns on their backs, made by cutting the skin with a razor and inserting small pebbles: another painful operation which must be borne without flinching. These are supposed to be the teeth-marks of the Poro "spirit". They are, roughly, the equivalent of an American undergraduate's fraternity pin.

Indeed, these West African secret societies—of course they are not confined to Sierra Leone—have their replicas on almost every college campus in the United States. Are the so-called Greek letter fraternities, one may reasonably ask (like Negro spirituals and jitterbugging), a part of America's African heritage? Are these Poro and Bundu societies the ancestors of Delta Kappa Epsilon and Alpha Omicron Pi?

There are many resemblances. Campus "hazing" often matches the ordeals endured by Poro and Bundu initiates to prove their hardihood; the rites of induction into fraternal mysteries (although, in the United States, actual circumcision is left out) have the same object and general pattern in both societies, and in both the principle of mutual help between members applies; both societies have secret passwords, insignia and codes. Of course there are differences also. There is only one Poro and one Bundu for all to join, and join all must. In America, only the invited can join a fraternity. Every campus has a large residue of youths and maidens who have not, for one reason or another, received "bids" and may feel themselves to be social outcasts. Such mental cruelty would shock Africans as sharply as their physical cruelty shocks us.

~ 7 ~

The Roman Empire left a legacy of imperial palaces, arenas
and temples; the British will bequeath secretariats, cinemas and
schools. Especially schools, which yearly become more splendid
in size, if not in looks. Unfortunately, architectural grace is a
concept almost unknown to modern empire-builders.

The school at Magburaka, for instance, is a clean, white
barrack. The dormitories are elongated rectangles with so long
a corridor running down one side that you could almost compete
along it for the 100-metre sprint. All is speckless, bare and painfully tidy. It has been left to the boys to add the only touch of
humanity. Each white pillow is embroidered with an uplifting
motto such as: "Charity Envieth Not", "Be Honest With Me
Dear", "Absent Not Forgotten", "God Never Lies", or, perhaps the most ambitious, two intertwined Union Jacks linked
under the phrase: "All Over the British Empire".

The headmaster, Mr. Hugh Clarke, is a Jamaican: he thinks
perhaps (though he has no proof) a Yoruba in origin, and certainly a most intelligent and cultivated man. In his opinion
there is too much benign but softening paternalism in British
Africa today: too much of what one might call the Wenceslas
touch. "Mark my footsteps, good my page, tread thou in them
boldly: thou shalt find the winter's rage freeze thy blood less
coldly." It would be better for the page to strike out a line of
his own and learn to contend with winter's rages. Paternalism
breeds self-pity, an attitude of mind very common among
educated Africans.

All Mr. Clarke's boys are boarders, and each pays a fee of
£7 10s. a year. For that, parents may pass their favourite son
into the ranks of the élite. With school behind him, a promised
land lies in front; the humblest boy can hope for glory greater
than the richest chief's. Even £7 10s. a year is quite out of the
ordinary peasant's reach. But that is no obstacle. A likely boy
is not merely the son of his father, he becomes the investment of
his family. Cousins, uncles, grandfathers, brothers-in-law, step-
brothers, all contribute to his fees. It is like putting money into
a club. The investment matures, the boy gets a job, and must

then contribute in turn to the needs of the cousins, uncles, grandfathers, brothers-in-law and step-brothers who helped him.

To Africans all this is fair, reasonable and fully in accord with tradition. Yet it hamstrings the young men who are being trained to take over their country's management. They must live and die in debt. And it is perhaps the strongest single reason for the all-pervading bribery and corruption which white officials condemn and successful Africans either deny or minimize. A man's first duty is to his family, not to the impersonal department or firm that pays his wages. So long as the African family system continues—and it is the core and soul of African life—so long will bribery and corruption, as we understand the terms, flourish.

Across the way from Magburaka school is an even grander Teachers' Training College, another barrack of a place, for which the British taxpayer has found about a quarter of a million pounds. Full of palatial halls and classrooms, with a craft room eighty feet long, it is intended mainly to serve the Northern Province, where whole districts are still roadless and can be reached only on foot. A few years ago, only three primary schools, taking in a handful of boys, existed in the entire Protectorate. Now it is reckoned that eight out of every hundred children get a schooling of sorts, though one that is often sketchy and short.

Most of the students at this College, when they go forth as teachers, will find themselves instructing pupils in open-sided mud-and-thatch village schools quite without frills. There will be no bedside lamps, flush lavatories and recreation rooms. Is it, then, wise to break these shoots off the branch that bore them and for two years to pamper them in such artificial surroundings, and then to plant them out again in stony ground?

There are two answers. One, that such treatment must raise expectations which can never be satisfied, and so bring the bulk of the students only to discontent and frustration. The other, that you must civilize your leaders, even if it hurts them. Some, at least, will continue to strive after enlightenment; at least they will know what the word means; their very discontent may detonate the charge that must be Africa's salvation.

I do not know which view is right. But looking at these

harsh, impressive structures—impressive in their sheer size and in the contrast between them and the brown mud houses of dusty little Magburaka—it seemed to me that perhaps their creators, like the pyramid-builders, have succumbed to a very human wish to stamp their surroundings with some indelible mark of their professional power and glory. Socrates, they say, instructed his disciples under a tree. All that you need in Africa is a shelter to keep out the rain and a good teacher. The native *barri*—a meeting-house with mud-block walls some two or three feet high and then an open gap between them and the eaves of a well-thatched roof—is the perfect architectural response to the climate, considerably better than those shockingly expensive, graceless structures built of alien and imported materials like cement and steel.

No, if it is just a place to teach children that is needed, or to teach teachers, the simple traditional materials, the cool temporary structures, would suffice, save for a single building proof against damp and insects—the library. The hidden object of these schools is perhaps less to teach children than to impress upon them the grandeur of schooling and to impress upon Africa itself a permanent symbol. Others have done that before. One thinks of Ozymandias' monument in the desert: "Look on my works, ye mighty, and despair." In a century or two, will these new buildings have become the nesting-place of bats, will goats graze among the crumbling walls? Or will they by then appear as ruins preserved for their historic interest among finer, nobler, grander edifices, packed with eager and intelligent youth? Whatever their fate, they are brave experiments. One only wishes that they were also beautiful.

∽ 8 ∽

The road to Mabonto winds up a valley over several rivulets where lilies with lance-shaped, creamy petals shine like stars in hurrying water. In the rains, each brook becomes a torrent and soil is torn off the steep, granitic hills. Forest not long ago protected them; now it has been clear-felled, leaving the soil exposed and ready to sweep down the sun-baked, storm-thrashed hill-sides in yellow cascades. Yet how rich these valleys look, with their flowing streams, their tall brown grass, their generous rainfall, their thick-foliaged trees! Down by the river a few gardens of tomatoes and coco-yams evince fertility.

The truth is, a sort of Mad Hatter's tea-party is going on. We are never told what happened when the Hatter and his guests had moved right round the table, dirtying *all* the crockery. That stage has been reached here.

The shifting cultivator clears his plot of land, exhausts its fertility and moves on to a new patch. Well and good—when time and Nature combined to replenish the soil. Man and land set up a low-level equilibrium. Time has now been foreshortened by European benevolence. Slavery, epidemics and famine, those triple guardians of the balance, have been disarmed. As people multiply, pressure on land increases and its resting period shortens. So crops grow lighter and, to counter that, each man tries to cultivate a bigger plot. This intensifies the pressure and makes matters worse. Cultivation spreads to places where it ought not to be, on hill-sides and slopes; what little forest remains is cleared; rain sweeps the soil away to leave exposed the bare rock; villages are abandoned and crumble away; where women hoed the yams, a lizard with an orange tail basks among the hot stones. So the cycle finishes.

Yet all this could be checked and even reversed. The valley we drove through, marked with erosion as if by leprosy, could be a paradise: the hills terraced, their crests forested, steeper slopes grassed, the bottoms regularly cultivated under a manured crop rotation. But to know how is one thing, to persuade another. Peasants seldom want to change their ways, and by the time they decide, if they ever do, on such a revolution, they may be too late.

We followed a narrow road that runs beside the Pampana river and through a gold-mining concession owned by Mr. Wherling, an Alsatian who has floated a dredger on the stream and lives here in a dark, indefinably Germanic bungalow with his wife and two young assistants. Sometimes the water rises twenty feet in a night, and only immense efforts prevent the dredger from being washed away. At other times the river falls so low that rocks must be blasted out and the jagged-edged chunks hauled up with winches lest they crush the dredger's sides. There is gold here, but it is elusive, and does not behave as gold should. No reef has been found. It is still a mystery whence the specks of metal come.

We drove back through hills that had taken on a misty hue of indigo and seemed to hold all the melancholy and disillusionment of immemorial age. The bush was dark and solitary, the sky soft and creamy as caramel; francolins whirred off the road and later, as darkness fell, nightjars took off on silent wings. So it had lain for untold æons, changeless and indifferent: rocks, grass, trees and river, a landscape without figures: for here, where man is not triumphant, beauty is absolute, but lacks a soul.

Many such lovely valleys lie off a main road lined with villages, each under the patriarchal rule of a grizzle-haired and often bearded chief whose authority seems (as yet) very little weakened by the education of the younger men. One I recall, who showed us his village—we were now in the country of the Mende tribe—owns fifty cows and at least as many wives, some of them "dashed" to him by sub-chiefs to keep relations sweet. In such cases, when the husband's powers can no longer rise to all these occasions, lovers are encouraged to live with the wives, provided they work on the husband's land. Thus the rich man secures free labour and becomes even richer than before. The children are his, too, and will grow up to work for him or, if they are girls, to command a handsome bride-price. To him that hath shall be given, here as elsewhere.

But riches are not everything; the old chief's health is poor. Disappointed in the European doctor in Bo, he went by bush-car to Liberia to consult a famous native practitioner.

"For some kinds of sickness," he said, "native medicines are better than the European."

"I hope the treatment was satisfactory?"

"Partly. I am cured of my swollen belly, but the syphilis is still troublesome."

I saw a bush-car later on—a fascinating contraption with wheels so large they might have come off a penny-farthing bicycle, and between them a little chair roofed with a tattered canopy. Old men of wealth and position are still pushed along forest paths in these vehicles. Younger chiefs have cars. One I met, near Port Loko, is planning to use a tractor to plough hitherto uncultivated Lophira bush for groundnuts. He has built a public swimming-pool, raised money to instal electric light and imported a sound projector with which he gives film shows in his chiefdom. A shy, young-looking man with a stutter, his name is Alikadu Modu and before he became a chief he worked for ten years as a shop-master for the United Africa Company. Now, with the help of an advisory council, he governs 40,000 people.

∽ 9 ∽

The train to Bo
She no agree for go:
The engine she done tire
For lack of plenty fire:
The train to Bo
She no agree for go . . .

This nostalgic little ditty was sung in Burmese jungles and Indian bazaars, and many who had never heard of Bo joined with men of the Sierra Leone Regiment to celebrate this misfortune to the train which runs from Freetown, 120 miles seldom completed in less than ten or twelve hours.

Bo, the capital of the Protectorate, is one of those towns created by Europeans out of a small village which accidentally found itself in a convenient position on the railway line. It has no native character and, so far as one could see, only one industry, the erection of innumerable Government buildings.

The country here is hilly—small, bumpy hills—and wooded, and you feel the airless, heavy presence of the forest all round. You feel, too, that no less stuffy air of hierarchy that broods over almost any small colonial capital. This does not seem to be so much the fault of the hierarchs, who are nearly always charming when you meet them and not at all encased in protocol, as of the system, which contains a certain schoolboy element, a kind of arrested development.

"Never since the heroic days of Greece," says Santayana, "has the world had such a sweet, just, boyish master." True; but not all aspects of boyhood beguile when carried over into manhood.

There goes the head prefect, alerting lesser fry; ingratiating juniors lard their talk with "sirs"; Smith minor has cheeked Bloggs major in the changing room. Here marriage makes things worse; Mrs. Bloggs takes umbrage and Mrs. Smith puts on airs—and how easily umbrage is taken, airs put on, in this steamy atmosphere, amid dragging days! Women are in harems, though they do not know it; their husbands' work is a thing apart, real life centres round leave at home. Here, orders of precedence rule; everyone changes for dinner; men wear ties; on the horizon fitfully flashes the beacon of the C.M.G. Yet all this has its strength also. This is a community transplanted, with standards and values and customs not merely intact but intensified: standards based on absolute honesty, hard work and a sense of order, ingredients in the best administration Africa has ever known.

I slept at Bo in one of a collection of chalets standing among lawns and trees, each with its bathroom, hot water, electric light —nothing could have been more luxurious. These Government rest houses, found now all over West Africa, are as a rule well-run, comfortable and very cheap. One of the evenings I spent here coincided with an all-night farewell party at the club to Mr. Appleyard, a Provincial Commissioner reluctantly retiring after thirty years: a shy, friendly, rather dried-up bachelor of a vintage which stands amazed at the new white palaces going up all round with upstairs bedrooms, electric cookers, immersion heaters and pram-parks. To old Coasters there is an element about these things of the sacrilegious. When they came to West Africa, it was still possible to regard the exploit as a bold adventure. They were going to the White Man's Grave, not to the white woman's paradise. If a man felt compelled to marry, he kept his wife in decent seclusion in England, bringing up children; if he was wise, he kept his freedom, and had plenty of money to spend. Middle-aged bachelors, in Britain rarities, abound in Sierra Leone. As they depart into a retirement they have in theory so long looked forward to but often dread when it arrives, not only a generation but a whole type disappears.

Disappears, that is, from West Africa, but not yet from our planet. There are many years ahead of Mr. Appleyard. (Contrary to their own conviction, retired colonial servants live, as a

c*

rule, almost indefinitely.) At first his thoughts turned, dubiously, to matrimony. Spectacled, bent, fiftyish, used to the comforts of good food and drink, to cheerful service from devoted and time-oblivious Africans; unpunctual, convivial, fond of company yet shy of women—could it be done? Should it be? And if so, how? The partner must be not too young, nor old either; shapely, decorative, *chic*; a good manager, tactful, a sympathetic listener, full of charm and *savoir-faire*; no gauche hoyden, no disappointed spinster, no hard-boiled career-girl would do. Such paragons, do they exist? And, if they do, are they not all snapped up by people twenty years younger? Discouraged, Mr. Appleyard has bought a new car and means to motor slowly home by starting, African fashion, in the opposite direction.

Next day one of the senior officials, Mr. Hodgson, invited to morning coffee a number of politicians whose leader is Dr. M. A. S. Margai, M.B.E., a tall, thin, pipe-smoking man of Mende blood in his late fifties with a dry, humorous expression. He was the first Protectorate man to qualify as a doctor, and a cousin, also now a politician, was the first barrister. Dr. Margai owns a lucrative nursing home but (like Sir Godfrey Huggins) has renounced healing for legislating. Should Sierra Leone reach independence before he retires, he would no doubt be its first Prime Minister.

The whole political development of the Protectorate has taken place in his lifetime. In 1898 the Mende rose in revolt against a proposal by the encroaching British to levy house-tax. Chiefs called out their warriors and set upon any British subjects—inhabitants of the Colony—they could find. About a thousand inoffensive Creoles were massacred, as well as some white missionaries. Two expeditions put down the outbreak, and thirty-three men were hanged.

British authority then slowly spread throughout the Protectorate, which is about the size of Ireland, in order to stop tribal warfare and extinguish slavery. It was only in 1924 that the Governor nominated the first men from the Protectorate to sit on a rudimentary Legislative Council. So Dr. Margai has seen many changes in a wink of time, and is now in command of a Parliamentary majority. His attitude, and that of his colleagues, is one of quiet jubilation. Politically, they at last have the Creoles where they want them, and Dr. Margai, his cousin and some of his friends have become, to all intents and purposes, salaried Ministers in charge of groups of Departments, following the pattern set in Accra.

In Africa there are only politicians, no parties; but since the whole business is a copy of the British system, and since parties are in Britain the correct thing, a politician who has won authority at once starts a party and provides it with a constitution, a secretary and a set of aims. Dr. Margai's is called the People's Party and its aims are unexceptionable: to advance towards self-government, to promote education, to accelerate economic development, to work for political unification. Its organizing secretary, and editor of the intermittent *Observer*, Mr. Cotay, is much more like a politician than Dr. Margai—loquacious, plump, a smooth deliverer of platitudes. "The People's Party includes Creoles as well as Protectorate members," Mr. Cotay emphasized. "Our general secretary is a Creole. We are democratic; we have no animosities."

Dr. Margai was realistic about self-government. "It will come, but we are not ready yet. We have not got the men to run it. We want our friends to go on helping us for some time to come. Above all, we want education."

That is the cry all over Africa. But how to pay for it?

"Taxes must be increased," said Mr. Cotay.

"House tax, Customs duties?"

"Oh, *no*; not the taxes on the people! Syrians should pay more. And diamond mines."

The Sierra Leone Selection Trust mines diamonds with great success near the Liberian border. It now pays in taxation over 40 per cent of its profits and produces one-fifth of the revenue. Mr. Hodgson pointed out that 40 per cent was about as much as the traffic would bear in a speculative business like diamonds, especially as losses both from theft and from illicit mining are already heavy and are growing quickly. One of the quirks of Sierra Leone's administration is that the only properly trained and officered police force belongs to the Colony and is not allowed to penetrate into the Protectorate, where the sole enforcers of law and order are untrained, illiterate Court Messengers under tribal control. In theory, Court Messengers guard the diamond mines. In practice, the only stolen gems ever recovered are found in their huts.

"There's a limit to what can be got from taxation," Mr. Hodgson observed.

The answer to that is simple. "Then we will nationalize the mines, and take *all* the money."

◈ 10 ◈

At Bo School, founded as long ago as 1906 to train the sons of chiefs, a curio survives: a founders' directive presenting ideas on education which have now a period quaintness, like Edwardian hats. No boy, it proclaims, is to be severed from his own people and customs. All must wear native dress and eat native food; learn methods of farming and building better than their own but not utterly foreign; be brought to an understanding of the virtues of honesty, responsibility and hard work. Good English and good manners are to be the corner-stones. "As it is robbery to place the cost of boys' education on a country and thereafter to place them in Government service," they must pay fees.

These traditions have crumbled slowly. The ban on shoes was lifted a few years ago. Carpentry and farming have given way to algebra and English literature, the passing of exams has become, as in all schools, the main objective and the number of School Certificates an efficiency barometer. The school's aspect has changed, too. For years, it rubbed along on mud-block buildings. In replacing them, Bo School has vaulted to the far pole. Here is the old dining-hall, an open-sided *barri* furnished with trestle tables that served for forty years; there the half-built new one, massive as a railway terminus and with three tiers of windows, all steel. (The top windows can only be opened or shut, presumably, with the aid of ladders.) Mountains of cement lie about, yet all the water is carried in kerosene tins from a distant stream.

I watched men laying a splendid floor of Gold Coast mahogany. An assembly hall? No, no, a chemistry lab. Wouldn't a concrete floor suffice? The headmaster shrugged his shoulders. The plans were drawn in Freetown and he had not been consulted.

We came to a sort of patio of solid concrete about thirty feet square, raised five or six feet off the ground, fat pillars supporting the roof. The purpose? No one knew. With orange trees in tubs and vines on trellises, it would make a splendid café.

"We thought," said the headmaster, "that the biology teacher might keep his rabbits here."

All this, and much more, is a gift from the British tax-payer—£117,000 voted so far and at least another £100,000 to come. Bo School has moved a long way from native dress and bare feet, good manners, sound English and improved farming.

For contrast, there is the Roman Catholic Mission School. Packed classes are taught in a long, mud-walled shed divided into sections by homespun curtains. The whole building cost £500. The boys learn their letters from cheerful Irish Fathers who get nothing out of it, materially, themselves. As to their pupils' intellects, you hear the same story everywhere: in early childhood they are sharp as needles but with puberty a dulling of the faculties occurs. The usual explanation is that, onwards from fourteen, a busy sex life uses up so much energy that the boys are too played out to concentrate.

As for the girls, no sooner do they show promise than, all too often, they drop into an *oubliette* of domesticity and are no more heard of by the nuns—mild, amiable, smooth-cheeked, simple Irishwomen encased in starched coifs and long robes, as if in cocoons. Why does their Church insist on this stifling, sweat-provoking uniform? One sees Fathers on trek far more suitably clad in shorts.

I was in Bo on Empire Day, when, by tradition, all the schools parade in front of the Chief Commissioner. It seemed as if every school-child in Sierra Leone was there. Round they trotted behind their banners, shepherded by sturdy teachers, whilst in the burning sun the poor Chief Commissioner, a slight figure under his gleaming topee, held a gloved and no doubt aching hand at the salute. Then came his speech, delivered at attention under the flag to a vast concourse of little black Sambos and their sisters; Noël Coward, one felt, had staged it all; but then an unrehearsed incident intruded. The Seventh Day Adventists had put into the field a squad of shock troops headed by a very formidable American lady, tall, blonde and handsome, a military forage cap tilted over one eye, a captain's sash covered with badges across her bosom and octagonal rimless glasses firmly set on stern eyes.

As the Chief Commissioner's speech ended, the captain rallied her men with ringing accents; surging round, they delivered with full-throated vigour an American college cheer, of the kind that involves acrobats led by cheer-leaders and the spelling out of various words.

"E-M-P-I-R-E—EMPIRE!" they holloaed; and again (for His Honour) "C-H-I-L-D-S—CHILDS! Rah—rah—rah!" In vain His Honour, a shy, correct and sober bachelor, tried to wave them down. Many more Seventh Day Adventists erupted from the ranks of youth and clustered in vociferous circles. In vain the hierarchs and their wives, ranged in order of precedence behind the throne, expressed disdain on frozen faces touched by an occasional icy smile; cheer after cheer volleyed across the field, and might have been volleying still had not some resourceful official thought to bring into action the even lustier strains of the Police band.

·◇· II ·◇·

At Kenema, near the Liberian border, almost the most attractive spot I saw in West Africa—deep forest, inviting hills, clear streams and fresh air—I met one of Sierra Leone's foremost chiefs, Kai Samba.[1] Small in stature, quiet, neat in his movements, self-assured but unpompous, he is more like a civil servant than a chief: good at desk-work, a speaker of excellent English (a copy of *Wingate's Raiders* lay on his desk).

"There are two schools of thought about the future of chiefs," he remarked. "One is, they should try to keep the leadership of the people at the centre, through politics. The other, that they should confine themselves to their districts and recognize changing times. I belong to the second school." And so he has re-

---

[1] There are no less than 161 Paramount Chiefs in the Protectorate, each assisted by a traditional council, the Tribal Authority. An attempt simultaneously to amalgamate and to modernize some of them began in 1946, when District Councils were set up, each one covering a number of chiefdoms. In 1951, these assumed powers to spend money on development. They meet under the District Commissioner's chairmanship.

signed from Executive and Legislative Councils in Freetown in order to give his full time to his chiefdom. Kai Samba is a very shrewd man. His people are intelligent also, but difficult. Quarrels flare up easily amongst them and often end in violence and sometimes death. The D.C. here has had to quell several riots, and has no armed police, indeed no trained police at all, to help him.

It is among the Mende that leopard societies are, or at any rate were, to be found. In 1891 the news reached Freetown that upwards of eighty men suspected of leopard crimes had been burned to death by Mende tribesmen in an impulsive purge. The result was the Human Leopard Society Ordinance of 1895, imposing heavy penalties on any person proved to have in his possession a shaped leopard skin, a three-pronged knife or a medicine known as *borfima*. After a Protectorate was declared over the interior in 1896, the new Governor set up a circuit court which, in seven years, condemned to death for leopard murders eighty-seven men.

In 1912 matters reached such a pitch—108 suspected murderers having been committed for trial—that a Special Commission was sent from England to try the accused men. It sat for over five months and condemned to death a number of the culprits, all of whom had confessed complicity. They were publicly hanged.

Later in my journey, in Nigeria, I was to hear much about contemporary leopard murders,[1] and because of the remarkably close resemblance between the two cults, although separated by thousands of miles and practised by quite different peoples, it is perhaps worth while to describe briefly those of Sierra Leone.

The basic reason for the murders is to procure human fat for the *borfima*, which seems to vary in its composition. One of the Special Commissioners described it thus:[2]

This package contains, amongst other things, the white of an egg, the blood, fat and other parts of a human being, the blood of a cock and a few grains of rice; but to make it efficacious it must occasionally be anointed with human fat and

[1] See pp. 287–290.
[2] *Human Leopards* by K. J. Beatty. Hugh Rees Ltd., 1915.

smeared with human blood. So anointed and smeared, it is an all-powerful instrument in the hands of its owner, it will make him rich and powerful, it will make people hold him in honour, it will help him in the white man's Court, and it certainly has the effect of instilling in the native mind great respect for its owner and a terrible fear lest he should use it hostilely.

Dr. Kenneth Little, in a more recent and thorough study of Mende customs, compiles a rather different list of ingredients. The medicine, he writes: [1]

is made out of skin from the palm of the human hand and sole of the foot and the forehead. There are also parts of certain organs such as the genitals and liver, as well as a cloth taken from a menstruating woman, and some dust from the ground where a large number of people are accustomed to meet. It also contains some rope from a trap from which an animal has escaped; the point of a needle; and a piece of fowl's crop.

All the above items are made up into a bundle and put into a bag, or they may be parcelled up in leaves. Attached to the bundle is a number of strings, perhaps as many as seven. Tied to the end of each string is a hook, sometimes of wood, sometimes of iron. When the owner of the medicine wishes to know if he can safely embark on a certain line of action, he will take the *borfima* out into the bush and throw it with strings attached into the undergrowth. If, on withdrawing the bundle, the strings come away freely and do not get caught, he feels safe in continuing. If, however, the hooks get caught in the branches and are difficult to withdraw, the matter is left over.

The *borfima* requires periodical "re-invigoration", otherwise it will turn on its owner and destroy him. Some *borfima* medicines have to be renewed annually; others more often. The success and power of this medicine depend on the parts of the body mentioned above. The oil, which is prepared from the fat of the intestines, is used to anoint the *borfima* itself and is also used as a rubbing medicine to bring good luck and to give the person so treated a fearsome and dignified appearance. The

[1] *The Mende of Sierra Leone* by K. L. Little. Routledge & Kegan Paul, 1951.

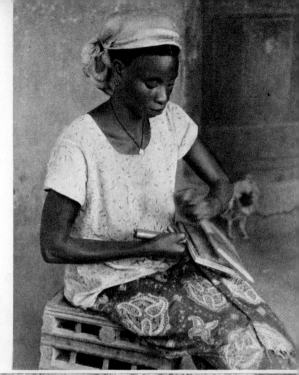

Girl carding cotton for home use

The favourite posture of Sierra Leone

A Sierra Leonian at his loom

Pit sawyers
near Kenema,
Sierra Leone

The ubiquitous
" dash ": a village
chief gets some eggs

" SG will make us all rich ! "

In the fishing quarter of Accra: a man mending nets

oil is sold, therefore, as a sideline and it may be bought by people who are not, in the proper sense, in league with the owners of the medicine. The report is that it is sold in small scent bottles for amounts varying from £5 to £20.

After deciding on a victim, nearly always a youth or maiden, some of the members disguise themselves in leopard skins and kill the victim with a three-pronged knife in such a way as to emulate a leopard's claws. Should they be disturbed, they escape and leave the apprehenders to spread the story that a bush leopard has made an attack—a story everyone is all the more ready to accept in view of the strong, malignant magic known to be at the leopard men's command.

If all goes well, the victim is divided up strictly in order of precedence. It was stated at a trial held in 1913 that one of two leading chiefs had eaten the girl's breasts, the other parts of the belly and scalp (chiefs are served first, just like Governors); the heart was "set aside to be sent to an important and educated member, who was represented at the feast but who did not wish to be present himself". One is left with a lively curiosity about this "educated member" who, like a king at a funeral, was "represented" at the cannibal feast.

A subsequent trial tells us more about him. Born and educated in America, he became a Minister of a Freetown Mission called the United Brethren in Christ, and some years earlier had been tried for a cannibalistic murder in another part of the country and acquitted by a jury of Creoles. At his second trial he averred in his defence that he was in the district only to give magic-lantern lectures in aid of his Mission. He was found guilty of leopard society membership, though not of murder, and banished. Perhaps this sentence was not irksome, since he was a practised speaker on sacred subjects who had raised plenty of money for his Mission in America. Possibly he turned his banishment to good account by signing up for a lecture tour in the United States.

Although satisfaction of the *borfima's* "hunger" appears to have been the main object of the sacrifices, the chairman of the Special Commissioners of 1912–13 makes an interesting guess at their inner meaning. "All the principal offenders", he writes, "were men of mature age past their prime, and I formed the opinion that when they devoured human flesh the idea uppermost in their minds was that they were increasing their powers of virility."

The last leopard murder to be detected by authority was at Kenema, rather over ten years ago. Cannibalism is in abeyance, but few believe it to be extinct. There is, indeed, no reason why it should be; *borfimas* no doubt still need ointment, the forests are deep, disapproving white men few and far between. Informers are nowhere honoured, and police do not exist. It would be strange if the last leopard man had eaten his last meal in Sierra Leone.

∾ 12 ∾

Round Kenema the deep forest stretches far into Liberia, which lies across a river and can be visited by bush-car or cycle, for there are no motor roads. Occasionally the D.C. here corresponds with his opposite number. Letters arrive by runner couched in flowery English and written in a flowing hand, evasive, it seems, in detail and signed each time with a different name, since Liberian administrators appear to change even more often than British ones.

In this steamy climate with its ample rainfall, and in forest soil packed with fertility, things grow profusely and need very little care. Cocoa and palm oil are the staples: ideal crops for Africa, for they demand no cultivation, you simply go out and lop the ripened fruits, which your wives carry home. To grow food crops, however—rice or cassava—you must first "brush" away the bush or forest, and this is hard work. Whole villages turn out for "brushing" parties but, even so, the bush is thick, heat oppressive and the price of palm oil and cocoa satisfactorily high; and so, in the words of the D.C.:

"These people live in one of the most fertile places in the world, and they're in danger of not being able to feed themselves. In this climate, fertility runs down quickly, and so the land is cropped for two years only, then rested for ten, or even longer. As the people multiply, they have to go farther and farther away to brush new land, so they reduce the period of fallow and the crops get lighter and harvests poor—it's the old story. . . . We urge them to practise rotations, make compost, terrace slopes, but propaganda just runs off their backs. Now we're trying to make them cultivate the swamps, where yields of rice are much higher; but they won't."

He turned to an ancient headman standing by. Everyone else was out brushing, save for a few old dames and small children and a man squatting in the shade and slowly, methodically, sleepily, sewing together slices of palm leaf into roofing "tiles".

"Will your people eat swamp rice?" asked the D.C.

"They do not like it. Swamp rice is not so sweet."

Mr. Dawkins grinned at him. "You know the real reason. Growing it is harder work."

"It is very hard," the headman agreed. "If the Government would send us a tractor . . ."

Talk of tractors has got about everywhere. The tractor is a talisman: it will do the work for you: it is the best of all the white man's ideas. Europeans are like insects, they itch and bite and prick and nag—do this, do that, work harder, never rest—but their tractors are different. Miraculously *they* brush, hoe, plant; on them a young man sits in shirt and hat proudly controlling so much noise and power; from the shade we shall be able to watch them working for us, and our bellies will be full. Send us tractors with their young men, and leave us in peace.

We left him, walking back through a cloud of heavy, drenching, sickly-sweet scent, like a concentration of syringa. *Robusta* coffee was in full bloom. Tight little clumps of waxy white blossom in the axils of green, glossy leaves created a screen of scent around the village.

Two pit sawyers worked at their task. They had heaved a tree-trunk to a platform overhead; with remarkable precision they were sawing it lengthwise into planks. Their long saw gave out steadily, rhythmically, its harsh note like a leopard's call, and the tangy smell of new-sawn timber mingled its astringent freshness with the coffee's cloying odour.

On the road, every man we passed bore on his head a tray and on the tray three or four calabashes of palm wine, frothing at their narrow necks, rivulets of foam running down the sides of

the fat yellow gourds. The men walked with slightly bent knees
to prevent jarring. How happy to live in a land where wine is
to be drawn from trees for the pain of climbing up and fixing a
calabash or bottle to the trunk! No tax, no hours, no bills, and
the poorest man can drink like a king. No wonder the Mende,
like other African peoples, spend a great part of their lives in a
pleasing state of semi-drunkenness.

Towards evening, when the bite is out of the sun, women go
fishing with very large butterfly nets. Naked, they walk up-
stream, sweeping their nets before them and occasionally scooping up a small silver barbet or other perch-like victim. The
catch appears meagre, but they enjoy the sport; the cool water
washes away the sweat of hoeing; the sun is amiable and sparkles
on the river; blue and carmine bee-eaters dip their beaks in the
water's edge; children, slippery as chocolate fishes, play and
scamper on the banks. This is an hour of freedom and pleasure;
the women gossip as they wade about and care less for the sport
than for the occasion. When the sun withdraws behind the
forest, outlining the dark, drooping crests of palms, they sling
their catch over their shoulders, wind their cloths around their
waists and tramp home to the evening meal—rice flavoured
with herbs, chillies and palm oil—partaken in the smoky, familiar fug of their dark, thatched houses, with all the family
gathered round the pot.

∿ 13 ∿

I spent my last day on a beach not far from Freetown. White
sand, azure ocean, drenching sunlight, palm trees by the water's
edge; and, meandering across the beach, a little stream so warm
that to lie in it, flat on the sand, was to be immersed in a hot
bath. Naked boys passed with a clutch of little fishes they had
taken in their miniature cast-nets. They stared for a while at
our curious, reclining figures, which must have looked to their
eyes raw, like unbaked clay, slug-like and unshapely, and passed
on, pressing the soles of their nimble feet into the wet sand.

The sea was clear, buoyant and gentle, the very sharks too idle
to molest humans, we were told. Green hills rose behind the

white beach; no houses were in sight; even the birds slept. The lapping of the sea was all that could be heard. It seemed like paradise.

"Yes, for a change," a woman agreed. "But tonight we shall go home and dine on the veranda and go to bed, and tomorrow all my housekeeping will be done by ten o'clock. There'll be morning coffee, and back to lunch; the afternoon's siesta and tea; then the beach again, or tennis at the club; then drinks, a bath, a dinner-party. . . . The trouble is that no woman here, unless she has babies, has enough to do."

We drove back to Freetown through clouds of evening dust. The shabby town sweltered, but a breeze cooled the lofty European bungalows. Seen from their verandas, the packed and shoddy little dwellings below became, as dusk fell, beads of light, lovely as a net of fallen stars.

Next day I took the launch across the bay to Lungi airport, half a day's journey from Freetown. At the Customs, a dejected but resigned Syrian was made to unpack every suit-case and spread women's underwear all over the counter; two tall Hausa traders sat in silence in a corner clasping their luggage, which consisted (as it always seems to) of a kettle each; a woman returning to England was in trouble over some avocado pears. They had been given her, a present, too late to weigh. An African official, full of charm and courtesy, put the basket on the scales and computed a crushing charge for over-weight.

"I'll leave them behind," the passenger decided.

The clerk looked shocked. "But you *want* them?"

"They're too expensive."

The young man was quite upset. After attending to another passenger he returned and smiled conspiratorially at the passenger.

"I have written you a label. But please don't tell the Manager."

Should she reward his kindness? If she did, wouldn't she be bribing an official—a serious offence against white law? If she didn't, wouldn't she be unreciprocal—a serious offence against black manners? She didn't want to be churlish, she didn't want to break the law. She couldn't refuse to take the avocados. . . . Unhappily, she wandered away. At the last minute, during the embussing ceremony, she darted back and thrust into his hand an assortment of loose change. He smiled rewardingly, and bowed; guiltily, she fled to the bus. It was wrong, no doubt, but she was glad that she had done it. She saw him through the window waving gaily at the departing bus.

THE GOLD COAST

A NOTE ON
THE GOLD COAST

POPULATION: In 1953 the total was 4,478,000—about 35 per cent higher
than in 1931. Of the three divisions, the Colony contained about
2,456,000, the Northern Territories just over 1,100,000 and
Ashanti rather over 910,000. The British-administered part of
Togoland, a Trust Territory, contained 416,000. There were
7,100 British and 1,930 Syrians and Lebanese. The Asante, Ewe
and Fante are the largest tribes.

CAPITAL: Accra, with a population of about 150,000.

AREA: 91,842 square miles, of which the Northern Territories (mainly
savannah) cover over 30,000, Ashanti (mainly rain-forest) about
24,000 and the Colony a trifle under 24,000 square miles. Togoland covers 13,040 square miles. The eastern boundary marches
with French-administered Togoland, the western with the Haute
Volta and the Ivory Coast, and to the south lies the Gulf of
Guinea.

TRADE: The economy is dominated by cocoa. Exports of this commodity were valued in 1953 at over £56,000,000 out of a total of
just under £90,000,000. Gold comes next in importance, then
timber and diamonds. Goods to the value of £72,767,000 were
imported—an increase over 1950 of nearly one-fifth—of which the
principal were cotton piece goods, foodstuffs and drink, vehicles
(bicycles included), cement and tobacco. As an index of prosperity,
imports of strong drink increased by one-third, and 2,658 private
cars arrived.

HISTORY: Commerce with Europe was started in 1471 by the Portuguese, who built Elmina Castle in 1482 and for the next century
monopolized the trade in gold. The first recorded English voyage
was made in 1553 by Thomas Windham. In the sixteenth and
seventeenth centuries the slave trade attracted first the Dutch, who
drove out the Portuguese, and then the Swedes, Brandenburgers,
Danes and English, who established themselves at Cape Coast
Castle in 1662. Trade was conducted by Chartered Companies
until the expense of maintaining forts and garrisons, and the growing intransigence of the Ashanti, led to the transfer of the settlements to the Crown in 1821. Friction with the Ashanti continued
throughout the nineteenth century (there were seven "wars" in all)
until their final conquest in 1900, and the expulsion of the ruling
Asantehene, or King, Prempeh. In 1850 the coastal areas were
separated from Sierra Leone and given their own Legislative Council, only to be handed back again to be administered from Free-

town in 1865, and again redeemed in 1874 and declared a Protectorate. In 1896 the advance of the French and Germans provoked the British into negotiating treaties in the interior and extending the Protectorate into the Northern Territories. In 1898–99 boundaries were defined, and in 1901 all the regions south of Ashanti were declared a Colony.

GOVERNMENT: In 1946 a reconstituted Legislative Council covering the Colony and Ashanti (not the Northern Territories) became the first African colonial legislature to have a majority of its indigenous inhabitants. After civil disturbances in 1950, an all-African committee under the chairmanship of an African Judge, Sir Henley Coussey, made recommendations which formed the basis of a new constitution introduced early in 1951. This provided for an Executive Council (or Cabinet) presided over by the Governor and consisting of three officials and eight African Ministers, headed by a Prime Minister (Dr. K. Nkrumah), and drawn from a Legislative Assembly of whose eighty-four members, seventy-five are elected by popular vote on an unrestricted franchise which includes women. A new constitution came into effect in 1954, providing for a wholly elected Legislative Assembly of 104 members and a Cabinet, normally presided over by the Prime Minister, consisting entirely of Africans drawn from the Assembly, over which an African Speaker (Sir Emmanuel Quist, Kt., O.B.E.) presides. Thus the Gold Coast achieved virtual self-government, with only defence, external affairs and the police reserved to the Governor. The Assembly legislates for the Northern Territories and Togoland as well as for the Colony and Ashanti. In local affairs, a rapid change is taking place from the system of Native Authorities, consisting of chiefs with their councils of elders, to a system of District Councils of whom two-thirds are elected by popular vote and the remaining one-third drawn from traditional authorities.

GOLD COAST

Miles 0   50   100

THE GOLD COAST

❧ I ❧

ACCRA is like a larger version of one of those towns of the American South that are full of growth, bustle and revolt against the legend of Tobacco Road. Here is the same flatness and sticky, airless heat, the same bare streets with ugly concrete buildings and, on the outskirts, a mess of shanties, leantos and squalid little cabins; the same treeless indifference to style and grace and the same human animation, colour and profusion. The country round is brown and unexpectedly dry, the native vegetation scruffy bush and tufty, fibrous grass, the soil poor and sandy. A narrow coastal plain with low rainfall here intervenes between the forest belt and a green Atlantic, torpid under tropic heat.

There is nothing torpid about the people. They like excess: excess of colour, of laughter, of wealth, of leisure; excess of guile, passion and generosity, of greed, fecundity and ambition. You feel this in the market, packed (like all markets) with chatterers but especially remarkable for the size, vigour and astuteness of the women traders, who hold a position unique, I should think, in Africa. Strong as buffaloes, large-boned, strident, gaily dressed in patterned cloths with little jackets, either plump and soft-fleshed as marshmallows or else lean as old leather, their faces look imperious and uncompliant, like the faces of cattle-dealers in English country towns.

Their god is money and they adore him constantly; their lives are happy because faith and works are one. They are down at their stalls by six in the morning and stay there till dark, concocting behind piles of printed cotton, silk and velveteen, or in dusty alley-ways between stalls of bright-hued vegetables and toilet preparations, chilli-flavoured stews into which they dip lumps of pounded yam and cassava, known as *fu-fu*, to stuff into the mouths of the children who cluster round. This is their life; all day long they bargain, gossip, argue, stir the pot, pound the *fu-fu*, suckle babies, greet friends. Somewhere a husband is working, idling or trading too: driving, perhaps, one of those

overcrowded lorries that hurtle over red roads up to the French
frontier or into Togoland, bearing mammies to distant bargains; or, nearer, carpentering on the margins of Accra's side-
streets at a bench set up in the shade of gin-shop or godown.
These husbands are, in a sense, adjuncts, like male spiders; it is
the market women who make the money and call the tune.

How much money they can make astonished me. Mr. Fitz-
gerald, general manager of the United Africa Company, told me
that one or two of his customers receive a monthly credit of up to
£2,000, and many more of sums up to £1,000 a month. A successful trader may see a profit of well over £100 a month—and
no taxes. Nearly all the mammies are illiterate and carry in their
heads intricate multiple sums. The trading firms have no security
beyond the woman's reputation; often they do not even know
her address. Yet it is the rarest thing in the world for one of
them to default, and if any mishap should befall, her debts are
always settled in full by her family.

I spoke to a mammy who wore a large straw hat on the back of
her head and put her arms akimbo on wide hips wrapped in a
cloth patterned in orange, claret and sea-green. Her close-
waisted bodice had flounces over the shoulders and buttoned
tight over generous dusky breasts. Her laugh was deep and
masculine, shaking her whole body; there was about her a
generosity like that of good burgundy, yet a hardness too; beside
such an Amazon I could but feel synthetic, bloodless and deeply
conscious of an empty quiver—like a discarded ice-cream cone
beside a cornucopia.

She spoke very little English, and roared with laughter at
everything I said. We soon got on to politics; they permeate the
air.

"CPP!" she said, striking her bosom with joy. "All the market
—all CPP! All SG! All Free Dom!"

These are magic passwords, SG for self-government and now
Free Dom. Once again she roared with laughter and slapped her
thigh. "SG makes us all rich!" SG swam before us like a vision
of a mighty god or emperor in cloth of gold and purple, pledged
to endow us all with joy, wealth and Free Dom—surely some
ambrosial, cockle-warming mead—with Kwame Nkrumah as his
chancellor.

Dr. Nkrumah will become a legend, as Aggrey did. To begin with, he is said to be the son of a market woman. Perhaps he, too, played about among stalls and open gutters from morning light till nightfall, learning how to bargain and sell. Perhaps that is one reason why the market women love him; and he, for his part, is the first African to bring women into politics. The constitution of 1949 enfranchised them, and Nkrumah saw in this a great opportunity. An angler of genius, he baited and hooked the plumpest fish in the electoral pool. The market mammies could break any politician; with their support, he has at his command the nervous system of the Gold Coast. Perhaps by luck, perhaps by intent, he is a bachelor, in Africa a very rare phenomenon. This serves to set him apart in women's eyes. It enables him, moreover, to aver from the platform that every woman in the Gold Coast is his bride. At public meetings, women shower him with gifts of eggs, fowls, fruit and other provender, and sometimes currency notes.

In appearance, Kwame Nkrumah is a slender man in his early forties, of middle height, with a mop of frizzy hair, big soulful eyes, a sultry, sensual expression and a trace of petulance, of *prima donna* touchiness, in his manner. He is, I am sure, a born actor, with all the magnetism, emotional sensitivity and *panache* of the good player. To say this is not to suggest insincerity. A true actor believes entirely in the reality of his characters. Nkrumah's part is that of the saviour of his people from foreign oppression. To give point to the part he has had to invent the oppression, but that was not difficult, nor in his eyes wrong. Nationalism is a passion, not an exercise in logic, and to passion's servant all means are justified.

He was born in a part of the western Gold Coast known as Apolonia, not far from Axim, the son of a goldsmith. He went to school—thirty years ago not many lads had this chance—and then to Achimota, where he took a four-years' course at the Teachers' Training College. He taught at Elmina and became headmaster of the Axim Catholic Junior School. Here he grew interested in politics and ambitious for wider scope in journalism. He went then to America. This was, no doubt, the decisive act of his career. He was not rich, but the African family system provides for the ambitious just as it relieves the distressed. In

1935, at the age of twenty-six, Kwame Nkrumah entered Lincoln University in Pennsylvania, to study theology and anthropology; he gained the degree of Bachelor of Sacred Theology in 1942. He was popular, it seems, with his classmates, who in 1939 voted him the Most Interesting Man of the Year and composed in his honour the following lyric:

> *Africa is the beloved of his dreams,*
> *Philosopher, thinker, with forceful schemes.*
> *In æsthetics, politics, all, he's in the field;*
> *Nkrumah, 'très intéressant', radiates appeal.*

The Lincoln year-book of the same period observes that "he graduated a fine and polished gentleman intent on the economic resurrection of his beloved native land".

Nkrumah decided to read law, and with this intention came to England after some eight years in the United States. In London, he made contact with many of his own countrymen and from them learnt of great political changes: above all, of the formation of a party pledged to work for quick and complete self-government. This was the United Gold Coast Convention, under the leadership of Dr J. B. Danquah.

Dr. Danquah was looking for an astute, hard-working secretary for his new organization, which he hoped would carry him high on a wave of liberation to the office of the first Prime Minister. The name of this unknown but promising young Gold Coaster was put forward, and in December, 1947, Mr. Nkrumah returned to his native land as general secretary of the U.G.C.C.

Alas for Dr. Danquah's hopes! The nest had taken in a cuckoo. The U.G.C.C. was managed in a way never before seen in Africa. This industrious young man introduced American methods of party management. He sent forth branch secretaries to rally country-wide support; beat the drum of race-hatred; and introduced himself to the public in a number of inflammatory speeches going for the Government with an envenomed rancour that, anywhere else but in a British dependency, would have landed him in jail.

By February, 1948, a boycott of European goods had been organized and, on the last two days of that month, rioting and looting broke out in Accra. An ex-Servicemen's procession was planned to march to Christiansborg Castle, the Governor's residence, then occupied by a most peace-loving civil servant from the Colonial Office, Sir Gerald Creasy—a man who would be reluctant, one feels sure, to crush a spider, though meticulous in doing so should his duty demand it. The police ordered the excited marchers to take a different route, but they paid no attention, and pressed down a road beside the sea leading to the Castle. A single British superintendent, Mr. Imray, supported by ten men with rifles, came out to halt the mob, perhaps 2,000 strong, which continued to surge forward, hurling stones. With great courage, and after the mob had disregarded all his warnings, commands and bugle-calls, Mr. Imray seized a rifle from one of his men and opened fire; the crowd fled, sustaining the modest casualties of two killed and four or five wounded, to join the looters who had meanwhile broken into European and Syrian shops in Accra.

For the rest of the afternoon and part of next day, a good time was had by nearly all, especially when the gin and whisky in the Kingsway Stores were discovered and passed, in part, over the wall of the prison, and when the doors of this old fort were broken in and drunken convicts escaped to join the fun. By afternoon, a battalion of the Gold Coast Regiment had brought the situation under control. The total casualty roll was fifteen killed and 115 injured, the great majority of these by stones and broken glass encountered during looting of the shops.[1] Excited telegrams were meanwhile despatched to the Secretary of State in London, with copies to the world Communist Press, claiming that unarmed ex-Servicemen had been slaughtered in cold blood, civil government had broken down and only an officer of the U.G.C.C., "with a short speech and wave of hands", had been able to restore order. Invited to Christiansborg Castle, this same individual met with "scenes of utter resignation". The D.C. then "summoned him to Accra to disperse the looters". The Working Committee of the U.G.C.C. declared themselves, in the name of the "oppressed, inarticulate, misruled and misgoverned people",

[1] A full account is to be found in the White Paper Colonial No. 231 of 1948, "Report of the Commission of Enquiry Into Disturbances in the Gold Coast", the so-called Watson report.

to be "prepared and ready to take over interim government". Their offer was not at the time accepted, and shortly afterwards six leading office-holders of the Convention, including Dr. Danquah and Kwame Nkrumah, were apprehended under an emergency order from the Governor and removed from Accra.

They were soon released; and now came Mr. Nkrumah's great opportunity. He was the man of the hour. The prestige of the U.G.C.C., too, stood high. Mr. Nkrumah, judging his moment, and in a flood of publicity, resigned from the Convention and announced that he would form a party of his own. Thus, in June, 1949, the Convention People's Party was born.

It was a bold, almost a foolhardy, act. Kwame Nkrumah had been back in the country for less than two years; twenty months, in fact. Hitherto unknown, he lacked influential friends and now incurred the enmity of nearly all the active nationalists. He was openly challenging the country's tried and seasoned political leader; a man of great ability, practised eloquence and high prestige. But Mr. Nkrumah was a match even for the shrewd old barrister. He denounced the U.G.C.C. as over-cautious, hidebound and out of date. He appealed to the young, the impatient, the semi-educated, the under-privileged, the half-baked.

He succeeded. In a very short while the new party had swept the country and Danquah's following had dwindled to a sad and angry rump. The red, green and white flag of the CPP flew in every village and had been painted on the bonnet of almost every bus and lorry. Kwame Nkrumah's portrait was everywhere; thousands flocked to hear him speak. Less than a year later he organized a country-wide general strike, remarkably successful considering that the technique, the whole conception was new, and a trade union framework lacking. Once more he was arrested, and once more turned this to his advantage. The Party gathered strength, directed from prison; a new constitution, devised by an all-African committee presided over by that wise and distinguished judge, Sir Henley Coussey, was quickly brought in; and Mr. Nkrumah was summoned from prison to preside as Leader of Government Business over the first predominantly African team of Ministers to assume the responsibilities of Government. On his release from prison he received the greatest ovation in Accra's history; and since then he and

Accra: in the old slave market

Street scene in Accra

A mass literacy class in the bush near the French frontier

The Prime Minister, Dr. Kwame Nkrumah, on his triumphal processio
from the jail to the Cabinet in February, 1951. *Photo: Public Relations De*

The chief of Bawku outside his house, whose walls are decorated with cowbones

A chiefs' meeting in the Northern Territories

A carpenter at his roadside bench

A skilled worker at the UAC Sawmills, Samreboi

those imprisoned with him for sedition wear, on public occasions, a white Gandhi cap bearing the letters "PG", for Prison Graduate.

I met Dr. Nkrumah in his office in the Secretariat. (He received an honorary doctorate from Lincoln University in 1951.) He was in a bad humour that morning, occasioned by a waspish paragraph about him in one of the London newspapers; was brusque to his European male secretary; and, while frank enough in answering questions, seemed so steeped in his serious purpose, his messianic message, as to see small place for friendliness or laughter. (This may be his public pose, however; I was told that off-duty he can be a light-hearted and amiable companion.) Ambition is his driving force. He means to be master not merely of the Gold Coast but of a pan-African union embracing all the territories of the Guinea Coast at present under French and British tutelage. He means to build a new Ghana, a great African empire, with himself as Cæsar. For this he will work, persevere, deny himself, scheme and sacrifice. For this he has forsworn the fat but enervating prizes sought by so many of his followers—wine, women and display.

The constitution, introduced in 1951, gives him a Prime Minister's position at the head of a Cabinet of seven African and three European Ministers.[1] Complete independence is his aim. Questions of defence and questions of trade he brushes aside—"those can be settled when the time comes". But—"we have the men to run the country ourselves". Office has sobered him, and the other leaders of the CPP. His speeches are now much less inflammatory and a note of caution has crept in: "We must not go too fast." This galls some of his more impatient followers.

Dr. Nkrumah's rise is something new in Africa, not because he seeks power—there is nothing at all new in that—but because the ways in which he has gained and now holds it are alien. African tribes had evolved, before the European advent, an

[1] These Europeans were subsequently (1954) replaced by African Ministers appointed by the Prime Minister; thus the Gold Coast became the first ex-colony to have an all-African Cabinet. Most of the senior civil servants are still Europeans, and the Governor remains responsible for foreign policy, defence and internal security. Complete "SG" will soon abolish these restraints.

D

elaborate and most effective system of curbing the abuse of power by their rulers through councils, elders and priests. All this has now gone by the board. As yet, Africa has no technique for curbing people like Dr. Nkrumah. He has the ball at his feet. With a few Western-trained, ambitious men at the centre, and at the periphery a mass of rather credulous and unsophisticated persons whose age-old social structure is in rapid decay, there seems to be no limit to what can be done.

People who recognize the dangers look to education to put matters right. There is little time. Two children out of every three still receive no schooling, and education for the great majority merely consists of learning to read and write. Everything really hinges on what the newly literate will read, on what will shape their minds. In fact, their reading matter is the newspapers whose editors, very often, obsessed by politics, use their "local rags" merely to traduce authority with vulgar abuse that, in other countries, would land them in serious trouble, and to whom objective truth is a stranger.

∿ 2 ∿

As Prime Minister, Dr. Nkrumah has little time to attend to details of party management. This is entrusted mainly to his lieutenant, Mr. K. A. Gbedemah, Minister of Commerce and Industries, to whom I was presented in a block of light, airy, prefabricated offices hastily run up to enfold a flock of new bureaucrats. Round each Minister hovers an attentive young European secretary, shining with correct deference and gallantly determined to find in his master the quality of a Palmerston or a Churchill.

Mr. Gbedemah, another ex-school teacher, is easier company than the Prime Minister. He displays an engaging alertness, a friendly smoothness of manner. You know where you are with Mr. Gbedemah; you have met his like before on party platforms, in public relations offices and in the sales departments of successful businesses. He is shrewd, fluent, well-dressed, self-confident; you feel that he enjoys ample food and drink and the sweets of office, which are indeed succulent, consisting of a salary of £2,500 a year (a lot in a country where the annual unskilled wage is about £70), plus a free car, a low-rented house, an allowance for a secretary and other perquisites. Ministers' Permanent Secretaries, incidentally, are all European.

By the test of results, Mr. Gbedemah's organizing ability must be highly rated. Perhaps the Party's most remarkable feat has been to keep its coffers full. Dr. Nkrumah's American experience taught him the value of propaganda, and also its technique. CPP vans tour the country carrying Assembly-men and other speakers right out into the country districts. They hold enthusiastic rallies; produce and money come rolling in. All this is built around the personal appeal of the Prime Minister, which this incident will illustrate.

At a market, a man was taking photographs, or at least appearing to do so, for seven shillings and sixpence apiece. For this the customer received no print, but a promise that the picture would be given to the Prime Minister, who would provide its original with a well-paid job when "SG" came. Needless to say, Dr. Nkrumah knows nothing of many of the things that are done in his name. The mere facts that they are done, and that people believe them, testify to his hold.

The third African Cabinet Minister remarkable for competence and personality is Mr. Botsio, Minister of Education, who has boldly taken on the task of introducing free schooling for all. Out of a population of some 4,500,000, well over 1,000,000 must be of school age. At present only about 300,000 go to school. The new Government has passed a bill to abolish the small fees hitherto paid in the lower standards, and to make a six-year primary course compulsory for every child.

Where are the schools to come from? There is no time to build them all, no materials, not enough money or labour.

"The children must be taught under the trees."

Who is to teach them under the trees? There are not nearly enough trained teachers as it is, far less an adequate new supply to draw upon.

"The older ones must teach the small."

It is a bold, determined spirit, and deserves to succeed. Whether the children will get much education out of it remains to be seen. Professionals are sceptical. But Teacher Training Colleges are being rushed up and expanded to keep pace, if they can, with the demand. Even so, there are under 2,000 young men and women in training, a quite inadequate number to cope with trebled forms. Nor is it easy to recruit more teachers in large numbers, since the pool of secondary school pupils includes, at present, less than 7,000 boys and girls. This is not a large reservoir of talent to feed all the professions in the country when immediate "Africanization" is the rage. Inevitably, the schools are having to fall back on young men and women with next to no training at all.

The Cabinet is said to be working together as a team with a great deal more success than anyone had expected, and for this much of the credit goes to Sir Charles Arden-Clarke, who presides. There is a rock-like solidity, as well as a shrewd, alert openness of mind, about this massive and good-looking Governor that has inspired among these touchy and at first suspicious nationalists that trust and respect which alone could launch the new system. Sir Charles Arden-Clarke started his career in Northern Nigeria; he knows Africa and loves it and has from the first believed that this experiment in Anglo-African partnership, leading to a British abdication in an atmosphere of mutual goodwill, can be made to work. He has not merely carried out official policy, he has himself done more than anyone to hatch that policy and give it shape. Dignity blends in his nature with humour and he is no "imperial icicle", as Africans have aptly named a certain type of British official. His capacity for prolonged hard work and his even temper in Accra's steamy heat astonish all observers. Both Britain and the Gold Coast have been fortunate in finding such a man at such a time; very few of its former Governors have matched his calibre.

∾ 3 ∾

Nothing struck me more, as I drove round the country, than the number of CPP outposts in so many small towns. The office may be in a tiny mud-walled room or the corner of a cocoa warehouse, but it is there, its incumbent generally a young man from that semi-educated no-man's-land lying between the peasant farmer and the university graduate: a small trader, a lorry-owner, a school-teacher, a sanitary inspector or produce weighing clerk. Outside stands a bamboo pole, and on each pole flies the CPP flag.

One sees these flags everywhere, and they have a deeper meaning that I at first realized. Flags have always been the prerogative of chiefs. A ruler wishing to enter the domain of another ruler must ask permission to carry through his flag, and to plant your flag in another man's territory is a challenge to battle. Flags, in fact, as in Europe, are symbolic, and the CPP uses them symbolically. No permission is asked to fly them, and each flag nailed to its pole in the village street is an open insult to the chief of the district.

For the CPP is not just a political party; it is the spearhead of a revolution directed not only, or even in the end mainly, against European overlords, but against the established order of things, the system of chiefs. For so long as time runs, the tribes of the Gold Coast have been governed by these potentates and their advisers. The British recognized them and endowed them with even greater powers, in some directions, than they held before—or perhaps it should be said, weakened the power of their traditional advisers, leaving them more untrammelled. At the same time, by themselves over-ruling, on occasion, a chief's decision, the chiefs' ultimate authority was undermined.

Times are changing fast. In this the main factor has been, and is, the British resolution not so much to let the people of the Gold Coast govern themselves (they did that before), as to induce them to do so on the British pattern. Just as Spaniards were ready to go to any lengths, in the sixteenth century, to ensure that Central Americans embraced Christianity, so are the British quite determined that, whatever the results, Africans shall practise parliamentary democracy.

It is strange, this swing-over from faith in God to faith in a political system, and no doubt historians will one day define the causes. For whatever reason, democracy is our religion and members of the Colonial Service a highly disciplined and paid cadre of missionaries trained to spread the gospel of elections, votes, local councils, parliaments, ministers, bureaucracies, free speech, high taxes and all the attributes of the welfare state. Because it is difficult (though not impossible) for illiterates to vote, and certainly impossible for them to study with suitable gravity and attention the claims of the various candidates, "education" (which in this context means learning to read and write) is a prerequisite to democracy. Reduced to its bare bones, the modern thesis is that everyone must learn to read and write so as to be able to vote and become a good democrat: a close parallel to the belief ascribed to an older generation that everyone must learn to read and write so as to be able to read the Bible and become a good Christian.

The outcome will of course depend on whether Africans really want the kind of democracy we think they ought to want. Our version derives from Greek philosophy and from the Christian doctrine that all men are equal in the sight of God. Souls are of equal value, and all opinions, at the polling booth, of equal weight; and the worst blasphemy is dictatorship.

But equality is not an African notion at all. In African theology, spirits reflect the inequality of the world they lived in. It would be absurd to postulate equality between the soul of a slave and the soul of a chief. On earth every man has his rights, certainly, but all men's rights are not the same. The chief, who is the link between the world of spirits and the world of men, has powers both divine and temporal; and Africans are hierarchical to the marrow, not egalitarian. "We do not want to be governed by principles, we want to be governed by men." So an African once said to me; and there he went to the heart of the matter.

The greatest obstacle to Dr. Nkrumah's grasp of absolute power is not the British—very much the contrary, the British are his props and supporters—but the chiefs of tradition.

Lip-service must be paid to custom and to Africa's hereditary rulers; behind it, the CPP leads the revolt against both. Yet this cannot be seen as a straight fight between old and new, reaction and progress. Some of the young chiefs are much better educated than their CPP rivals and just as anxious for independence and reform. Some of the CPP's supporters are elderly rogues who see which side their bread is buttered. The issue is rather between two sets of men contending for power, one traditional in outlook, one exotic. In this the CPP appears to hold all the aces. Nkrumah, Gbedemah, Botsio and the rest are playing the hand with skill. Wherever a chief has made himself unpopular, either through too much graft or too much discipline, CPP agents first whip up, or perhaps merely canalize, popular discontent, and then organize a campaign to de-stool (that is, depose) the offender.

De-stooling is an old custom. In no part of Africa do people so often dismiss their rulers. (Perhaps it is this safeguard that has maintained the system amid so volatile a lot of citizens.) In olden times, however, de-stooling was a great deal less frequent than it is today. It is the CPP's notion—a sound one, like most aspects of their public relations—that frequent accusations of corruption and abuse of power, true or not, discredit the whole institution of chieftainship; so they bring cases left and right. Even a most respected member of the Executive Council, relied upon by a succession of Governors for advice, was a victim of such charges. The committee of enquiry set up by the Government cleared him, but his position had by then been made so intolerable that he resigned.

·❧ 4 ❧·

As a result of leadership, skill and hard-hitting propaganda, the CPP won 90 per cent of all votes at the first general election, held early in 1951. Sincere democrats are perturbed, and wait in some anxiety for a rival party to emerge. There are plenty of opponents. Chief amongst them is Dr. J. B. Danquah, who nurses a hand still bleeding from Nkrumah's bite.

He invited me to tea in a two-storey concrete-block house in Accra which seemed full of people—relatives, children (all African houses are full of children) and fellow politicians and barristers. A grizzled, neatly-dressed man in his late fifties, Dr. Danquah is a veteran of politics and one of the most experienced lawyers in a country where the ambition of almost every young man of brains is to practise law. In his eyes Dr. Nkrumah is not only a traitor but an upstart. Dr. Danquah himself is a member of the chiefly family of Ofori Atta: a "royal", in contrast to Nkrumah the "youngman"—an engaging Gold Coast term for any commoner, even if an octogenarian. He is famous for a lifetime's devotion to the ideal of self-government, and now sees others reap where he has sown. He is celebrated also for his part in a *cause célèbre* which started in 1944: the Kibi murder trial.

The Omanhene, or chief, of the state of Akim Abuakwa, a distinguished knight called Sir Ofori Atta, died and was buried at his capital, Kibi; and six months later a second funeral custom was held. By tradition, hundreds of slaves should have been sacrificed; by British law, not even a single beggar's head might fall. There was a compromise, and one sub-chief disappeared. His relations complained, rumours reached official ears, some human bones were found and in due course eight men were put on trial for murder before a Turkish judge.

Eye-witnesses were persuaded to talk. The sub-chief had been seized, they said, and a dagger thrust through both cheeks and tongue in the traditional fashion. The object of this custom is to prevent the victim from swearing the "great oath" which, uttered in time, redeems his life. The victim was beheaded and his blood "washed the stool" of Sir Ofori Atta, who had been to England to be knighted by the King.

A jury of eight Africans and one European found all eight men guilty of murder. Their appeal failed. So did a further appeal to the Privy Council, and an execution day was fixed for six of the murderers, the other two having been reprieved by the Governor, Sir Alan Burns.[1]

The lawyers for the defence then proceeded to conduct an elaborate game of cat-and-mouse with the British legal system. There was an application to the Supreme Court for the quashing of the coroner's inquest, another to the Attorney-General for his fiat for the issue of a writ of error, and one to the Supreme Court for a mandamus compelling the Attorney-General to issue his fiat. The Privy Council was appealed to three times. Every application failed, but this did not deter the defence, who buried the original charge of ritual murder under a thicket of legal technicalities far beyond the grasp of any layman, black or white.

The executions were delayed from month to month. This was a softening-up process. The defence then made contact with some of the more easily ignited Members of Parliament, they enlisted the Press, they instructed deputations to the Secretary of State. In Britain (though scarcely in the Gold Coast) public opinion grew concerned over the mental agonies of convicted

[1] A full account is given by Sir Alan Burns in his book *Colonial Civil Servant*.

men kept for so long in suspense. That this suspense was due entirely to the tactics of lawyers for the defence was overlooked; the blame was subtly shifted to the shoulders of an inefficient Colonial Government. Little attention was paid to the sufferings of the condemned men by their own lawyers, who waited until the last hour of the last day to file every petition. At one point Dr. Danquah, a relative of several of the accused men, was charged with interfering with a witness, but won his acquittal.

In the end this tireless campaign was partially successful. On the very day before the executions were at last to occur—two years after the first trial—the Governor commuted the sentence on two more of the men. One had died in jail; three were executed. So ended a case that for nearly three years had been the talk of the Gold Coast. No one had realized, until the defence lawyers discovered them, that so many loopholes existed in British colonial law. It was said that the law was brought into contempt by the Kibi murder case; to the ordinary citizen, it certainly appeared more like a complicated legal game of blindman's buff than a system of punishing crime.

As for Dr. Danquah, the closing of the case did not quench his belief that his relatives and the other convicted men were victims of a plot to discredit his distinguished family, which has produced many leaders in public life—and the Gold Coast's first woman doctor. Nor did he abandon politics. He has kept alive the rump of the United Gold Coast Convention and lately merged it with the National Democratic Party, another small opposition group, to form the Ghana Congress Party. He now acts as spokesman for the Opposition in the Assembly. Intellectually, he outstrips most of the CPP members, but as a rabble-rouser he cannot compete. No wiles and tricks of politics are hidden from him, but he is unlikely ever to gain the power Dr. Nkrumah wields and will never relinquish save to a better demagogue than he.

One of the measures he has attacked with fire and eloquence—but without effect, so tiny is the Opposition—is a CPP bill to take the land and revenues attached to the Stools away from the various chiefs, and put them under District Councils. Two-thirds of the members of these Councils are elected; thus the CPP expects to bring them all into its fold. The chiefs are to be

D*

preserved for ceremonial and religious purposes. This will indeed be to emasculate them.

The measure is supported by European officials on the grounds that it "democratizes" local government. Dr. Danquah is probably nearer the mark when he avers that it will enable the CPP to win country-wide control at district level to match its central authority. Bad chiefs can at least be de-stooled. In theory, a bad set of district councillors can be unhorsed at an election. In practice, this is difficult when there is no one else to vote for, and inadvisable when enthusiastic members of the CPP are ready to set roofs alight, mutilate cocoa trees, slash lorry-tyres or beat up rebellious voters. It is safer to put the cross in the right place.

Support for chiefs who have lined their own nests is not a popular cry at a time of revolution. Dr. Danquah, for years the firebrand of Accra, the nationalist prophet, the British thorn, now finds himself in peril of ranking as an old reactionary. I left him with the feeling that here is a highly intelligent, cunning, delightfully mannered, puzzled and disappointed man, who has lived to see younger hands snatch from his the standard of freedom and the trumpet of fame, just as the walls of the beleaguered city started to crumble.

∽ 5 ∽

Dr. Danquah's political partner is a man as unlike him as possible in almost every way, except that both are barristers. Nii Ollennu, founder of the small National Democratic Party, is a tall, young-looking man with great charm and vitality who has gone into politics less from motives of ambition than from a genuine wish to help his people by offering them an incorrupt and honest government. Hard-working, sincere, he is a good and fluent talker, but no demagogue. Nii Ollennu is, indeed, just the sort of man that British idealists would wish an African leader to be. Corruption in public life disgusts him, nor does he endorse what seems to him to be a cynical British acquiescence in a sorry state of affairs.

Corruption, I suggested, is a hard charge to prove.

"It could be done," he said, and quoted several instances. It is no secret that large presents are given at public rallies to

Cabinet Ministers. To bring into the open less public and more improper goings-on would stir up so much mud that the European elements in the Government, handling race relations as tenderly as a piece of antique porcelain, sit tight and say nowt. In so doing, they impair the respect of those Africans, like Nii Ollennu, who have taken most to heart the lessons of integrity and public service learnt from Britain. There are Englishmen who find this bitter, and some are quietly leaving the Gold Coast.

Yet those who stay have their answer. Human nature cannot be changed in a day, politics is the art of the possible—all the clichés, which have become clichés just because they are true. What, after all, is corruption? The word is sinister, the deed may be venial. Bribery has an ancient lineage, springing from the universal West Coast habit of giving and receiving a "dash".

No man wishing to address his chief, no chief visiting a paramount or colleague, no youth waiting on a future father-in-law, no one seeking a favour or returning a courtesy—in short no man at all, in the ordinary intercourse of life, would omit his offering of yams or kola nuts, palm wine or fruit, a cloth or a cow, according to his wealth and status. To ignore this custom would be a gross breach of good manners and an open insult to chief, host or colleague. Whether the dash is paid in kind or in the newer medium of money is immaterial. In European eyes a man who, with a case to lay before a chief, first offers him a sheep or a pound is guilty of bribery. To Africans he is merely behaving in a decent, civilized way. Only an oaf would so insult a chief (or a magistrate for that matter) as to make demands on his august attention and offer nothing in return, not even a mark of respect. If bribery is to us a crime and to Africans a courtesy, integrity in this context is to us a virtue and to them a solecism.

But old wine in new bottles may turn sour. Chiefs were trained to give as well as to receive, and schooled in moderation. Most of the men who are replacing them are not. They may have passed the right examinations, but moderation is not in the syllabus. There is no custom to guide and little public opinion to restrain, but family demands and a taste for new-found pleasures to egg them on. They are moral freebooters, for the most part. And so what started as a tribute becomes an exaction. The finest of lines divides the voluntary offering of a few eggs from the whispered word that if ten shillings to the Party funds is not forthcoming there will be unpleasantness.

On different occasions I was told of many such practices, by their nature hearsay and, if published, libellous. Others are based on assumption. What can one say, for instance, of a member of the Government who, on a salary of £1,200 a year with no private means, is known, in the last year, to have spent £800 on sending his wife to England, to have acquired a new American car whose price is about £2,000 and to have lived expensively in a large rented house with numerous servants?

Other cases can be more precisely pinned down. Here are two which I believe authentic.

The Native Authority of a certain district was reformed so as to bring in the "progressives", including an educated young man who was appointed chief in place of an old reprobate. The young man persuaded his colleagues that their appointments would not become effective until their names had been published in the *Official Gazette*, and that, to arrange this, the District Commissioner required £100. He collected the subscriptions and, a little later, took delivery of a new American car.

A month afterwards, the D.C. (who told me this story) received a letter signed by ten members of the Native Authority asking when their names were to be published, since they had paid the fee. The young chief was confronted with this letter. All lies, he said: a plot by jealous enemies. The D.C. sympathized; such spite was cruel; fortunately, redress was possible. He would forward the letter to the Law Officers, who would have its authors prosecuted. After some further exchanges, the chief admitted that the £100 had gone towards his new car.

Soon these European D.C.s, who are disinterested, will be replaced by Africans who live embedded in a matrix of relatives and must spend their whole lives, not just their working hours, among the people. They would be men of iron resolution and implacable principle who resisted the pressure that must squeeze any African in such a post. And men of valour, too. Behaviour which seems anti-social to the majority is sometimes punished swiftly and brutally in this part of the world.

The second instance occurred in Kumasi and was front-page

news for a while. Two junior Ministers in the Government, £1,200-a-year men, called on an African magistrate and advised him to treat more tenderly those CPP members who were brought before him on various charges. The CPP, they incorrectly said, now controlled the appointment and promotion of the judiciary, and his career would not prosper if he kept on sending good Party members to jail.

The magistrate took notes of the interview and went straight to the police. The two Ministers were convicted of contempt of court and sentenced to a year's imprisonment. The African judge who tried the case was very caustic in his comments. So far, the judiciary has managed to keep clear of politics, and its reputation for integrity, in a land not kind to reputations, is high.

A man with thirty years' experience of the Coast said to me: "There are three reasons why this country will never fundamentally change. One, there's no code of morals; two, the climate; three, the family system. And life's been too easy, the people have never learnt to work."

Others think remarks like this to be the barkings of reactionary old bulldogs. Universities, schools, Missions, adult education teams are diverting minds into new channels. Given a little time, there will be enough men with a new outlook to change the whole aspect of West Africa.

Such is the belief of Dr. K. A. Busia, himself one of the "new" men, and the third member of the triumvirate which controls the Ghana Congress Party. He is an Oxford man who became one of the Gold Coast's first two African District Commissioners. Later, he became a student of anthropology, took his degree at Oxford and now holds a readership in the University College, where he hopes to build up a department of African cultural studies. As to politics:

"We have only put in our second eleven, if that," he said.

Nii Ollennu, Dr. Busia, Dr. Danquah—an oddly assorted trio; can they, together, challenge Nkrumah and his team? It seems unlikely. None of the three has a popular appeal comparable to the Prime Minister's, and their uneasy partnership lacks a policy. Prestige, money, political acumen are at present all on the side of the CPP. It is early days yet, however—early and prosperous, and the surface of things can change very quickly in Africa. If prices fall, if storms blow over lotus-land, an angered people may seek a change of government.

Now that "SG" is achieved, the nationalists burn to hasten to its consummation the policy of replacing whites by blacks, especially in the Civil Service. The cry is that "expatriates" must go, and go quickly. The expatriates are willing, but the timing is everything. If, for political reasons, they are replaced too quickly by untrained men—and sufficient trained and worthy Africans do not exist—then standards of efficiency will fall below the safety mark. Many Africans (the Prime Minister certainly included) know this, but are urged forward by the more ardent among their own supporters, and especially by the popular Press.

Accra has five daily papers of a sort. Some are single sheets and the printing is generally atrocious; in some respects their standards are low, but they pass with *éclat* the first test of any newspaper—there is a fitful flamboyance about their prose style (combined with a complete disregard for libel laws) that compels one to read on.

Only one of these five dailies, the *Accra Evening News*, uncritically supports the CPP, and its circulation of 8,000 is about the same as that of a paper antagonistic to the Party, the *Daily Echo*, edited by a Liberian.

Two years ago the *Daily Mirror* group in London started the *Daily Graphic* in Accra. This, the first West African venture of any British newspaper concern, has been a great success. Better printing, better editing, better journalism all round have won it a circulation of 40,000, five times higher than any of its rivals'.

The total circulation of the Accra papers—much of it of course outside Accra—is reckoned at 150,000. Considering that each copy is passed many times from hand to hand, this figure probably covers at least half a million souls.

The inter-racial team working in the Information Department is probably the busiest and best to be found in any British dependency. Commanded with military efficiency by a dapper and hospitable Irishman, Major Jimmy Lillie-Costello (whose French wife is a superb hostess to people of all races, to visitors and locals alike), its first objective is to make the African Government it serves—the men and the machine—known and understood all over the country. To that end its vans, its radio diffusion system, its films, its publications are devoted mainly, and most effectively, to spreading the word of the present Ministers, but also to bringing news of wider horizons to the Gold Coast people: who by and large, and not unnaturally, prefer to read about the peccadilloes of their neighbours rather than the deliberations of the United Nations.

❧ 6 ❧

The crest of the University College is a rampant cock, the bird of dawning, surrounded by fourteen bosses representing guineas. For Guinea Coast gold was considered so much purer than any other that a sovereign minted from it was worth an extra shilling. So Achimota has taken the guinea as a symbol of that generous spirit, that resolve to put a little extra into life, which the University College strives to instil.

"Only the best is good enough for Africa," quoted Mr. Balme, the Principal, when he laid on Legon Hill the foundation stone of the first of many buildings that are to replace the present scattered collection of temporary prefabricated hutments sprawling over Achimota hill. He added: "That is a very expensive remark." Part of Achimota's mission is to inculcate devotion to that extra shilling's-worth, and dissatisfaction with the second-rate, in a continent almost lacking the concept of quality. It is an alpine task, yet most faculty members seem confident, buoyant and full of pride in what they have done already, and what they feel sure they will be able to do. Either they have a great deal of imagination, or practically none at all.

The scientists, I think, have least. (It is always startling how little imagination scientists can have outside their work, which needs a great deal.) Priests and priestesses of botany, chemistry, geology, physics, for the most part pale, spectacled and (one feels) vaguely neuter, they cut sections and titrate acids among fume-cupboards and microscopes with exactly the same detachment and unruffled accuracy, murmuring in the same flat voices, wearing the same shapeless suits and saggy trousers or skirts, as they display in Sheffield or Bristol. That they are in Africa means little more to them than unfamiliar plant and insect species, specimens from different rocks, trouble with a fungus that grows on the lenses of microscopes. The laws of chemistry and the structure of crystals do not change because you are in the tropics. The modern scientist inhabits the only truly international world.

Such an austere and unromantic outlook is most useful here. The scientist has only one set of standards, and these he never relaxes or adapts. A formula is right or wrong. So is a student, be he black or white, young or old, proud or humble. There can be no patronage, no relativity, and few allowances made. Students must conform to standards of accuracy that are universal and fixed.

This they do with no sign of inferiority of intellect. On the contrary: identical examination papers are just as strictly marked here as in London, and students do rather better in them. They are more eager to learn than London students and they work harder. It was interesting to hear from Mr. Balme, who has taken seminars at Reading, Manchester, St. Andrews and Cambridge, that students introduced to philosophy ask exactly the same questions, whether they are British or African.

"Our students prefer theory to practical work," a botanist told me, rather sadly, for they did not bring interesting specimens to be identified. You can see why. Plants are dull, ordinary things, everyone knows them, but in the cell structure of a leaf, or the process of photo-synthesis, lies a bewitching mystery that Africans are glimpsing for the first time. He added, more sadly still, "They all want to be doctors."

They are serious, hard-working and intelligent, these students, great users of an excellent library; fond of drama and debate; ambitious, eager to get on and deeply contemptuous of anything "bush" or of work done with hands. Outwardly, nearly all are Christian or Muslim, but one of their mentors said: "Scratch, scratch, and there's the African—fetish, ancestor worship and all. The babies are baptized, but on the eighth day they are 'outdoored' and tribal marks cut on their cheeks. They want a foot in both camps. Don't think that a degree obliterates the African. Why should it? They don't want it to. This is only a beginning, you know. Come back in a hundred years' time and we'll have something to show."

Achimota has at present only 340 students, guided by a faculty of 110, nearly one instructor to every three students. These embryo African universities must have the highest ratio of instructors to students in the world. This is expensive, and could be done only with the help of the British taxpayer. The new site at Legon Hill is to provide for 800 students, in the first instance, at a cost of £5,000,000, and ultimately, at cost unspecified, for 5,000. The faculty is, with a few exceptions, European. Acceptable African candidates for chairs are badly needed and very rare.

The growth of a native university (as it soon will be) has awakened a new interest in the native culture of the Gold Coast, and many of the students now want to study the arts, institutions and above all the history of their country. Dr. Busia's department is to develop these studies. He has already teams of students recording songs and dances and others preserving on paper a record of customs which are dying out. History sets a more difficult task. The youth of the Gold Coast, with nationalism in its blood, now seeks a glorious past to give it confidence among the nations and the promise of a future even more sublime. In the land that has never known the arts of writing or of architecture, a history, glorious or otherwise, is hard to delineate. But in the vanished empire of Ghana the nationalists have found their quarry.

You cannot be long in the Gold Coast without hearing this word. There is a Ghana party, Ghana societies, Ghana buses, bars and restaurants, at one time there were Ghana schools, there is even a Ghana design—a best-seller—on cotton cloths.

Probably no one will ever know the exact site of this ancient city, but it is believed to have stood about 300 miles west of Timbuktu. The time and manner of its rise are no less uncertain. Legend, recorded by Arab travellers, places at the head of the earliest state a line of "white kings", Semitic probably, whose rule ended in the eighth century in favour of a dynasty drawn from a branch of the Mandingo tribe. Probably the power of Ghana reached its peak in the middle of the ninth century, when it may have spread to the Gambia River in the west, the Niger in the east, and in the south to the upper reaches of the Senegal and the Baule, a Niger tributary.[1]

[1] For a summary of all that is known about Ghana, see *Caravans of the Old Sahara* by E. W. Bovill (International African Institute).

The wealth of Ghana was built on gold, and the gold came from a district known as Wangara, whose location is also obscure. Probably it traversed that cluster of tributaries, like a hand's fingers, leading into the headwaters of the Senegal. Here came Barbary merchants with camel-trains of beads, salt and a resinous wood used for sweetening water stored in skins. Halting by the river, they beat their drums to summon the Negroes, who refused to emerge until the merchants had arranged their goods in piles along the river-bank and withdrawn from sight. Then out came the Negroes to place a heap of gold beside each pile of goods, and again retreat. If the merchants were satisfied, they took the gold, beat their drums and departed; if not, they withdrew again and waited for the Negroes to add more gold. This "silent trade"—said to have been practised by Phœnician merchants trading down the Guinea coast—endured for many centuries and, though it has ended, the people of this region continue to trap in pits the gold which the Senegal river carries down from the mountains and deposits when it floods its banks. This method has been followed with little change for perhaps 2,000 years, and survives even into the age of machinery.

In Ghana, gold was at times so plentiful that two *dinars* (the *dinar* is the weight of thirty-two grains of barley) were needed to buy one of salt. Nuggets were the king's property, dust the people's. This rule was observed in Ashanti down to the time of the British incursion and is one of the reasons advanced for linking the modern peoples of the Akan states with the ancient Kingdom of Ghana. One of the king's nuggets was said to be so large that he tethered his horse to it.

About the time the Normans invaded England, the armies of a fanatical Muslim sect, the Almoravids, conquered Ghana, looted its capital and stripped of wealth and power its reigning king. The city's trade lingered on until, in 1224, the surviving Arab and Soninke merchants marched into the desert to found a new trading centre a hundred miles away. The old one withered totally away, leaving no traces.

Ghana, then, under its Negro kings, was an ancestor to be proud of; but there does not seem to be the slightest evidence that its borders at any time extended to within a thousand miles of Accra, nor are there any ties but those of fancy to bind the present people of the Gold Coast, many of whom migrated from the east within the last few centuries, to the citizens of an empire that fell a thousand years ago. Not that it will matter in the least if the Gold Coast takes the name of Ghana, or any other name it pleases. The fear sometimes voiced at Achimota is rather that evidence might be fabricated or twisted to prove the descent, just as backing for the racial theories of National Socialism was winkled by dubious means out of German historians. A State university whose professors contradict official dogma does not often continue to enjoy official support, and colonial universities will soon have to depend for funds wholly on the goodwill of politicians.

On the way back to Accra, driving across the brown, sandy plain quietly baking under a pale and cloudless sky, we passed a white mansion standing on an eminence above the road, bare but imposing.

"My uncle," said Ashong the driver, waving a proud hand. "Big, rich man."

Uncle is a vague term. The owner of the house has become a chief of the Ga people, and Ashong is a Ga man.

"The house cost £28,000," Ashong added, with an exactitude probably illusory. "My uncle has half a million pounds in the bank. It is his bank."

The sum may be approximate; all the same, Ashong's uncle has done well. Starting life as a sea-cook, he visited Japan and China, and was quick to see that Oriental goods would go like hot cakes in his native land. But he lacked capital. He had, however, a friend who worked as a cleaner in the Supreme Court. The Court's grand new buildings were so greatly admired in Accra that a picture of them had been reproduced on the writing-paper used by the Legal Department. The brilliant idea occurred to him of ordering goods under this engraved letter-head. The Japanese, impressed by the grandeur of their correspondent's offices—clearly his business must be even more prosperous than the United Africa Company's—gladly extended credit to so important an agent. Ashong's uncle made his fortune, and is now a newspaper proprietor and a well-known member of the Legislative Assembly.

Most of Accra is new, straggling and untidy. Harsh white concrete buildings are going up. There is a peripheral taggle of brown grass plots, barbed wire, scaffolding and boxy houses dumped down like forgotten parcels.

The fishing village in the heart of Accra has been there for centuries. You are back here in an older Africa that never dies, however many forts, churches and offices may be added by transient foreigners. While the easy-going inhabitants doze in the sun, scrawny hens pick over garbage in unpaved streets, naked children piss into the gutter, fat short-legged goats like corgies roam about between palm-thatched, mud-block houses. In the shade of a tiny veranda on the narrow street a plump young woman is plaiting into innumerable pigtails the wiry hair of a companion who sits cross-legged at her feet. An old man lies on the ground fast asleep; a woman with flat, scaly breasts that dangle to her waist squats against a door, pounding food in a hand mortar.

A flight of old stone steps leads down to a beach packed with fishing-canoes. Most have names painted on the prow. "Look Sharp" rubs timbers with "Wait to See the Truth". They are dugouts hollowed from the light *wawa* tree. A naked youth emerges from the metal-coloured ocean and runs with light feet up the steps, glistening like a new farthing and shaking the water from his hair. His muscles flow like mercury under the silky skin, his athlete's body is in perfect running order. He looks at the canoes; no doubt one of them is partly his; these men fish six days a week and rest on Tuesdays; this is a Tuesday afternoon.

Back from the beach, in an open square, the nets—each one immensely long and heavy—are stretched out to dry and men are patiently repairing them, knotting the string with a quick twist of the fingers. This way of fishing can have changed little for hundreds of years. The people who practise it, the Ga, came to this coast, it is believed, from Nigeria in the sixteenth century under a great leader called Okai Koi. ("There is no nation now dwelling in the Gold Coast," says Ward, "which has been in the country much longer than the European." [1]) The Ga were a strong, warlike people who might have challenged the Ashanti had they remained united, but they fought amongst themselves and, because of this, were in 1660 defeated in a great battle. Okai Koi, when he saw the fight lost, called his chiefs together and painted one side of his body with white clay and the other side with charcoal. If his body fell with the white side uppermost, he told them, victory would follow, but the black side signified disunity and failure. Seating himself on his stool, in front of all his captains he shot himself. His body fell with the black side uppermost, and his enemies inherited the overlordship of the plain. It is said that this battle was fought on a Tuesday, and that is the reason no one fishes on that day.

We passed the house of a fetish priest and stopped to call, but he was away trading; his priestly functions take up only a portion of his time. At the start of the herring season he must sacrifice a cow—it used to be a human—to the spirits of the sea. The catch last year was light, Ashong told me, because of the powered dorys with which the Government is carrying out experiments. This ill-mannered, hustling way of getting fish annoyed the spirits, who have taken their revenge by keeping empty the nets of the poor fishermen.

The old slave market—or one of them—lies a little way outside Accra, close to Christiansborg Castle. It is a pity that no one has sought to preserve it. You enter through a doorway bearing the date 1809 to find yourself in an open unroofed court in whose centre a flight of stone steps rises to nothing; the rest of the building has tumbled down. A young boy lies full length on one of the steps, peering into a school primer. Below lies the rump of an ancient car, a mere battered chassis; there it will stay, no doubt, until in the course of years it slowly disintegrates; and one day, perhaps, archæologists grubbing in the red dust, unearthing a buried city, may date its heyday from the indestructible portions of old cars, as we date earlier cultures from flints and sherds.

"My aunt lives here," Ashong said, waving in the direction of several toothless old women peering out of a hovel excavated from the crumbling wall.

[1] *A History of the Gold Coast* by W. E. F. Ward (Allen & Unwin, 1948).

Sun and rain have done their work of spiritual as well as physical ablution. One feels no sense of evil here, no emanation of misery. Despair has been baked from the stones as blood has been washed out of the dungeons, and now old men can sleep in peace on heaps of stones and boys con their primers in tranquillity. Africa obliterates; she does not remember.

◅ 8 ◈

The harmattan, a steady north-east wind from the Sahara, spreads over everything a soft fuliginous mist thicker than heathaze but thinner than fog. You can see through it, but it blurs shapes and blunts colour; everything becomes a pallid brown, dark red or dull yellow. Even the sun, which on usual mornings leaps in glory from behind a ruler-drawn horizon, is at first obscured. Dawn starts as a dirty saffron glow in a sky of indigo, and when the tone deepens to a lurid ochre, as if a storm gathered, you know that the sun has risen and hear the guinea-fowl greeting raucously a new day. Later on, the sun defeats the harmattan and the plains grow bright but hazy.

The dust gets into engines; three stops for carburettor-cleaning were forced upon us between Tamale, the capital of the Northern Territories, and Bawku, on the French frontier. We crossed two ferries. Their pontoons can manage one lorry at a time only, and they do not hurry; ferry-men pull listlessly, arm over arm, at the wire hawser, and at each end of the journey there is a good deal of business with ramps and planks. There is always a queue. A week before, unlucky drivers had waited three days to cross the White Volta. Every lorry is packed with passengers and upwards of a thousand people were gathered there, with very little food and no latrines; the foulness of the crossing can be easily conjectured; luckily, Africans seldom seem to mind the waste of time.

A mile or two from Bawku the French boundary, a tributary of the Volta, runs through a shallow gorge, and in the evening I watched herd after herd of cattle from the French side being driven up the bank into a quarantine area, where they must stay for three weeks to receive inoculations for rinderpest. Here, at the start of their journey, they look bony and sad enough; their horns appear to weigh down their heads; but the poor brutes have another 400 miles to go, at first across this brown, baked, desiccated plain and then through forest full of tsetse-fly, only to be slaughtered at the end. They arrive all skin and skeleton, yet cocoa-growers, avid for meat, will pay as much as £40 a beast.

South come the cattle, north go salt and kola nuts, neatly packed in baskets shaped like fat cigars. You chew the kola, as the Indian chews betel, and its bitter flavour stimulates the nerves and sweetens mouths parched by this dry atmosphere; it is also said to stop you feeling hungry. When a friend calls, you break a kola nut and offer him the segment next your heart as a sign of friendship. With kola nuts you pledge brides, settle debts and pay respects to chiefs; men will give their last penny for a nut, as Europeans for a cigarette.

Bawku market is packed with grain, fruit, vegetables, oils. Here is shea butter, sold in little conical piles: oil expressed from the nut of the shea tree (*Bassia parkii*), which you see dotted all over these plains, about the size and conformation of a pear tree, and preserved by law. The market offers woven mats of dyed raffia palm and, on the stalls of the Lagosians, bales and bales of cotton and enticing displays of ointments, lotions and pills. The men of these parts wear loose trousers caught in just below the knee and a tunic or *jibbah* made of heavy but supple home-woven twill, as a rule striped in white and indigo. The cheapest of these costs thirty-five shillings—a high price in a land of poverty.

This is harvest time. Women bring the grain in big baskets to the market, Southern traders pay a low price, and many growers fail to keep back enough for their own needs. Bawku merchants store the grain in their houses and sell it back to the improvident, who are by then half-starving, at two or three times the price they gave for it. The District Commissioner spoke with enthusiasm of a co-operative society which has been started, with Government initiative and support, to buy grain, store it and sell it back at cost price when the hungry time comes. It also advances money to peasants for the purchase of ploughs and oxen. The scheme has started well, but depends for future progress on finding the money to build rat-proof stores.

From the market-place at Bawku you can take a bus to Mecca and back for £30.

∽ 9 ∽

I dined that night with the D.C. in one of those spacious, thick-walled houses built of native materials and in traditional style. You climb up a long flight of steps to enter, for the house is perched off the ground. The rough clay walls are plastered over and the big living-room seems full of arches; the whole effect is one of dignity and space. We sat over drinks on an open veranda like the bridge of a ship. The sky above was star-encrusted and a new moon was half obscured by feathery cassia trees. A moon-flower clambered up the walls of the dark veran-da, its heavy waxen blooms, trumpet-shaped, filling the air with a scent of extraordinarily strong sweetness, like jasmine, only sharper and with more strength. All this to attract moths, they say, that pollinate flowers by moonlight—moths whose sense of smell is so fine that males will beat themselves against a window to reach a female trapped inside, with only her scent to draw them on. What a deluge, an ocean of scent must then immerse them when the moon-flower opens; so overwhelming one would think they must drown. Each bloom unfolds, releases all its passionate fragrance and withers in a single night.

Mr. Ian Baillie, a tall and serious young Scot of northern energy and purpose, ignored the moon-flower and spoke of the people he administers. Their hardest trouble is that they are too thick on the ground. (How familiar this has become!) The land is fertile but very light; to over-cultivate without frequent resting quickly tears out its heart. The people multiply, and so over-cultivation is what it gets.

Cannot some of the people, one asks, move elsewhere? The country looked very empty when we drove up from Tamale, 170 miles south: orchard bush, with scattered trees that might have been knobbly old apples, and tall, golden-yellow grass with graceful, feathery panicles that might have been oat-grass. Signs of human life were few.

The people will not move, it seems. There are reasons: short-age of water, insect-borne diseases, wild animals, perhaps above all a general lack of pioneering spirit. The Government is pioneering for them through a body called the Gonja Development Corporation, which intends to open up several blocks of land with bulldozers and heavy caterpillar tractors and then bring in new settlers who will be presented with the usual gifts—thirty acres of cleared land, houses, piped water, a hospital, night schools and baby clinics—of the Santa Claus State. A start has been made at Damongo, west of Tamale, on 32,000 acres, where the first few settlers have been installed: whether fruitfully or no, it is as yet too early to say.

Here in the north-east lies some of the most productive land, and the most thickly populated, in the Northern Territories. Much of it needs to be saved quickly, or it will be gone. And so "land-planning areas" have been mapped out and Agricultural Officers drafted in to act as "executive officers" of the mainly African committees which have been set up in nominal charge.

The first task of such an officer is to decide what land is so far gone that the people flogging it must be evicted and helped to start elsewhere. The land they quit he lets fall back to grass, or has neem trees planted. He and his men then set about the rest of the area with tractors, ploughs and scoops to change its very shape and bring it under law and order. They terrace every slope to keep the soil in place, make dams to preserve rainfall and arrest the water-table's fall; in the shallow valleys they make bunds for rice, they introduce the unknown art of hay-making and they lend the peasants bullocks and ploughs.

All this sounds easy; naturally, it is not. There are practical obstacles and psychological ones. People cling to their land, however emaciated; to their homes, however hungry; and to that special bit of soil that holds the bones of their fathers and so links them with their ancestors, their tribal past, the spirit world. Tribal authority in these parts has two arms: the secular, exercised through chiefs, and the spiritual, exercised through priests who are also the guardians of the land. It is to his *ten'dama*, his land-priest, that the young man must come for land to cultivate, and to whom falls the task of keeping the spirits well-disposed. And it is often the land-priest who is the biggest enemy of land-planning, as the following story shows.

One of the "resettled" peasants, equipped with ox and plough, inadvertently ploughed a few yards over his boundary on to land under the *ten'dama's* care. That year the rains were poor and crops failed. The fetish, through the mouth of the land-priest, blamed the offending settler and demanded the sacrifice of his ox and the banishment of his plough. And so the Government's loaned ox had its throat cut to allow its blood to drip over a stone sacred to the fetish. Such obstruction will be slowly overcome, but there are other obstacles—apathy, climate, jealousy of the successful, political change.

The Northern Territories hold over a million people, one quarter of the Gold Coast's inhabitants. The first land-planning scheme to be launched near Bawku involves the resettlement of fifty families. A million pounds has been set aside for four such experiments in this northern area, and they will merely scratch at the necessity. Only the heaviest and most expensive tractors will stand up to this gruelling climate and to the rough handling of semi-trained mechanics. If farming in the Northern Territories is to be even partly mechanized enormous sums will have to be sunk and, from an economic point of view, no returns expected.

Where is the money to come from? The hard-pressed British taxpayer, who is finding a part, cannot find it all. The Gold Coast Government provides the bigger share, and a question troubling the North is this: under complete self-government, will politicians from Accra and rich Ashanti cocoa-growers be willing to sink large sums of their constituents' money to benefit people they are apt to regard merely as a source of cheap labour? Only those with a view of human nature even Pangloss would consider over-confident believe that the Northern Territories will get the heavy subsidies they need.

These tribesmen are for the most part sturdy, honest, hard-working folk more often possessed of the simple virtues needed for survival than of the guile and subtlety needed for politics. Police and army draw most of their recruits from among their numbers. Education is embryonic, and to find nineteen representatives for the Assembly in Accra required a pretty thorough scraping of the barrel. Whenever the Assembly meets, an exodus occurs of almost every English-speaking chief with even a sketchy understanding of administration. There is one Northern Minister in the Cabinet, Chief Braimah, in charge of Communications and Works—the only Minister outside the CPP. He holds his own well.

Many Northern leaders watch the approach of self-government with misgiving. They want independence, of course; but to exchange a British District Commissioner for a politician's nephew from Accra does not necessarily seem to them a step in that direction. They do not trust the forest-dwellers very far. Cautious by nature, in effect they say: "Let us go forward slowly". Caution is out of fashion, and Northern opinions carry little weight in Accra.

◦ 10 ◦

Round Bawku, the country is gently undulating and absolutely bare of trees. These have all gone for firewood, and the people burn the stalks of guinea corn. The harvest is in and the hedgeless, haphazard fields, dotted over this great plain as if a giant's thumbnail had nicked off little flakes of skin, are bare and sandy, scarcely to be distinguished in colour from the coarse brown grass. Bundles of corn-stalks lean against clay huts ready for thatching, for this is the season—the dry season—when roofs are re-made.

These people are dwellers on the margins of life, so much is clear. The country they inhabit is the real Africa: the veld, the arid bush, the dusty plain, stretching for countless miles from the Transvaal to Turkana, from the Orange River to the Congo and on to the Sahara and the Sudan. Here is the ceaseless fight against drought, desiccation, storm and fever, the struggle just to live and little more; here the political intrigues of capital cities, the balancing of constitutions, the shady deals of the ambitious, seem like shadow plays. There, men are hungry for power; here, for food; and not all the constitutions in the world will add an inch to the rainfall or a head-load to the yield of guinea corn.

It is strange that this bare and dusty landscape receives as much rain as Sussex, but all in five months, and mainly in heavy storms which bear the soil in red torrents down sluits into rivers and do more harm than good on the way.

Like most cattle-owners, these people do not live in towns or villages, but in family homesteads, each one surrounded by a circular wall of rammed clay. Seen from outside, there are bulges in the circle made by the backs of huts built into the wall. These huts are thatched, and often swathed all over with a vine producing calabashes (a relative of the cucumber and the American squash). It must be useful to grow your jugs, cup and pots on the roof. All around the homesteads stand the tall stems of that variety of yellow-flowered hibiscus known as tie-tie, for the reason that its name suggests.

There is an inner and an outer circle in these homesteads, each circle a wall ringed with huts. Opposite each hut stands a granary, a small round clay structure like the old-fashioned bee-hive, raised off the ground. The women fill these granaries from the top, seal them, and then neatly thatch them all over. Relatives, perhaps younger brothers or married sons, occupy the inner circle of huts. Just by the entrance stands the fetish table where sacrifices are made. There are huts, too, for cows, and tiny huts for chickens. If not all under one roof, the family and its possessions are inside one wall.

And what families! We paid a call at random, and thirty or forty occupants crowded round. The women were naked save for a bunch of leaves tied fore and aft, and every single woman, young or old, granny or teen-ager, large or small, appeared to be in an advanced stage of pregnancy. I wondered whether I was the victim of a delusion similar to the late Lord Northcliffe's, who, when his mind was failing, became convinced that every woman in Germany was about to give birth. Or could it be in part a result of malaria, with its enlarged spleen? This suggestion was dismissed out of hand. With laughter, pride and not a little complacency they all proclaimed their fertility, which indeed, judging by the flock of little ones already in existence, was scarcely in doubt.

Ancestor-worship still permeates these people's lives. No important event can take place without the sacrifice of a hen or a sheep on the family shrine to win the blessing of an ever-watchful, never-dying father. Death has indeed no finality; it is a stage only in a journey, and the dead hold places of authority in the councils of the living. The importance of having sons is absolute, for without them there can be no one to sacrifice at your shrine and, on the dissolution of your body, you will be cut off and dishonoured, the chain of kinship snapped.

Between Bawku and Navrongo you can still feel a long way from civilization. Of the hordes of children that dart about the homesteads few, if any, go to school. This does not say that they are not educated. They are merely taught different things: how to greet an uncle or court a girl, to herd cattle, hunt guinea-fowl, plant groundnuts and cut up sheep for sacrifice. From infancy, every child must do the right thing. Even a baby must not lie upon a sleeping-mat until a sort of godfather has cut a particular root from the bush, placed pieces of it in certain positions under the mat and carried the baby three times if a boy, four times if a girl, to the top of a roof or wall at sunrise, and then laid it on the mat. Until a boy's head is shaved and sacrifices offered, he must not make love. Once qualified, he must take tobacco and guinea-fowl next day for the young lady; then more tobacco and more guinea-fowl—a costly business. At last his advances lead either to a love affair, or to marriage.

If marriage is to be the case, the girl's family must welcome him by offering him cold water; but should the women start to break shea-butter nuts, then, rejected, he must go home. The two fathers eventually agree on the number of cows to be paid. Then the girl's father cuts a cock's throat over the family shrine and throws it down. If it falls on its back, the ancestors are satisfied; if on its front, they are displeased, and the soothsayer's advice is needed. Eventually the bride's father sacrifices a ram, and after the feast the young man takes the girl home. She is not yet his, however. For three nights she shares a sleeping-mat with her husband and one or two of his friends, who may not touch her, in spite of one of their own sayings: "Can a hen sleep with a grain of corn and not eat it?" At last she goes to her husband's home.

Even then she is not securely married, for if the husband's family find her lazy, sulky or troublesome, they can return to her parents the calabash in which she brought her beads and waist-strings. Her father sends to the husband's family to ask what is wrong. "Does she steal or fly?" (Is she a witch?) "No, she does not steal or fly, but we do not want her." And her parents are bound to take her back.

A hundred other rites and prohibitions wrap these people round from birth to death, and beyond. The complexity, the strands of kinship, the elaborate etiquette—as formal and rigid as that of any French court or monastic order—which the simple savage is obliged to remember, never ceased to amaze me. And it may be that the informality, the brash impulsiveness with which a white man often acts, the lack of ceremonial and reserve, subtly offends the African in ways which he himself may scarcely understand.

While good manners are the first requisite of tribal life, their excellence is often due less to consideration for one's fellows than to fear of them. To give offence is highly dangerous, perhaps lethal. Every mishap—a child's vomiting, the escape of a hunted antelope, a broken cooking-pot—is the result not of misfortune, for there is no such thing, but of an enemy's spite. Thus an offence today, however trivial or unintended (treading on a person's shadow, passing behind him when he eats), may lead tomorrow to a snake-bite or an ailing child. It is often said that a primitive tribesman lives in constant fear, but few Westerners can imagine how his mind is like a floating leaf sucked and eddied hither and yon by a stream's currents, moved and saturated by unremitting suspicion. He suspects everyone—living wife and dead father, friends, neighbours, relatives—suspects them constantly of malice, however affable they may seem to his face. After all, *someone* caused his cow to have a dead calf, *someone* made his wife slip on the river-bank and break the water-pot. The roots of suspicion have grown into his soul, as a tree's roots entwine themselves in masonry. It will take more than official benevolence, democratic elections and an up-to-date Public Relations Department to disentangle them.

"Education", of course—schooling—literacy—contact with Western ways—these work the change: but slowly. In such remote parts only, perhaps, one in a hundred has any such contact. And even those who have, do not change in the wink of an eye. The anthropologist R. S. Rattray described as follows a ceremony he attended in a cave sacred to a fetish in these northern hills.

To my wonder and astonishment I saw well-dressed Africans, men and women who, I later discovered, had motored hundreds of miles from Kumasi, Kwahu and Mampong. . . . All the pilgrims now began to undress. The Coast women disrobed and put on shorts; hats, shoes, white pith helmets and clothes were piled up and scattered over the boulders. We were now called to come forward, and climbed up the rocks until we came to the low entrance of the cave. This we were asked to enter backwards. Soon the cave was packed so full that many were sitting on their companions' legs and laps. I know I had a person on each knee.[1]

Each man in turn spoke his petition to the priest, who recited it to an altar at the back of the cave. The petitions quoted by Rattray are interesting: one man had a store and two taxis, and asked for fewer bad debts; another had cocoa trees, and wanted more profit; a third was a clerk with four wives, and prayed for more money; a fourth drank too much gin, and hoped for temperance.

When I state that these supplicants were educated men and women, some of whom owned large businesses, well-furnished European houses, and not a few of them their own cars in which they had come hundreds of miles to visit this pagan god, the power and influence of the old beliefs may readily be imagined. . . . Nearly everyone asked for "money" or "profit".

The Northern Territories are famous, in the south, for the "temples" (generally rocks, caves or trees) of several strong fetishes. Pilgrims still come here to consult the fetish priests, bringing for sacrifice sheep, goats and fowls.

❧ II ❧

I met eight chiefs one morning; they had invited Mr. Baillie to a palaver in a small court-house some twenty miles from Bawku. The banging of guns, the crowd's cheers and a vigorous serenade from a two-man orchestra—one wielding a rattle, the other a sort of banjo with a tiny bow—marked the arrival, on horseback, of each chief in turn. They sat in a row on a bench, backs to the wall, and put their problem to the District Commissioner.

[1] *The Tribes of the Ashanti Hinterland.* R. S. Rattray (Oxford, 1932).

It was this. Since time immemorial, each district has been governed by its chief, appointed in the traditional manner by councils of elders. Each has been equal to the others, although all acknowledge a paramount living in the hills. (These chiefs belong to the Mamprusi, a race of conquerors who came from the east in the fourteenth or fifteenth century.) Now they have been told that all eight must join together in a council of equals in which none shall be greater than his fellows. Very good. A paper has come from the Chief Commissioner to say where this council shall meet and what its duties shall be. Very good, also. But one of the eight has been singled out to be the first President. He will walk in front into the council chamber. How can it then be said that all are equal? Will not this President be seen to be first by all the people? And will not the other seven then lose face? [1]

Mr. Baillie faced the line of puzzled potentates on a small folding chair and listened attentively to the interpreter beside him. The paper signed by the Chief Commissioner was produced. It appointed as first President the chief of Tonga. Was the Tonga Naba then the biggest man? Seven chiefs in turn said that they did not agree. The Tonga Naba said nothing.

"All the chiefs of the district are equal in the Government's eyes," Mr. Baillie assured them. "The Tonga Naba was put first because the meeting-house is in his district. But each of you will take it in turns to be President for one year. If you can agree amongst you on the order, the Chief Commissioner will accept it. If you cannot agree, then we will keep to the order on the paper. Which is it to be?"

The chief of Tonga was a big, burly man wearing a heavy homespun tunic striped in blue and white and a very impressive pair of red-and-black leather riding-boots. After a consultation he spoke up for his colleagues.

"We are satisfied that the Government does not see one chief amongst us bigger than the others. We will keep to the order on the paper."

[1] There are six District Councils in the Northern Territories, each having one member for every 10,000 people. (This one, the Mamprusi, has eight elected and four traditional members.) The members of these six District Councils, plus sixteen other persons, comprise the Northern Electoral College, which sends nineteen of its number to the Legislative Assembly in Accra.

A ferryman on the Volta river

Ashanti cocoa-farmers waiting for lorry to pick up their produce

An Ashanti girl

Ashanti schoolgirls display one of the old-time dances

A village in the Northern Territories

Celebrating the enstoolment of a chief in an Ashanti village

The banana department of the market near Odumasi, by the Volta river

Elmina: a corner of the old Dutch castle

Fishermen hauling in their nets

So the meeting ended: amid another burst of gunfire from ancient muzzle-loaders and a spirited performance from the orchestra, the chiefs rode away on their scrawny ponies, upright in high-cantled saddles with their feet thrust into leather bucket-stirrups. Dust rose in hot plumes behind each little party; some had many miles to go. But honour was satisfied. The most caste-ridden Englishman is not more sensitive to subtle distinctions of status and precedence than Africans. In their eyes, equality exists only among slaves.

These people are in theory Muslims, but they attend no mosques, answer no calls to prayer, perform no daily ablutions. The Prophet seems to have retired into a shadowy field of legend among the birds and beasts native to Africa. The seventh month, for instance, is named after Kpini the guinea-fowl because, when the Prophet was hunted in the desert by his enemies, a guinea-fowl dropped water on his head out of a tree. "Lead me to the well," he commanded, but the guinea-fowl flew away. Then the Prophet met a pig covered with mud and gave it the same directions. The pig obeyed; and Mohammed ordered his followers from that day to spare the pig, but to pluck and beat the guinea-fowl whenever they pleased.

One of the Mamprusi's war customs seems to have been a sound one. The king appointed a "minister of war" and had his leg tied to a stool. As the warriors, for reasons of prestige, dared not run away and leave their elder to be killed, their line never broke; and for their part the elders, any one of whom might be picked out as "minister", never urged the young men into battle unless the prospects of victory were bright.

◆ 12 ◆

Beyond Paga, a small market town five miles from the French frontier, we left the car and walked a few hundred yards across the baking, dusty plain to reach a small grove of stunted trees. Here, in the shade, old men in striped tunics, women naked save for the usual twin bunches of leaves, and a horde of children sat on their haunches, staring at blackboards propped against the trunks of trees. By each board stood a smart young man in blue shorts, a clean white shirt and tennis shoes. A sudden

E

burst of chanting issued from one of the groups. These blue-shorted teachers are pupils of a school in Tamale which trains instructors for the mass education campaign.

This school was started, and is now directed, by two American missionaries of the Assembly of God. Lloyd Shirer and his wife, from Pennsylvania, rode into Tamale from Kano in Nigeria, a month's journey, on bicycles, thirty years ago. They found a tiny Government station, half a dozen stores, a market and not much encouragement from anyone: the Muslims were hostile, the pagans indifferent and the Government distinctly lukewarm. Tamale was reckoned to be unfit for European women, and the officials disapproved of Mrs. Shirer's arrival.

The Shirers settled down to found a mission of the good old-fashioned sort, now out of favour, whose converts were obliged to forswear all heathen practices, to live austerely (no smoking, drinking or fornication, and only one wife) and to read the Bible. Mrs. Shirer, ensconced in a native mud hut—unlike most Europeans, missionaries do not consider a high standard of comfort essential to health and efficiency—began her life's work of translating parts of the Bible into several vernaculars, while her husband cycled over native paths through mud and dust, according to the season, to spread the word of God. They went on leave twice only in thirty years, and again cycled to and from Nigeria.

Two children were born to them and raised at Tamale, schooled by their mother with the aid of a correspondence course from Baltimore. Every morning at eight o'clock she rang a hand-bell, and followed with undeviating rigour a fixed time-table. As one brought up also in Africa, although in an atmosphere somewhat less devout, I could appreciate the will of steel behind that hand-bell. In my case, in spite of all resolves to keep to schedule, something was always cropping up: a piece of vital farm machinery broke and had to be patched up or its function circumvented; a man with a gashed leg, or a woman clasping a baby seared by fire, appeared at the door of the schoolroom and demanded first aid; a reedbuck sighted among the broccoli called for an immediate *battue*. No less distracting was my mother's own eclecticism. Projects and experiments followed each other like shooting stars in August, and into each she threw without reserve all the enthusiasm of an incandescent spirit. A witch's cauldron in a lean-to shed at one time boiled load after load of guavas and Cape gooseberries for jams and jellies. Confined by a home canning plant, they were dispatched in queer-shaped packages to distant customers, and the residue, stored in the bathroom, eventually exploded like so many bombs. Marmalade followed, a sideline from acres of citrus planted on the farm, only to give way to (I think) geraniums for essential oils. Meat being short, two sheep a week appeared to be cut up and distributed to neighbours; a co-operative store sprang up next to the schoolroom to enable the labour force to buy necessities at cost price; in the midst of arithmetic, someone would rush in to say that soldier ants were biting to death the imported English pullets; a pony stricken by horse-sickness would have to be sponged day and night with cold water.

Life was never dull, but it was not conducive to study. My teacher's enthusiasms invaded the schoolroom no less than the farm. A passing interest in theology involved us in a learned two-volume commentary on the book of Isaiah; another time it was a treatise on the Illuminati, or, again, a study of the Vedic pantheon. My mother's nimble and resilient mind quailed before some of the more prosaic studies, and for Latin and algebra she enlisted the help of a young neighbour, fresh from his own school. Twice a week he rode over to conduct the lesson; but he was not of the studious type, nor was Latin a favourite with him. At school he had been, I think, captain of the rugger fifteen; and, at this period, two wet years running had brought flocks of wild duck to the *vleis* (impervious pans which turned into ponds) on the farm. Alas! that examiners did not, later on, consider an interest in bird-shooting, or a grasp of the rudiments of rugger tactics, an adequate substitute for Latin grammar or differential equations.

The education of the Shirer children, I was glad to hear, had been a great deal more orthodox. Robert only once played hookey to spend a morning in the bush. He was soundly beaten and made to stand all day in the corner without food; never again did he dodge the hand-bell. He in due course became a student of theology, his sister a teacher: both worthy citizens and servants of God.

The Rev. Lloyd Shirer is now forcefully in charge of mass

education in the North. No better choice could have been made. He speaks three vernaculars and has received from the Dagomba tribe the compliment of installation as a chief, under a name which means "the fixer of things". At his installation ceremony he was presented with a robe and sandals and warned that he was to have "no river, no bush, no locust tree"—meaning no land, for this belongs not to the chiefs but to the people themselves under the guidance of the land-priest. (The chiefs explained: "The people belong to us, the land to the *ten'dama*.")

Mr. Shirer finds his chieftainship expensive. Each December a three-day ceremony is held when he must wear his robes and "greet" his colleagues with presents, either of kola nuts, cloths and sheep, or of money to buy these commodities. He is "greeted" in return, and last year came back with eight sheep. A cow is killed for the feast and a certain elder entrusted with its tail. His office is hereditary, and his collection of tails provides a chronology of Dagomba history, for he knows, by word of mouth, how many tails were added in the lifetime of each chief, and can thus reckon the number and span of Dagomba rulers.

"We try to provide a mental climate in which the experts can put their story over," Mr. Shirer said. "For years, specialists have failed because they've used the wrong technique to convince simple people." Here the intention is to weld technique and message into one. The region round Paga has been chosen for the first mass education drive because it forms part of a "land-planning area". The Government land-renovators cannot succeed unless they win the interest and co-operation of the peasants, and this they cannot do unless the mass of the people, not just the chiefs and a few clerks, know what is to be done, and why. Literacy is thus put in its place as a means to an end, not as an end in itself.

◈ 13 ◈

No clouds and no game—those are the two missing pleasures. Your eye searches the rolling, khaki plain for a sight of zebra or gazelle shimmering in the haze of heat. Here is a patch of bush that might, but does not, hide a fat, wrinkled rhino; over among those trees you look in vain for the absurd pole-necked giraffe.

Nowhere can your ear catch the shrill, sharp whistle of a reed-buck, your eye the wart-hog's pricked-up, hurrying tail. It is extraordinary, how much sheer interest is added to a journey by the unseen presence of game. The whole wide landscape is charged with a latent excitement that may at any moment fuse into a flash of delight. But you are denied that here. There is game still in West Africa, and in the North a few lions and elephants, but they are scarce and wary, and I encountered none.

We stopped to get a puncture mended at Navrongo. A "fitter" came—a young man in trousers. Every small town and village has its "fitter", in name at least; in nine cases out of ten an ex-soldier. A large, admiring crowd gathered to watch him change the tyre in the shade. The fitter declaimed, gestured and brandished tools; the mundane task became an event of high dramatic importance, a test of skill, a wrestling with the puncture-causing devil. The event was far too enjoyable to be hurried through, and took the fitter over an hour.

Outside Navrongo stands a huge white empty hospital, flanked by bungalows, erected at some fantastic cost, unfortunately in such a position that flood-water drains into, instead of away from, the building. The designs were drawn in Accra by persons who never visited the site until the hospital was too substantially in existence to be moved to a drier spot a little farther up the hill. Bare, bleak and out of scale with its surroundings, it stands there like some temple of the future, lacking gods or priests.

The priests of the past must be hard put to it to keep the tenth commandment when confronted with these lavish outpourings of public money. They have to manage with so very little themselves. Drinking orange squash on an open porch outside their simple, home-built living quarters, the White Fathers near Bawku, these black-bearded and white-robed priests, who are all French, spoke of their work in this vast and (one would think) unrewarding land. As it was growing dark a young, beardless Father came in on his bicycle. He had been comforting the dying, he said. At this time of year, when dust-storms sweep about, cerebro-spinal meningitis breaks out. It is a painful disease and nearly always fatal, and the Fathers are kept busy going from hut to hut. The people welcome them, but very few receive the Sacrament or Christian burial. Converts in these parts are not easily made. The Fathers do not seem at all discouraged; they cycle about in the sun, laugh, run schools and have a great serenity. They go home on leave once only, after ten years, and from then until the end of their working days must live and toil in Africa.

Tamale is a flat, sprawling, mud-and-thatch town smothered, at this time of year, in red laterite dust, the streets packed with people. (In one of them is a small general store called Gloria in Excelsis Deo.) It is baking hot and far from healthy, yet Europeans love it. "This is the real Africa," they say approvingly. The simplicity appeals, the spareness, the dignity derived, in life as in art, from elimination of all but the esentials. The virtues of the people—their honesty, candour, manliness and, above all, their goodwill—redeem the starkness of their land. They have not yet learnt to resent the European, and their good manners would in any case prevent them from abusing him; and that makes up for all the heat and flies and fever in the world. But on "Education Ridge" a flock of new academies has recently arisen in an effort to retrieve years of lethargy: the trade school, a Teachers' Training College, a boys' and a girls' secondary school. These presage revolution in the still dormant North.

Round about grows the coarse-stalked, reddish *andropogon* grass of the savannah, with here and there patches of rustling guinea corn and mounds ready for yams. Drifts of a tall, pink, campion-like flower called Tamale pride (*Oldenlandia oppoitofolia*) line the roads out of the capital. At night, fruit-bats tinkle in the trees, emitting without respite a high, piercing, mechanical note like two metal skewers striking each other. Ping, ting—ping, ting-ping, ting: each bat sounds the same note endlessly. What does this metronomic pinking signify? By day, the bats hang upside down in trees, silently; now they are presumably about their business, eating fruit, mating, flying about. In the darkness they are invisible, but I flashed a torchlight into the branches of a tree and saw them flitting ominously round and round, their aim a mystery, still squeaking out their plaintive, plangent, tinkabell chorus.

From Tamale I flew south in one of the little Doves in which

West African Airways efficiently, though sometimes bumpily, conveys its customers. Coming in from Accra, the Dove disgorged a six-foot, fifteen-stone, burly African captain of the West African Frontier Force, smoking a curly meerschaum pipe. He alighted with two tennis racquets, a squash racquet and a hockey stick under his arm. A fellow-officer who met him asked what he had been doing in Accra.

"Oh, just swanning around," he said.

∽ 14 ∽

Kumasi has been called the garden city of West Africa. In this moist, steamy climate with its high rainfall and forest soil, plants proliferate, flowers bloom, wither and bloom again continuously and grass grows tall and green. The scarlet of poinsettia and hibiscus is everywhere; so is a profusion of hydrangeas, the ostentatious, waxy trumpets of the frangipani, the blare of bougainvilleas; with here and there a bed of mildewed roses, clearly depressed by all this riot of tropical vigour.

Despite all this, Kumasi seemed to me less like a garden city than a throbbing pulse of trade, a place of getting and spending. Its most impressive sight is the lorry park, where hundreds of trucks—it might be thousands—packed as close as herrings in a basket, load and unload their freight. Every moment of the day a truck draws out for the north, crammed with passengers perched on piles of kola nuts, bales of cloth, drums of palm oil or petrol; or another rolls in with loads of sheep, cattle, groundnuts, onions, shea butter. Here is the terminus and point of departure for all traffic with the north, and into French territory. Lorries loaded with cocoa rattle in, also, from surrounding villages, and go out with trade goods. Lorries and buses are indeed the life-blood of the Gold Coast, as trade and money are its ruling passions.

All this has developed, within fifty years, at the court of the Ashanti kings. Never can a city have changed more in half a century. The rude magnificence of the Ashanti capital in former days amazed every traveller. Gold was the key-note. The king, his captains, his wives, servants, slaves, every courtier and office-bearer was encrusted with this metal that struck back at the sun himself with glory. Gold breast-plates for the messengers, gold rams' heads dangling from gold-handled swords, gold horns for the trumpeters; even the executioners wore on their breasts golden hatchets.

Gold, garish colour, turbulent throngs easily pricked into frenzy—these were the visual aspects that impressed travellers like Bowdich, who saw the Ashanti court at the peak of its glory.[1] He and his companions, forming a mission from the Governor at Cape Coast, were fêted with bands, volleys and a wild dance performed by warriors in monstrous uniforms ornamented with feathers, bells, the horns and tails of animals, shells, knives, amulets, chains and tassels. A hundred bands struck up with drums, flutes and horns; at least a hundred state umbrellas, each large enough to shelter thirty persons, were sprung up and down. Made of brilliantly coloured silks and set with mirrors, each canopy was crowned with some golden emblem—an elephant, a crane, a sword—or with a stuffed animal. Chiefs and notables wore silken cloths of every hue and pattern thrown over the shoulder like a Roman toga (as the cloth is still worn today); their blood-encrusted, golden-handled swords were sheathed in leopard skin or shagreen, and from their left wrists hung lumps of rock gold so heavy that each man had to rest his arm on the head of a boy.

Passing through close-packed ranks of seated warriors hung about with knives, brass bells, iron collars and leopards' skins, and estimated by Bowdich to number 30,000, the embassy at last approached the presence of the king.

His manners were majestic, yet courteous; and he did not allow his surprise to beguile him for a moment of the composure of the monarch. He appeared to be about thirty-eight years of age, inclined to corpulence and of a benevolent countenance; he wore a fillet of aggry beads round his temples, a necklace of gold cockspur-shells strung by their largest ends, and over his shoulder a red silk cord suspending three saphies cased in gold; his bracelets were the richest mixture of beads and gold and his fingers covered with rings; his cloth was of a dark green silk; a pointed diadem was elegantly painted in

[1] *Mission to the Ashantee*. T. E. Bowdich, first published in 1823.

white on his forehead; also a pattern resembling an epaulette
on each shoulder, and an ornament like a full-blown rose, one
leaf rising above another until it covered his whole breast; his
knee-bands were of aggry beads and his ankle-strings of gold
ornaments of the most delicate workmanship, small drums,
sankos, stools, swords, guns and birds clustered together; his
sandals, of a soft white leather, were embossed across the instep
with small gold and silver cases of saphies; he was seated in a
low chair, richly ornamented with gold; he wore a pair of gold
castanets on his finger and thumb, which he clapped to enforce
silence. The belts of the guards behind his chair were cased
in gold and covered with small jaw-bones of the same metal;
the elephants' tails, waving like a small cloud before him,
were spangled with gold, and large plumes of feathers were
flourished amid them. His eunuch presided over these attendants, wearing only one massy piece of gold about his neck;
the royal stool, entirely encased in gold, was displayed under
a splendid umbrella, with drums, sankos, horns and various
musical instruments, cased in gold, about the thickness of a
cartridge paper: large circles of gold hung by scarlet cloth
from the swords of state; hatchets of the same were intermixed
with them; the breasts of the Ocrahs and various attendants
were adorned with large stars, stools, crescents and gossamer
wings of solid gold.

Beneath all this glittering splendour, the skeleton of savagery
protruded. Kumasi had three execution grounds, the king a
staff of a hundred executioners; the British expedition which
took the town in 1896 found a grove full of the bones and skulls
of literally hundreds of victims. They also found, and took
away, a brass bowl five feet in diameter in which was collected
human blood to be offered to the stools of dead kings. To divert
Bowdich's embassy—a sort of comic turn—a man shortly to be
sacrificed was paraded before them.

A knife was passed through his cheeks, to which his lips
were noosed like the figure 8; one ear was cut off and carried
before him, the other hung to his head by a piece of skin;
there were several gashes in his back, and a knife was thrust
E*

under each shoulder-blade; he was led with a cord passed through his nose, by men disfigured with immense caps of shaggy black skins, and drums beat before him.

Very possibly this man was suffering the early stages of that dreadful torture known as "the dance of death", the punishment inflicted on anyone taken in adultery with one of the King's many wives. The wife herself was beheaded, together with her parents and maternal uncles. The fate of her lover is described, in a passage not for the squeamish, by Rattray, who had the details of one of the King's executioners, an active participant in the rite.[1]

The delight in cruelty, bloodshed and excess which so startled early travellers found its most sanguine outlets at the annual

[1] "The culprit, through whose cheeks a *sepow* knife has already been thrust, is taken to that part of the town known as *Nkram*' (lit. 'In the midst of blood'). Here he is seated, and the famous Gyabom fetish is placed upon his lap. The nasal septum is now pierced, and through the aperture is threaded a thorny creeper, by which he is later led about. Four other *sepow* knives are now thrust through various parts of the body, care being taken not to pass them so deeply as to wound any vital spot. He is now led by the rope creeper . . . to Akyeremade, where the chief of that stool would scrape his left leg, facetiously remarking as he did so 'I am scraping perfume for my wives'; next, to the house of the chief of Asafo, where his left ear is cut off; thence to Bantama, the village near Kumasi containing the royal mausoleum, where the Ashanti generalissimo resides. He personally severs the victim's right ear, and then scrapes bare the right shinbone; then the man is taken back beneath the shade of the *atopere* tree. Here he is compelled to dance all day, keeping time to the rhythm of the *atopere* drums. After dark he is dragged to the spot outside the royal palace where the King and outraged husband sits surrounded by all the chiefs and court attendants to witness the final dispatch of the victim. His arms are now hacked off at the elbows and his legs below the knee; then his eyelids are cut off. He is ordered to continue dancing, but as he is unable to do so, his buttocks are sliced off and he is set down on a little pile of gunpowder which is set alight. A slab of skin is then cut off his back, and this is placed before him with the pleasantry: 'Since your mother bore you and your father begat you, have you seen the skin of your back?' The small executioners, sons of the chief executioner, now approach their father and complain: 'Father, he has taken our knife.' They receive the reply: 'Go and take that which is yours.' With these words they are let loose on the dying man and cut pieces of flesh from various parts of his body. The chief executioner now reports to the King that the man is nearly dead and receives permission to cut off his head. . . . The executioner's fee for this day's work is an *asia* weight of gold dust (26s.). A punishment somewhat similar was inflicted on a murderer. . . . I may add that my friend the executioner was normally a most delightful, humane and benign old gentleman" (*Religion and Art in Ashanti*. R. S. Rattray. Oxford, 1927).

yam festival and at the funeral of a king. The yam custom was a cross between harvest-home and saturnalia. For three days licence prevailed to cover any familiarity, indecency or assault; "each sex", Bowdich observed, "abandons itself to its passions", and the king provided free rum for all. Executioners paraded, clashing their knives on the skulls of past victims, and in the "custom" witnessed by Bowdich about a hundred slaves were sacrificed in Kumasi in such a manner that their blood flowed into the holes from which the yams had been lifted. Without such a sacrifice, the next season's crop would fail.

Even the yam festival paled beside a king's funeral. On the instant of his death, his male relations rushed out into the town as if demented, firing at anyone they saw. Laws were suspended, chaos reigned. A round-up of slaves for sacrifice was held, and soon all the vultures in Africa seemed to have gathered, for only the heads were buried, the trunks were left to rot in the bush. Royal wives, dressed in their finery, drank themselves insensible with palm wine and were strangled. As the king was allowed 3,333 wives—a lucky number, Bowdich says, carefully kept up— the holocaust would have been great even for Ashanti had they all been sacrificed; perhaps only those as it were in use were expected to share their husband's grave. On the death of Sai Quamina, in 1799, the custom was repeated once a week for three months and 200 victims were killed on each occasion.

Sai Quamina's mother was even more bloodily mourned. The king gave 3,000 victims, each of the larger towns contributed a hundred, and the villages two each. Even burial did not end the bloodshed. The king's bones, carefully scraped and cleaned, were laid in a mausoleum, and there many sacrifices took place to keep the royal spirits satisfied. As, at a king's death, every custom made for lesser fry during his reign had to be repeated, the slaughter must have claimed so many thousands of men and women as to have been a factor in keeping population numbers stable. Bowdich comments on the looks of exultation cast on the victims awaiting sacrifice and the transports of frenzy displayed by captains and warriors. They enjoyed it all, that is certain.

Yet the people were not mere savages. Their king's rule was wide and firm, yet wisely decentralized; their armies disciplined and nearly always victorious; the dynasty stable; the currency controlled. (Gold dust belonged to the people, but nuggets must be brought to the king, who then allowed the blindfolded finder to take one in three from his hand; the treasurer's weights were one-third heavier than anyone else's; by these means the Treasury collected a sort of universal $33\frac{1}{3}$ per cent purchase tax.) Family life was secure and well regulated, inheritance was assured and men lived under a law which, being exceedingly savage, was scrupulously observed. The king's powers were great, but not untrammelled; without the consent of his council he could do little, certainly not go to war. In Bowdich's day his inner council consisted of four "caboceers", and he never gave a judgment without first consulting them.

As abruptly as the scythe fells the nettle, British rule put an end to the public enjoyment of these savage indulgences. No more funeral customs, no more yam festivals, no more "washing" of dead chiefs' stools with slaves' blood. So far, so good; but what of the instincts, the dark desires of which these indulgences were but an outward expression? British rule has not eradicated them. Education, one may suppose, is doing so. In many cases, where education is sufficiently prolonged and thorough, no doubt it is; but will a few years of indifferently taught lessons in the three R's change the deeper levels of the mind in a single generation?

Fifty years is little time in which to jump from the slaughter of 3,000 victims and a three-days' saturnalia to an Empire Day parade with an improving speech by the Chief Commissioner, which seems to be the best we can offer in the way of pageantry. How dull life has become, how monotonous, how anaemic, how inert! Impatience with British rule is due, I am sure, as much to this as to anything. It is called a revolt against imperialism, but in truth I think it is, in part at least, a revolt against *ennui*, and that when the British Empire finally crumbles we might write as its epitaph: "We bored them to death." What will follow? A revulsion to more natural ways? Perhaps the end of British rule will see not a tidy, democratic, bourgeois state run by an imitation parliament, full of the things we so much enjoy —adult suffrage, housing committees, sewerage schemes, welfare clinics, reform schools and women's institutes—but reversion to an older, harsher, more haphazard and satyric order, expressing the passions of Saturday night rather than the intentions of Sunday morning.

∾ 15 ∾

The Asantehene's palace is a low stone bungalow with a gravelled drive flanked by two sandstone lions. It is a male residence; the Asantehene's wives live in a compound of swish huts close at hand and do not appear in public. I am ignorant of their number, but it certainly does not approach the traditional 3,333. The reception of a modern visitor is very different from that accorded to Bowdich. No drums, no crowds, no retinue, no umbrellas, no display. A lone secretary, quiet and courteous, shows you to a stiff English arm-chair under two life-size photographs of English royalty, wearing crowns. Everything is tidy, clean, and without taste, good or bad—perhaps no one has cared enough to impart it. The bungalow seems to hold itself aloof from those soft, warm, human noises which accompany the flow of life in an ordinary village or home.

Nana Sir Osei Agyeman Prempeh II, a man of middle height and middle age, wears a simple cloth of white and indigo, plain leather sandals and no ornaments. His face is lined and strong, with a broad nose and forehead,[1] his self-command flawless, his English fluent. He has held the Stool for nearly thirty years and watched the progressive dissolution of Ashanti tradition and the slow undermining of chieftainship. Now, in the winding up of indirect rule, he sees the final eclipse of his own authority. He is to become a "constitutional" chief, allowed to preside at formal openings of the council and then obliged to withdraw. The lands and forests of the Stool are to be handed over to a council of "youngmen" whose fathers' heads might have adorned his own father's grave.

Now he must watch, in dignity and silence, a *volte face* of British policy, formerly based (it seemed securely) on the recognition of chiefs and their traditional councils as the lynch-pins of

---

[1] It is stated by Mrs. Meyerowitz (*The Sacred State of the Akan*) that the parents of a boy eligible for kingship used to soften his bones with hot wet cloths and massage the skull in order to make it wider, as this was believed to confer the aspect of dignity.

administration. All this is going, or has already gone. There is
no blinking the fact that, by sponsoring the new constitution, the
British Government has abandoned indirect rule and thrown the
chiefs overboard. The Asantehene is too intelligent a man not
to understand that change is inevitable and the "youngmen"
bound to have their say, and too true an African not to wish for
self-rule. He did himself, in fact, go to meet these changes by
supporting proposals to elect "youngmen" to the Asanteman
Council and appointing them to Native Authority courts. But
one can bow to the inevitable, or surrender to it. If surrender
cannot be helped, it needs to be recognized that certain faithful
allies suffer, and cannot withdraw from the scene. Their only
course is then to make terms with the victors and accept a new
position in the scheme of things. It may be that an innate
African respect for tradition, and an equally embedded reluc-
tance to embrace logical conclusions (qualities held in common
with the British) will help to keep the chiefs off the scrap-heap
and on some kind of pedestal, even if their power and wealth
disappears.

The Asantehene, at any rate, seems to waste no time on
regrets.

"It is a good thing", he said, "for district councils to take over
political powers from the chiefs. Up till now, the 'youngmen'
have been like spectators who shout to football players to put the
ball in goal. Now they will have to go and do it for themselves.
And they will have to stop accusing the chiefs of stealing the tax
money, and promising to do away with taxes, when they take
over the Government."

In olden days the Ashanti union, embracing now some 800,000
souls, comprised a number of separate states, each with its court
and ruling family, loosely bound together by a common allegiance to the Golden Stool. With the exile of Prempeh in 1896,
the union might have fallen apart; but a common tradition,
language and loyalty held it fairly well together until, in 1935,
it was officially revived under the Ashanti Confederacy Council.
Now, in place of the twenty-four Native Authorities of which it
was composed, there are twenty-four district councils, two-thirds
of whose members are elected "youngmen". The chiefs will be
forced to withdraw from the political management of their divi-

sions. In one sense this is to revert to the older situation, when the chief was a religious more than a political leader. But religion, in those days, counted for more than politics—governed politics. With the old religion shrivelling away, the chiefs are being ordered to feed on empty husks while the fruits of authority go to the new politicians.

Next to the Asantehene in importance is the Queen Mother, who need not be the true mother of the king; in fact, she is more often a sister or cousin. I was taken to see her by Mrs. Quashie-Idun, the wife of an eminent Judge. We walked through an outer courtyard full of women pounding *fu-fu* and stirring cooking-pots. Children crawled about on earth hardened like cement by the footfalls of generations. A few fat, tame vultures hopped about among the kitchen refuse. On the far side of the courtyard was a low stone bungalow, one room thick, with a narrow veranda. These were the Queen Mother's private apartments.

She sat upright on a sofa: thin, ageing, alert, with hair cropped short as a man's. Her face was intelligent but mask-like; she might have been an idol cast in bronze. The office of chieftainship appears to breed a type of woman as different from the plump, full-breasted matrons of the bush as oil from granite: a hard, formidable type, like the horsey Englishwoman or the harsher kind of female army officer.

Two old cronies crouched at the Queen Mother's feet. A young man in a loin-cloth stood behind her with a fan, and a cluster of naked children stared in through an open doorway. The fan-bearer unlocked a cupboard and brought out a bottle of wine. Mrs. Quashie-Idun and the Queen Mother, who does not speak English, exchanged greetings. Sitting opposite each other, they represented two extremes. Mrs. Quashie-Idun is one of the best-known women in the Gold Coast. She serves on committees and supports every good cause—Red Cross, infant welfare, Mothers' Unions, nursery schools—in spite of having to look after five children of her own. Her outlook seemed to me exactly that of a conscientious Englishwoman of county family married to a public man at any time during the fifty years preceding the last war. In Africa, the new order, perhaps. The Queen Mother most certainly represents the old.

When a king dies, it is the regnant Queen Mother who, after

consulting the elders, chooses his successor. Her choice must be confirmed by the full council of elders and chiefs. Her jewellery is silver, as the King's gold; when she dies, the eight openings of her body are filled with silver dust; her stool rests on a sheep-skin to symbolize peace, as the King's on a leopard skin to suggest fierceness. Any woman in trouble may come to her, for she is the champion of women's rights. Girls are brought to her at puberty and she presents a gift to those found to be virgins. Her cooks must prepare meals for the spirits of dead Queen Mothers, each of whom has her stool. Queen Mothers of the past seem to have had a sound feminine leaning towards the practical. Tradition holds that it was a Queen Mother who introduced the hoe in the fifteenth century and others who brought in, at different times, basins, bowls and brass lamps.[1]

Is the Queen Mother—I asked her—still consulted by the women? Do the girls still come to her and does she continue to carry out the rites of her office? Her lined, leathery face remained impassive, expressionless. Her butler poured more wine. Women still come to her, she answered; young girls receive gifts; as for the ceremonies, some continue and some do not. It was an ancient custom for all the people to greet the King and the Queen Mother on every forty-third day, bringing sheep, yams and corn, hens, eggs and palm wine. The talking drums sounded, the people gathered and, in the mausoleum of dead kings, the Asantehene himself, in bare feet, offered meat and drink to each of the blackened ancestral stools. Afterwards, he paraded under his state umbrella, attended by Court officials with golden staves, by fan-bearers, elephant-tail switchers, heralds, sword-bearers, horn-blowers and many others, to receive the homage of his chiefs. A lesser version of this festival (the *adae*) took place every twenty-first day, and, in the districts, each divisional chief had his own *adae*. One way and another, festivals with feasts and dances came thick and fast in old Ashanti.

But now, the Queen Mother said, there is no *adae*. During the troubles of 1948 a rumour spread that the CPP meant to organize demonstrations against the Asantehene. To avoid trouble, the "stool washing" was held in private; and so the drumming

[1] See *The Sacred State of the Akan* by Meyerowitz.

and dancing and feasting are over, perhaps for ever. But the Golden Stool itself is still paraded on ceremonial occasions. The repository of the Ashanti soul, it was summoned from heaven by a great magician and floated down in a clap of thunder to rest on the knees of the federation's founder, Osei Tutu. This happened in Kumasi, ever since a hallowed place.

That the Golden Stool is still deeply revered is shown by an incident which happened in 1941. A divisional chief brought to a meeting of the Confederacy Council a stool with gold bands on it. His fellow chiefs were so outraged at his presumption that they obliged him to offer twelve sheep in atonement to the offended ancestors. The Stool has its own house near the Asantehene's palace, and near the mausoleum which holds the blackened stools of his ancestors. Part of the sacred hill where the old mausoleum stood is being levelled by bulldozers to make a site for a new 500-bed hospital.

∾ 16 ∾

I drove to Mampong, north of Kumasi, with Mr. Oduntun, director of the Government's information services in Ashanti: a young man with an eager zest for his job, a flair for administration and an endearing modesty of manner. A conscientious, upright individual who neither smokes nor drinks, Mr. Oduntun is a product of Methodist endeavour in which that Mission might well take pride. His father was a Methodist minister, and his grandmother, who lived to be ninety-three, had been brought up a literate Christian. Mr. Oduntun took his degree in Modern Greats at Oxford and has returned with a sword of idealism unsheathed to help build Jerusalem in his green and hopeful native land.

The road to Mampong cuts through the close, dark, humid rain-forest. Trees tower up: grey-boled proud mahoganies, silk-cottons buttressed like cathedrals, and many others. Walk in a few paces, and you inhabit a world as dark and strange as the ocean bed. No sun, no colour, and at first silence, but not for long; the ear soon picks up a symphony of little rustles and stirrings of twigs and leaves, odd breathings and ticks; if you sit motionless on a log, you hear a soft, insidious, irregular plop—

plop—plop—plop, like the footsteps of a phantom hunter. It is only the big, flat leaves of a certain tree making their gentle landfall on a floor of rotting vegetation. All this is a "closed forest", meaning that it has reached the climax of its long, slow growth. New species cannot break in, old ones smoothly reproduce themselves. The forest has reached equilibrium and, left to itself, would scarcely change.

Red dust thickly gilds trees, shrubs and undergrowth bordering the road. This rust and green curtain is here and there flecked with holly-berry red—"Ashanti blood", a creeper whose flower has four scarlet bracts. According to legend, the nation will go down when "Ashanti blood" loses its colour. There is no sign of it yet.

We are here in the heart of cocoa-land, and at the height of the cocoa boom. This must be one of the easiest crops to live by in the world. You simply plant seedlings in the forest—for they must have shade—let the trees grow and in due course lop from their convenient branches brilliant orange pods containing purple beans. The pods have to be fermented and dried on trays in the sun. Then you bag the beans, and a buyer with a lorry collects them from the side of the road. Exertion is reduced to a happy minimum, and at present you enjoy the heartening price of £4 a bag, instead of the seven-and-sixpence you got before the war.

Of course there are catches. The biggest of them all is swollenshoot disease, of which I was to hear much. In places it has spread like a bush fire and killed tens of thousands of trees. Another is the danger of a falling market. High prices do not last forever, and the growers may not take a fall stoically. A third, not widely realized, is the rapid cutting down of forest to make way for food crops. Except where it is preserved—and less than one-fifth of it is—the closed forest is melting away at the rate of 300 square miles a year. If this continues there will be little left outside the Government reserves in a generation, and of course the rate of destruction is growing as the population rises.

We passed through many forest-encircled villages straggling along a thread of road. In each, standing proudly up among the swish huts, are to be seen several new, superior bungalows built of concrete blocks and painted like a gay old lady. One house has blood-red steps, pale pink pillars and walls in the sickly green tint of pistachio ice-cream. The colours strike a European eye as incongruous and somehow off-key; you seldom see a pure, strong, straightforward sky-blue or grass-green.

A surprising number of houses are roofless and full of vegetation; through the frameless window embrasures you can see undergrowth and a young palm or two poking up inside. Are these houses going up, or falling down? You cannot tell.

"It is the cocoa boom," explained Mr. Oduntun. "A man decides to spend his money on a house. But money runs out before the house is finished, and so he has to wait until the next cocoa season. If it is good, he will be able to add the roof." If it is bad, or if he owes too much money, the roof never goes on at all and the house, or what there is of it, crumbles away.

These, it appears, are country villas; most successful cocoa-growers live in town, leaving their trees in the care of relatives and hired labour from the Northern Territories.

"And what do they do," I enquired, "in the towns?"

"They litigate."

As football pools to the British, so litigation to the Gold Coaster. A good lawsuit will go on not just for years, but for decades. The subject is generally land. A Judge told me of a typical case. It concerned rather less than an acre of land, worth perhaps £10, and had worked its way already through two native courts and the High Court to the West African Court of Appeal, on its way to the Privy Council. It would cost each of the two parties at least £1,000.

"It's a question of face," the Judge said. "People will mortgage everything they have, borrow right and left, immerse themselves in debt, rather than give up—and lose face."

An almost fanatical pride, accompanied by a passion for revenge, would seem to be a characteristic of the Ashanti. In confederacy days, a man would give his own life in order to discomfort an enemy. If he swore on the king's head that his enemy must kill him, that enemy must do so, or else forfeit all his property and generally his life as well. On the other hand, if he observed the oath and killed the swearer of it, he and all his family would be ruined by the case which the victim's family would bring against him, and he himself would run the risk of death by torture. Lawsuits appear to have taken the place of these Borgian feuds, or rather to be the modern expression of them.

We reached the village of Bonwire, famous for its weavers, to find it *en fête*. Women in bright-hued cloths were dancing up and down the main street waving handkerchiefs and chanting a song of praise for a new chief. "His yard is full of chickens. Peace to the chief, and peace to the inside of the belly," Mr. Oduntun translated.

The street was lined by small shops, and almost every one carried a licence to sell beer and spirits. Piles of bottles outside each door indicated that business was excellent. A bottle of gin costs eighteen shillings. In the cocoa season it is quite usual for a man to walk in, put down his money and drink the whole bottle straight off. He may have received £40 or £50 in cash that morning for his cocoa. About £37,000,000 is being paid out this season to cocoa-growers, of whom there are about a quarter of a million.

In several of the little shops, weavers were at work in dark corners on their narrow looms. They weave in silk, making the *kente* cloths for which Ashanti is famous, to be worn only by chiefs and Queen Mothers. In his book on Ashanti arts, Rattray illustrates sixty-three different designs.[1] Each follows a traditional pattern, and some, like Highland tartans, belong to certain families. Some have meanings, or commemorate a past hero, or recall a legend. Royal cloths—heavy, thick and brilliant in colour—have been made in Bonwire for perhaps 400 years and are still made here, although the cost of silk yarn—all imported—is now so high that a *kente* cloth costs at least £50.

Most of these craftsmen are employed by one of the master weavers of the town. One of them showed us his establishment: in his yard, half a dozen weavers at work, their yarn stretched out in front of them tied to a stone; and a double flight of steps leading to his pride and joy—a new, concrete-block house with an upstairs. The master weaver led us into a long, narrow living-room with a veranda on both sides. The colour scheme was arresting: chocolate-red walls picked out in yellow ochre. Had Euclid suffered from nightmares, he might have designed the

[1] *Religion and Art in Ashanti.* R. S. Rattray. Oxford, 1927.

linoleum on the floor. Local carpenters had made, and made well, the heavy mahogany furniture, but in shapes that almost caricatured the late Victorian. On the sideboard stood a jeroboam of eau-de-Cologne.

◇ 17 ◇

One expects to be surprised in Africa, but it is as startling to come upon two white palaces designed by Maxwell Fry amid clearings in the aboriginal forest as it would be to find one of the Great Pyramids in Surrey.

One of these two groups of buildings near Mampong houses St. Monica's, a girls' school run by sisters of the Order of the Holy Paraclete, which, unexpectedly, has its headquarters in Whitby. The nuns are tall, gaunt Yorkshire women, well wrapped up against tropical airs in long white robes, black capes, black stockings and sun-helmets. Strange, how you never see the topee now, save on the heads of nuns or Government officials in full uniform. Time was when no white person dared venture a yard from his dwelling unless heavily encased in cork and flannel. There were even spine-pads to button on the shirt and back-flaps to hang from the brim of the helmet. No one was bold enough to test the theory that the sun brought instant death until, in the war, men of the R.A.F. abandoned not only hats but shirts as well, the better to build airfields, and thrived. Now the topee has disappeared. With it has passed an epoch, a *weltanschauung*. It could, indeed, be argued that the topee, like the Golden Stool, had certain magical properties, that in it reposed, if not the spirit of the British nation, at least a great deal of its self-confidence. Stiff, formal, inflexible, it was a fitting headgear for a ruling race. Now, bareheaded or in a light squashed felt, the ex-priests of empire talk of partnership and write to friends about openings in England.

The nuns of the Holy Paraclete, however, stick to their topees and their task, which is to make English schoolgirls, on the way to becoming Christian mothers, out of Ashanti girls. No more, for these young things, the pledging with yams and palm wine, the sacrifice of cocks before ancestral shrines, the rites of puberty and agonies of circumcision; for them clean frocks and pigtails, prayers and basket-ball, *Little Women* and the arts of needlework. They were practising, when I arrived, for an end-of-term performance of *Antigone*, a drama they might very likely grasp more thoroughly than a bunch of English schoolgirls. To modern Europeans, used to wars which totally disintegrate the warriors and perhaps themselves about to be vaporized, all that fuss about the burial of a body may seem a little overdone. An Ashanti, on the other hand, would fully share Antigone's horror at Creon's behaviour; and incest is to them, as to Athenians, a crime against the gods which only death can expiate. As for Teiresias, give him a bag of beans and a mass of amulets and charms, and there is the monkey-faced old witch-doctor everyone knows.

A few miles off, a Teachers' Training College for men run by the Presbyterians occupies another cluster of bold, angular and rather harsh Maxwell Fry buildings, the inner walls imaginatively coloured in pastel shades, the outer ones as white and hard as good teeth. It is refreshing to see a group of buildings that is not *extempore*, flung together, and obviously destined soon to fall apart. As places to live and work in they have two faults, I was told. They are hot, because they have large windows and no verandas, and they are dry, because they have no gutters to collect rain-water off the roof. And so the students were fetching water in buckets from a stream nearly a mile away. These are serious practical drawbacks to buildings which cost nearly £100,000 to house only 120 future teachers. But to the eye these scholastic temples are arresting because they are original and try to lead into an African architecture that will be permanent and notable. But why is one irresistibly reminded of an international fair, why does one look round for the Palace of Industry, for the statue of a young giant and giantess striding to work with a baby and a blunt, unserviceable tool?

The smallest room is the library, and it has very few books in it; as the Principal explained, you cannot buy many with a grant of £15 a year. But a handsome bell had just been installed in the clock-tower at a cost of £150.

⌁ 18 ⌁

Bosumtwi is an unexpected lake, lying in a deep cup in hills whose slopes are thickly forested: smooth and silky, smoke-grey and very quiet. The villages clustering round its banks cannot be seen until you are on them, and the calm of its surface is unbroken by canoes. For Bosumtwi is a sacred lake, the home of a powerful god to whom canoes, metal and nets are all tabu. In Accra I had heard a fisheries officer lecture a class of clerks who were to manage the new district councils on the need to break down such customs, in order that people should have a balanced diet. All the educated clerks agreed. But on the shores of Lake Bosumtwi they would be helpless to enforce such views. The people fish from log rafts which they propel with their feet, since wooden paddles, as well as canoes, are tabu.

Sometimes the lake god fires his gunpowder, and then a strange, muffled explosion occurs. The waters turn black, a queer smell is given off and fish in their thousands rise to the surface and float there in a stunned condition. The prosaic European suggestion is that gases generated in layers of rotting vegetation at the bottom for some reason explode and blow to the surface a lot of decomposing black scum.

An especially powerful fetish used to hold sway on the lake shore. It was seen by Rattray to consist of two life-size clay models of women's breasts with a knife between and a wooden idol above, with other wooden figures arranged round it.[1] Its function was to detect witches, who were plentiful and at night would suck people's blood through the walls of the houses. The fetish priests grew too powerful; their rites became suspect and the fetish was suppressed by the Government.

Some fetish objects, of course, are beneficent and there is no secret about these. In Ashanti they are known as *suman*, or charms. What Rattray called "the greatest *suman* in Ashanti"[2] consisted of an ordinary broom, with chips of an old flintlock gun stuck into the handle, stained with dye, eggs and the blood of many sacrifices. This the witch-doctor had brought into

[1] See *Ashanti* by R. S. Rattray. Oxford, 1923.
[2] *Religion and Art in Ashanti*. R. S. Rattray. Oxford, 1927.

contact with every tabu object within reach and spoken to it many forbidden words. After that it held the power to protect him from a great number of misfortunes. A scapegoat, in fact.

One is struck by the inconsequential, muddled composition of charms. A jumble of black-and-white threads twisted together with porcupine quills, three leopards' teeth, two seeds of two different trees and some iron rings is a charm against medicine which might cause a man to fall down while dancing—a most sinister mishap. Another has strips of red flannel knotted into it and a pair of small antelope horns, pieces of leopard skin, a bit of porcupine's tail and a padlock. This prevents pains in the back. A third consists of antelope horns plastered over with "medicine" and packed with clay containing a rusty needle and a red feather from a grey parrot. If the needle is stuck into a lime at midday or at sunset, and the right words spoken, it will kill an enemy. And there are literally hundreds more.

I discussed magic with Mr. Oduntun over tea in a rest-house in the forest above the sacred lake. While we talked, the light began to fade, the silent waters darkened and angry, ancient gods and hungry spirits did not seem far away.

Mr. Oduntun is one of those few at once released from superstition by his Western training and gathered up into the Christian fellowship. Thus equipped, it is within his power to find a way across the wilderness between two worlds. What most perturbs him is the streak of morbidity running through the African character.

"It soaks into all our songs, even into the stories we're told as children," he said. "Nothing seems worthwhile, because death is everywhere. Death and cruelty. We laugh, but our hearts are full of fear. I believe this is our worst enemy. We must shake it off, if we are to achieve greatness."

I heard the same opinion, curiously enough, that evening from a disillusioned European doctor in Kumasi. He added:

"In Sekondi there's the grave of a doctor who, according to his tombstone, saved the people from an epidemic. Who was he? How did he do it? Where did he come from? Why did he die? No one remembers anything about him. Soon his tombstone will fall down, and then his name will be obliterated forever. That's what frightens me in Africa—there's no continuity, no building with one brick upon another. Just indifference. Things slip back and have to start afresh each time. Life has no rhythm, no routine—each day is disconnected—half your work is futile because you know that although people will do what you tell them, and often do it well, as soon as your back is turned they'll shrug their shoulders and forget everything you said."

A woman doctor supported him. She, too, was disillusioned; she had been engaged two years ago to start a children's clinic in a country district, but the site was not yet even cleared, and so she worked on at Kumasi hospital, mainly on children's malnutrition, a very common complaint.

"We treat them and feed them and put them right," she said, "and they go home, and what happens? Within a year they're back again with the same trouble. It isn't that the mothers don't *know*. We explain over and over again, and back they go and fill the children up with nothing but starch, starch. . . .

"Often women come to us only when the witch-doctor's failed. Last week we had a woman who'd been in labour for three days. Earlier in her pregnancy she'd been to consult a big fetish in the Northern Territories, and the 'doctor' had stuffed her full of leaves. The baby was born dead, and so I suppose we shall be blamed. . . .

"And then the inefficiency! No fuel for the cooker—electricity failures—Kumasi was completely out of aspirin for two months! The other day we ran out of mepacrine—it had all been sold as penicillin by the African staff. Even doctors sell the drugs here!"

Doctors especially find it hard to tolerate any relaxation of standards which have been so rigidly clamped to their minds. The stealing and sale of drugs by hospital staffs—a custom almost universally practised—they find hard to stomach. Yet to most Africans this seems a perfectly reasonable thing to do. For as long as time runs, people have been visiting the medicine-man to seek relief from sickness and misfortune, and no one has ever thought of withholding payment. Now a sick man goes to a different doctor for the same reasons; why should payment not be given and received?

Europeans perhaps expect too much. It is not so long since the English surgeon was a barber, as rough and almost as superstitious as any witch-doctor.[1] The England of the surgeon-barber was the England of Christopher Wren and Daniel Defoe, of Marlborough and Walpole, the Adam brothers and Queen Anne—not a wholly barbarous land. Yet Africans are expected to jump from the witch-doctor to St. Thomas's in one generation.

∾ 19 ∾

Three years ago, an immemorial pelt of forest covered these valleys and hills. Narrow paths wound under a dark canopy among lichen-covered trunks and long, rope-like creepers. No roads had been driven in. Today you may walk into a two-storey house more full of *confort moderne* than the average villa. Parquet floors shine with polish, flowers à la Constance Spry catch the sunlight from wide windows; electricity, push-and-pulls, refrigerators, fans, are taken as a matter of course. A clearing has been scooped from the forest and filled with these gleaming residences. One feels that, like the Golden Stool, each house has floated down from an engineer's heaven and come gently to rest at Samreboi, very likely with its châtelaine, in a newly pressed silk dress and varnished finger-nails, seated at morning coffee inside.

Out of the window you can glimpse the reason for it all—the long roofs of sawmills, M.T. parks, a power-station, a water-tower, new roads vanishing into the enveloping trees. This is the United Africa Company's timber venture near the western border of the Gold Coast. Housing alone has cost them £200,000 and is by no means done; the hospital £45,000; the roads most of all—the startling figure of £3,500 a mile, and fifty miles at least will be needed. The most fantastic thing about Samreboi is that the concession will last only twenty-five years.

The U.A.C. is known for hard-headed, even ruthless efficiency and would not spend its money on speculations or frills. Presumably these heavy overheads are necessary. The tropics have to be paid for: torrential rains that render makeshift roads unusable, threats to health which make good housing desirable. And

[1] Surgeons and barbers were separated into two Corporations by an act of George II, in 1745.

without good housing white technicians, it appears, will not come. After their first question—"How much will I make?"—the next is: "What about housing?"—sensible, for they bring wives, and wives stay indoors. What a contrast between today's pioneers and their fathers! Mud huts, camp beds and foot-slogging were their portion, but I doubt if there is one who would exchange them for all the sweets of Samreboi. For these concrete luxury cages keep out more than snakes and sandflies. They keep out the people, save as servants—in fact they keep out the whole of Africa.

Into this technicians' Eden, a few "old Coasters" have penetrated. Such a one is Mr. Petley, who has served for thirty years in Africa, survived most of its diseases and emerged properly contemptuous of this new age of morning coffee and air conditioning. His generation stuck to gin and thrived on it. He took me to see some tree-felling along one of the new roads. And very lovely it was, a red road twisting down to clear, stone-cobbled streams and up over the next rise through shaggy forest and the clean-boled trees. He knew the native names for nearly all. To the stranger these are euphonious but meaningless—*niangosi, terrietia, lophira.* I can remember the deep and mellow crimson of the *kaku,* red almost as a Canadian maple, blazing out among its green companions, and the big umbrella leaves, like huge horse-chestnuts, of the *musonga.* Foresters have identified about 500 species in these forests, of which fifty-seven, they say, are usable.

As soon as the Company cuts a road, squatters crowd in to cultivate the rich, fresh soil on either side of it. They clear-fell the forest, and the Company has no power to stop them. At the present rate, there will be no timber a mile back on either side of every road long before the concession expires.

Worse still, no replanting is required by the Government. Where squatters cultivate, there can be no natural regeneration. And so, unless some great change occurs, in a surprisingly short space of time all this expanse of natural forest will be gone.

Can nothing be done? It seems not. A new-comer must ask the local chief's permission to cut trees and plant crops. As this request always carries a dash with it, permission is seldom withheld. Before the concession went through, the Company had to win consent from all the chiefs concerned, each of whom expected his dash—in some cases as much as £200 and the customary gin. It was Mr. Petley's task to conduct innumerable palavers. Chiefs are sticklers for etiquette, and one meeting ended in failure because a European gave offence by crossing his legs.

Fetishes and fairies are proving a practical problem. The men refused to work in one part of the concession because a fetish has its seat there; even after the sacrifice of a cow, some bolder individuals who ventured in were taken with fits. The forest is heavily haunted by goblins and monsters. The goblins are of three kinds: red, white and black. They converse by whistling; all are about a foot high, and their feet turn backwards. Black *mmoatia* are harmless, but white ones can be as malicious as gremlins; they steal food and palm wine, drive goats away and torment people.

There is a far worse creature in the forest, a real monster, covered with long hair, bloodshot of eye and given to sitting on branches dangling its feet. However high the branch—whether the height of a man or a steeple—the monster's feet can just touch the ground. Sometimes an unwary hunter will find himself tangled up in the dangling legs, and that is the end of him. Mary Kingsley encountered this monster in Nigeria, near Calabar; one side was putrefying, and if a man accidentally brushed against it in the dark, he was doomed.[1]

Alas for the monsters and goblins! Canadian lumberjacks, brought in to train English and African alike, have no time for them, and the noisy donkey-winches, caterpillar tractors and big timber trucks are driving them into the limbo of lost mythologies.

As you drive south from Samreboi towards the sea, the forest thins and you come to villages again. You have entered the Colony, that region which has been much longer in touch with Europe than Ashanti or the Northern Territories. In each village, women traders offer bright piles of tomatoes and garden eggs, chillies and red peppers, lumps of *fu-fu* wrapped in banana leaves, yams, kola nuts and a collection of oddments ranging from laxatives (a big sale for these) and throat pastilles to hair

[1] *West African Studies*, Mary Kingsley.

oil, soap and Stilbœstrol pills for fertility. It is a mystery who buys these things, since everyone seems to be a seller. Women with their hair done in dozens of tight little plaits wash cloths beside their houses. Everyone looks very clean. Skins glisten with health, and you never see a cloth soiled or crumpled. The courtesy and friendliness are remarkable. I stopped to take some photographs, and a burly carpenter at once stepped from his thatched, open-air workshop to show me round. (Every village seemed to have its carpenter, making doors, beds and tables for neighbours.) His store was full of solid mahogany chairs and bedsteads priced at a few pounds, and very neatly constructed.

A woman was making pots between the houses. She shaped them by hand in two sections, joined them, and dried them in the sun—no wheel, no kiln; simple, if not durable, vessels. They are used for palm wine, and cost one and sixpence each. As she can make twenty-five or thirty in a day, she is on to a good thing —provided, of course, that she can sell them.

Did she, I asked, with so large an income, contribute towards the household expenses? Roars of laughter rang out. Of course not, the potter said, when she had recovered from her paroxysm; what woman would be so foolish? Her husband must pay for all the food and give her money. I remarked that, in England, wage-earning wives generally had to contribute. The Wassaw ladies were at first incredulous, then sympathetic; wives in England must be very badly treated, they said; but clearly thought it was the women's own fault for being soft.

The children surged home from school, literally hundreds of them. Seeing a white face, they dashed up and started to practise their English—"Good morning", "Goodbye", "Good night", "God help you". At the sight of a camera, they clustered in front of it in a body, re-deploying like acrobats if the camera shifted. "You take me, missus; you take me." As it was impossible to take anything except a mob of children standing at attention, I returned to the car, which was like an oven. The children still swarmed round, conducting an incoherent conversation, whilst others rushed off to the stream to splash in the cool water, chirping like a flock of birds.

Back on the coast at Takoradi, you find yourself in a different world altogether: a world of transport, industry and trade. I was told that the quickly growing town now contains 1,000 Europeans and 2,000 prostitutes. (No connection: most Europeans bring their wives.)

Takoradi is the headquarters of the railway, the only one (I think) in West Africa that pays. In part this is due to the Gold Coast's situation as a small, compact country about the size of Britain, with no long, unproductive hauls and a flourishing trade, but in part also to the skill and energy of the forthright Yorkshireman who has managed it on business lines. His wife has been on the Coast for twenty-four years without a single day's illness or bout of malaria. Beside her, Mr. Salkeld is almost a weakling; he had malaria once, and was away from work for nine days. Her secret (though it is hardly that) is hard work. Mrs. Salkeld gardens. She does not instruct Africans to garden, she does it herself. The place is a mass of tubs and boxes, for the soil here is so inclement that very few plants will grow in the ground. Most women get discouraged by the ants, lizards, frogs, earwigs, beetles and many other creeping things that ravage gardens, but Mrs. Salkeld does not allow the lower orders of creation to dishearten her, and there are few kinds of plant, shrub or creeper that she has not coaxed into existence here.

Mr. Salkeld, meanwhile, employs on the railway over 8,000 men, who in 1943 were organized into two trade unions by an expert sent out from Britain. (It is a peculiarity of African unions that none arose spontaneously out of need, as in Europe; all have been founded by British labour missionaries.) After the general strike of 1950 the dues—a shilling a month—were no longer deducted by the management. As a result, membership fell to one quarter of the previous figure, and now the unions are, at least for the moment, purged of politics.

Takoradi is at present full of cocoa and timber. The year's cocoa output must be cleared within three months, or the damp turns it mouldy. The whole crop is now handled by the Cocoa Marketing Board, set up in 1947 to buy it from the growers and then dispose of it in world markets. The Board fixes a price for the season; the grower then knows what to expect, and all the middle-men can do is to act as agents for the Board, buying on a small fixed commission.

Selling on a rising market, the Board has made such good profits that in three years' trading it has put by the tidy reserve of £51,000,000 for use as a cushion against the day, perhaps not far distant, when cocoa prices will fall. This plan, while prudent, is unpopular with growers who want the cash here and now. The Board's officials know that the money would vanish in a snap of the fingers were it to be paid over, and have tried to meet criticism by returning some of the profits to the growers in the shape of scholarships for cocoa-growers' children, to which they have devoted a million pounds, and a contribution towards the new University College, which is taking a further million. They have also loaned money to the Government for the building of new deep-water quays at Takoradi, and have paid £7,500,000 to the growers in compensation for "cutting out". Insurance against riots and civil commotion has cost the Board £1,500,000.

The Board's managing director is still a European, but a strong feeling prevails that the whole staff, as well as the directorate, should be "Africanized". Nothing is more natural. Cocoa is an African crop from pod to quay, and until Africans control it at every stage they will continue to suspect that they are being cheated. The difficulty is that there are at present no Africans with the needful knowledge of world trade. The crop goes to seventeen countries, of which the United States is the most important. The financing of the business, the short-term day-to-day loans, the selling forward, the dealings in currency are far beyond the capacity of African traders, who as a rule cannot, for lack of training, read an ordinary balance sheet. The general notion that these things can be picked up quite easily by anyone with a secondary school education is likely to prove illusory. And the days of easy profits are probably over.

While it has lasted, the cocoa boom has been good. New cars to be seen everywhere, new bicycles, new clothes, new upstairs houses, are its testimonials. In a Takoradi store, a smartly dressed African shopper chose, with taste, an excellent Brussels lace priced at eighteen shillings a yard, and was much chagrined to find that only two yards were left in stock; she had wanted twelve yards to trim a cocktail dress. The cost would have been £23.

<o> 21 <o>

The coast between Axim and Accra is studded with old castles built by Europeans who sailed here in caravels and pinnaces and set up forts to protect their trade in gold. The oldest of them, and the finest, is Elmina, founded in 1482 by Don Diogo de Azambuja, at the head of an expedition of 500 soldiers and seamen and a hundred workmen and engineers. Among his captains was certainly Bartholomew Diaz and possibly Christopher Columbus. The Portuguese brought all necessary materials with them, stone already dressed and timber morticed, and they rushed the fort up in record time. They named it Sao Jorge da Mina, probably because of an abundance of gold. "In Beauty and Strength", Bosman justly observed more than 200 years later, "it hath not its equal upon the whole Coast".

Throughout the sixteenth and seventeenth centuries, forts and castles changed hands continually as the Portuguese (who had to keep off the Spanish) gave way to the Dutch (who had to keep off the Swedes, Danes and Brandenburgers), and the Dutch to the English (who had trouble with the French). After the Dutch captured the castle of Sao Jorge da Mina in 1637, they carried out many alterations, and it stands today much as they left it, with tremendous granite walls and battlements whence one can survey the flat surrounding country and the ridged green sea.

Now it has become a training-college for Police. An enormous sergeant-instructor, with tribal cuts on both cheeks, showed me round. We explored a large courtyard, paved in stone and encircled by severe grey barracks that have a certain grace and a good deal of Dutch solidity. All is tidy, in good repair and well kept. Policemen's wives cook for their families behind the high battlements where cannon once were mounted. In one quarter lie the Portuguese dungeons and chapel, cool and dark, with walls fantastically thick. (The permanence of Portuguese building in this land of impermanence is astonishing; our modern concrete blocks and pressed tiles will all have crumbled when these monumental walls still commemorate the questing sailors of Henry the Navigator.) The Portuguese left a deep impression on native art and introduced a great many plants which are now staples of Africa—citrus, rice and sugar-cane, for instance, and maize, tobacco, cassava, guavas and pineapples. Plantains and yams are also exotic. Before the Portuguese came, people must have lived on game, guinea corn and palm oil.

The first English fort was not built until 1631 at Kormantine, ten miles east of Elmina. The English came, as everyone knows, to trade and not to govern, and for the first 150 years the slave trade was predominant. This was not, of course, a European invention, but an institution as old as history. Europeans established an export side to what had hitherto been mainly a domestic business—thereby, of course, greatly stimulating production. They were the shippers. Chiefs and Kings were the suppliers, and African traders the middlemen.

The Ashanti, after their rise to power at the end of the eighteenth century, became, with the King of Dahomey, the greatest slavers on the West Coast. As their military strength waxed they pressed ever harder on the coastal peoples, who had by that time allied themselves with different European nations. The Dutch had an *entente* with the Elmina people, the British with the Fante. It was the invasion of Ashanti armies into Fante country in 1805 that led to the first clash between the British and this powerful inland people, and drew the British into West African politics.

The Ashanti attacked a small English fort near Cape Coast, whither 2,000 Fante had fled for safety. The outcome was a truce. Colonel Torrance, the British commander at Cape Coast, handed over two chiefs wanted by the Ashanti, who tortured them to death; one of them, Otidu, was old and blind. "From the hour Torrance delivered up Otidu," the Asantehene is said to have observed, "I took the English for my friends, because I saw their object was trade only, and they did not care for the people." After his victory the Asantehene waded into the sea at Winneba and took the name of Bonsu or whale, because he had found no one to withstand him.

Further invasions completed the conquest of the Fante and

F

brought Ashanti power down to the sea. In the midst of these disturbances the British Government abolished the slave trade, and the Guinea companies were faced with the alternatives of turning over to trade in goods, or abandoning their castles. The status of Africans changed from that of potential captives to potential customers. Wars became bad for business instead of good for trade, and the existence of an aggressive Ashanti military power a barrier to the peaceful opening up of the hinterland.

At first treaties were sought with the Ashanti, and the expedition so well chronicled by Bowdich secured the Asantehene's mark. But the Fante did not accept their position as vassals and in various ways embroiled the British at Cape Coast, who, in the Asantehene's view, broke at least the spirit of the treaties. The British settlements fell into such a bad way that in 1821, after a Parliamentary enquiry, they were taken over by the Crown. War with the Ashanti broke out a year later. The British Governor, Sir Charles Macarthy (whom we heard of in Sierra Leone), took command. Advancing with a force of less than 500 men, he found himself face to face with the main Ashanti army. His men held the enemy until their ammunition ran out, and might have escaped, had not the officer bringing up supplies failed to prevent the flight of his carriers and delivered only four kegs to the battlefield, three of which were found to contain macaroni. The small British-led force was annihilated and the head of its commander taken to Kumasi. But, two years later, the main Ashanti army was decisively defeated near Accra. Peace was signed, and trade slowly expanded. At last, after a long line of mediocrities, a British representative came who was firm, dignified, tactful and keenly interested in the people. This was Sir George Maclean. By his personal influence he raised British prestige and spread British influence from Volta to the Pra. In 1850 the Government bought the Danish forts, including Christiansborg, for £10,000, and inherited a vague responsibility for certain inland regions.

Throughout the second half of the nineteenth century trouble with the Ashanti, sometimes breaking into war, bedevilled the Coast and hampered trade. The Dutch at Elmina found their trade so disorganized that they sold out to the British, and the castle was formally handed over in 1872.

This act, presented to the Ashanti as a *fait accompli*, touched off another and more serious war. An army from Kumasi, at first repulsed, defeated the forces of the Fante alliance and drove thousands of refugees into the rain-sodden streets of Cape Coast. At this critical moment Sir Garnet Wolseley arrived. Three battalions of British troops came after him, and four months later Wolseley and a contingent of the Black Watch entered Kumasi and, forming up in the main street, gave three cheers for the Queen. For the first time a foreign army had entered the sacred capital. The military glory of this great and bloodthirsty nation was ended. The omens had indeed foretold it; a short while before, a tree planted by Osei Tutu's high priest, the architect of the Confederacy, had toppled down.

The British intention, however, was to show their strength, not to occupy Ashanti, and Wolseley immediately withdrew. Heartened by this, the Asantehene and his captains returned and proceeded to build up again the strength of his armies, quite undeterred by the British, whose vacillating policy was born of a dread of further wars. This led, inevitably, to the war that was dreaded. In 1896 a second expedition marched to Kumasi under the command of Sir Francis Scott. The Asantehene, Prempeh (a nickname meaning tubby), capitulated and removed his sandals as a gesture of submission, but expressed his inability to pay the indemnity. He, the Queen Mother and other members of the royal family were seized, in a manner the Ashanti considered treacherous, and exiled to the Seychelles. A few years later, the British Governor's obtuse demand for the surrender of the Golden Stool led to a third Ashanti war, and the siege of the gubernatorial party in Kumasi fort. Finally, on January 1st, 1902, came the end of the chapter. Ashanti was formally annexed and became—for the time being—a Crown Colony.

Below Elmina castle, I watched a fleet of fishing-canoes land their catch. If the shade of one of those "Portuguese masters" who built the castle had stood at my elbow, I daresay he would have noticed very little change. Out beyond the line of breakers, all the crews dived in and swam to shore, save two men from each boat, who paddled and hauled the canoe through the surf and up on to the sandy beach, bearing with them a long rope attached to the net. Then the glistening, muscular, almost naked fishermen lined up and began to haul the loaded nets slowly in, singing as they did to an old, melodious, rather melancholy chant and shuffling their feet in the hot sand, while on the beach clusters of market women waited beside their little cooking-fires. Shoals of naked children played in the warm surf and several paddled miniature canoes, exact replicas of their fathers', inside the breakers. These strong and carefree children are as native to the sea as porpoises; they are fishermen to the nails of their toes and the valves of their hearts. Each of the long seine-nets took about an hour to draw in. At last the catch appeared: a silvery writhing mass caught in a purse at the very end. Men, women and children fell upon it and helped to ladle the struggling fish into baskets. Floppings and pantings grew gradually weaker as the fierce sun struck the fishes' silver flanks. Turtles were thrown down on their backs and waved their fat legs helplessly.

Market women buy the catch on the beach. Some of it they smoke, the rest they carry to a line of waiting lorries and start at once for Kumasi and other inland towns. The fish is not cleaned, and must be very high by the time it gets to market; but people seem to like it this way, as English connoisseurs prefer pheasants.

The price on the beach that day was £4 a basket. The catch made six baskets, which was poor; on a good day fishermen bring in twenty or thirty. Even so, this poor catch meant £24; and an energetic crew can bring in two catches a day. One-third of the takings goes to the crew of eight, the rest to the owner, who, of course, must maintain the canoe. To replace one, a fisherman told me, cost £150, and a net twice as much again. Very few people save, and so a fisherman in need of a new canoe often gets into debt with a market woman, who advances him the money and ends by owning all his gear. Then the market woman takes two-thirds of the catch. Many have made fortunes in this way.

∽ 22 ∽

A minor breakdown halted us on the outskirts of a small town. While a "fitter" was found to "weld" (i.e. solder) a part, I watched a constant stream of mammy-lorries rattle by, each one crowded with people, baskets of produce, fowls, sheep and goats.

Sometimes they stopped to disgorge passengers. Two comely women alighted and put their shopping down while they arranged plaited quoits of plantain leaf on their heads. Then each helped the other to raise and arrange her load: first a large enamel basin full of yams, then a heavy bunch of plantains, on top of all a live fowl. A young lad followed with a toy drum on his head. Later came a young man and his wife. He lifted down a heavy box stippled in many colours bearing the painted legend, in very large letters, "Say Ho", and placed it on his wife's head; she wriggled her shoulders to settle it in position, and they walked off towards the small town. From the next bus emerged an itinerant photographer with a heavy wooden camera and tripod and a sample of his wares, a picture-frame full of portraits of affluent citizens in stiff white collars and tight black coats.

Each bus that clatters by in its pillar of red dust has a motto painted over the driver's cab. These texts suggest a fascinating blend of piety and cynicism. GOD NEVER MISTAKEN rumbles by, followed by POOR MAN NO FRIEND. COVETOUS ARE NEVER IN WANT is somewhat contradicted by the lengthy observation: HE WHO WISHES THE DOWNFALL OF HIS NEIGHBOUR WILL NEVER SUCCEED IN HIS UNDERTAKING. A healthy caution is displayed in SEE BEFORE YOU SAY and in FEAR WOMEN AND GROW OLD; and clearly WHATEVER YOU DO, PEOPLE WILL TALK reflects some bitter experience. A cryptic note occurs in IF YOU LOSE THE BALL, DON'T LOSE THE MAN; a message of comfort in SWEET NEVER DESPAIR; and of optimism in SEA NEVER DRY, GOVERNMENT NEVER SPOIL, COMPANY NEVER BROKE. EVERYTHING BY GOD is devout, but I liked best the touch of frankness in the text GOD IS MY SHEPHERD AND I DON'T KNOW WHY.

The country grew more hilly as we turned inland, full of valleys which, when wooded, must have been rather like parts of Surrey; and soon we were in the diamond-producing country whose capital is Kibi. A general concession to mine diamonds over all this part of the Colony has been given to a South African company called the Consolidated African Selection Trust, known as CAST. But anyone, by paying £100 to the Stool, can get a permit to dig over twenty-five acres. Diamonds may be found anywhere, and, at sixty-five shillings a carat, large fortunes may at any moment be made by the poorest of peasants digging holes for yams.

The richest local citizen is a Nigerian, who is said to have paid £1,500 (these figures are and must be only hearsay) to have the fetish lifted from an area exempted from the concession because of its sacrosanctity. He then obtained the concession over it himself. Instead of mining it, he hit upon a much easier way of making money. For £5 to £15 each, he sold tickets affirming that the holder was employed by him as a digger. It was thought that between 1,500 and 2,000 of these had been sold. Armed with a ticket, pick and shovel, a man could dig safely anywhere; for if questioned by CAST agents or police he need only say that he was going to or coming from work. I was sorry not to meet this enterprising Nigerian, who was away on holiday. No doubt he could afford a good one, having probably cleared at least £10,000—and no income tax.

In the meantime the concession is being quickly and illegally worked out. The Government estimate is that between 15,000 and 20,000 men in this division are intermittently engaged on illicit diamond digging. It has become a sort of fever, and food production suffers. Syrians drive out in taxis from Accra on Saturday afternoons to buy the stones. A lucky digger may get £10, £20, or even £100, and that night he celebrates. Next morning there are empty bottles all down the street and not many sober heads in Kibi. On Sunday and Monday the citizens sleep it off, and by Tuesday they are ready to dig again.

The Syrians are of course obliged to smuggle these "hot" diamonds out of the country. This is not difficult. The Gold Coast has about 1,200 miles of boundary with the French, guarded only at two or three crossings. The stones are said to find their way to Cairo and the cities of Morocco, where buyers gather from Russia and the East. Occasionally a Syrian who attempts to get his goods out by ship or aircraft is detected by the Customs—invariably because he is betrayed by an informer—and then a case may be proved. Not long ago a Syrian flying to Paris was found to have several thousand pounds' worth of diamonds tucked away under the skin of a ham.

The town of Kibi does not flaunt its wealth. Its unpaved, uneven streets have the usual open gutters and rows of swish houses, each with its veranda, on which merchants display their wares and young men treadle away at sewing-machines. There is no water supply and no electric light, and everything is roofed with rusty corrugated iron. The women carry food about on their heads in enamel basins. You see no dogs in West African towns; they have all been eaten. A film of dust lies over everything. Yet, with rich takings from cocoa and diamonds, tens of thousands of pounds must be buried in yards or hidden away among the rafters. The only direct tax is six shillings a head for men and two shillings for women, annually.

～ 23 ～

The Stool's present occupant is Omanhene Ofori Atta, nephew of that Knight whose funeral led to the famous murder trial. When I called to pay my respects, a meeting of the council of elders was just over. The elders sat on upright chairs along one side of the room. Some were indeed ancients, white-haired and stooping, but others were in the prime of life. All are the heads of certain lineages or clans. The Omanhene, a tall, burly man of middle age, sat behind a large, flat-topped desk supporting on it many files and a telephone. At his right hand was a young man in spectacles: a son, the chief explained, just called to the Bar in England, who had come back to help his father. (Under the law of inheritance common to all Akan states, he can never sit on the Stool; a maternal nephew must succeed.) One of the late Omanhene's daughters is a fully qualified doctor.

A formal exchange of courtesies took place through an interpreter, in order that the elders should understand. The Omanhene was careful to explain that he could reach no important decision without their approval, and that they in turn could not advise him contrary to the sense of public opinion. As he, the chief, must consult the elders, so must each elder consult his clansmen. Thus no unpopular measure, the Omanhene said, could be forced upon the people; and if the chief was tempted to become an autocrat, by the decision of these very elders sitting round with silent tongues but keen eyes he could be de-stooled.

"Our traditional system", said the Omanhene, "is democratic. We think it is more democratic than the system which the British have introduced." Some, at least, of those who have seen the customary system working would support his claim.[1]

This chief's council continues to function unofficially, but now it has no statutory powers. These have been passed to the new District Council, one-third of whose members have been chosen by this group of traditional advisers, while the remaining two-thirds were elected early in 1952. The elders' main objection to this new system is that it is less democratic than the old, since the new leaders are less likely to draw out with patience and impartiality the views of the people, than to harangue the people on the rightness of their own.

Formalities over, the Omanhene, a fine figure in a green-and-purple cloth, led me along a corridor to his private house and took his seat on a throne-like chair, resting his sandalled feet on a leopard skin. The rest of the room was European in style: linoleum-covered floor, a lot of chairs and tables, the walls hung with photographs of past chiefs and relatives. A servant came with glasses and a bottle of champagne. We drank, and the Omanhene talked in fluent English of the state of the nation—the cocoa crop, here badly hit by swollen shoot disease, the grow-

[1] For instance Mr. W. E. F. Ward, who, in his *History of the Gold Coast*, gives the following description: "A tactful chief sits patiently and attentively listening while the elders round him are excitedly debating. Occasionally he interjects a few quiet words, but for the most part his impassive demeanour contrasts strongly with the eager oratory and the passionate gestures all around. To an outsider it seems that the conflict of views is irreconcilable; but the chief has gauged the sense of the meeting. When he begins to speak there is a hush. His speech closes the discussion; it is received with quiet approval, all excitement and opposition vanishes and the meeting passes to the next business. . . . A chief has no opinion of his own; he can only express the opinion of his people, and from this it follows that he can express no view until he has a chance of finding out through formal discussion what his people's view is.

"This characteristic of chieftainship is found in chiefs of all grades. The village headman is a member of the council of a higher division; the chief of the division is a member of the council of still higher rank; and ultimately the highest sub-chiefs are members of the national council, presided over by the paramount chief. From the paramount chief downwards all must consult their people and express their people's opinion, not their own. Their position as representatives of their people is more like that of a member of a Russian Soviet, or of a British trade union delegate, than that of a British Member of Parliament" (pp. 94–95).

ing lawlessness, the de-stoolings, above all the new Government. He makes no secret of his hatred of the CPP. Coming back the other day from Accra, he stopped his car, jumped out, pulled up a pole and tore the CPP flag to pieces.

Here in Kibi we can see clearly the issue that divides the whole Gold Coast, as it divides most of Africa: chiefs versus *evolués*, aristocrats versus upstarts, tradition versus innovation. "We are living through a revolution," as the Governor said. "All revolutions throw some queer fish to the surface—and some scum. We are lucky to have got off, hitherto, with so little bloodshed."

Argument rages fiercely. These are a passionate people, as their history shows—passionate, quarrelsome, independent, alive. In former days each state or tribe was closely knit together by the web of kinship, and generally at war with its neighbours. Now, for the first time, a bar is being raised horizontally between old and young, peasant and literate, country and town, which divides the people of one tribe, even of one family, from each other, but unites those of different and previously warring tribes. No one can foretell the outcome; the full effect will not be seen for perhaps two generations. Then, when European influence has retreated to the commercial sphere from which it emerged, we shall see what Africa will make of this great, yeasty, indigestible mass of new ideas. At present it is like a boa-contrictor that has swallowed a goat.

It may be that a new Africa, based on the European ideas and dreams for which it is so avid, will be the issue: an Africa of the materialist, the bureaucrat, the trade union, the lawyer and the technician; or it may be that the goat will leave the boa-constrictor stronger, but oddly unchanged. "The white man brings his cannon to the bush," said a former king of Ashanti, "but the bush is stronger than the cannon." Whether it will be stronger than the book is yet to be seen.

∾ 24 ∾

At Tafo, east of Kibi, at the West African Cocoa Research Institute, scientists are studying the cocoa tree in all its aspects, but more especially are they seeking a defence against its greatest scourge, the swollen shoot disease.

F*

A small scale-insect called the mealy-bug carries the virus from tree to tree. Soon leaves change colour, swellings appear and the tree dies. The disease is quite incurable, but its diffusion can be checked by cutting down and burning trees in their first stages of infection. To begin with, "cutting out" was voluntarily, although never willingly, done. Trees must be destroyed before they show obvious signs of sickness and while there are pods on them still to ripen, and worth a great deal more than the few shillings of compensation paid by the Government.

This remedy did not keep pace with the virus, and so the Government made cutting out compulsory. The growers' natural discontent was turned to good account by politicians who condemned it as a trick to impoverish poor, down-trodden Africans perpetrated by the ruthless British, who had sold the Gold Coast to America and were destroying all the cocoa before completion day so as to hand over a worthless asset. Resistance to cutting out soon became fierce and general, and when the CPP was voted into office in 1951 its leaders revoked the order and suspended cutting out. The virus, unconcerned with politics, resumed its spread.

Cocoa accounts for nearly two-thirds (in value) of all the Gold Coast's exports, and provides a living for perhaps one-third of its people. Its disappearance would bring general ruin. As the disease developed, so did a certain nervousness among politicians. Three foreign scientists, invited to give advice in 1950, had reported that cutting out was the only preventive. A clear choice confronted the CPP: to revoke its policy and eat its words, or to ruin the country for which it now found itself responsible. Courageously, Dr. Nkrumah executed a *volte face* and announced that cutting out must be resumed and, after a while, made compulsory. The disease is spreading still, but at a much slower pace, and there is now hope that it may be controlled.

From the scientist's point of view, cutting out is an admission of defeat. His object is to find a way to prevent the virus from attacking, or the trees from succumbing to the attack. There are two possibilities. One is to breed resistant strains of tree. To this end plant-breeders have introduced varieties from Trinidad and the Upper Amazon, some of which show signs of resistance and produce no less than ten times more pods than local trees. The possibility thus opened up is a tremendous one, but will take a long time to realize. Cocoa trees take five years to come into full bearing.

The second possibility is to control the spread of infection by chemicals. A drug called Hanane, produced by Pest Control, a Cambridge firm, is undergoing tests which look very hopeful. You "plant" a capsule near the roots; the tree absorbs the drug and its sap kills the mealy-bugs that carry the disease. As Hanane is a derivative of mustard gas, it needs to be handled by trained men under expert supervision, which makes the cost of its application high. And strains of mealy-bug resistant to Hanane might evolve, just as certain bacteria are gaining resistance to penicillin, or ticks to arsenic. It is too soon to claim Hanane as the answer to swollen shoot disease, nor can it replace cutting out. But at least it offers hope.

Tafo is a little world apart, encased in forest, content with its own social life, its club, its bridge- and dinner-parties. Trees press almost to the doorsteps of its fine new houses, and it has its own network of roads, its own power-station.

It has also a most attractive reservoir, a bird-frequented lake. Before this was made, the local chief's approval had to be won, and when it was ready for use he was invited to give it his blessing. He came with his elders in his ceremonial robes, and a sheep was sacrificed to propitiate the river-god. The silver lake reflecting the tall timber, the chiefs' multi-coloured robes and umbrellas, the chocolate torsos of attendants, the crimson blood—all combined to form a scene inspiring to photographers, of whom three were at work: a professional from Accra, and two of the Tafo staff, who were experienced and keen amateurs.

But the chief demurred. He felt sure that the spirits would not like a sacrifice to be photographed. Biologists, however, could not be expected to defer to so unscientific a view. The chief's objections were politely over-ruled. And not one of the pictures of the sacrifice was recognizable.

I asked one of the three, who told me this story, how he could account for such a happening.

"There is no satisfactory explanation," he said. "It was a hot day, we'd had a good lunch; perhaps our hands were shaky, or perhaps we didn't pay enough attention to the stops."

"And the photographs of the sacrifice were the only failures?"
"Oh, yes; all the others came out."
Perhaps a coincidence; yet my informant did not really believe
so. Frankly baffled, he shrugged his shoulders, smiled and
added: "It just happened, that's all."

❧ 25 ❧

I spent the next night on the banks of the Volta River, whose
upper reaches I had crossed and re-crossed in the Northern
Territories. Here it flows through gorges, its banks thickly
forested, and flecked with the red foliage of the *kaku* tree: a wide,
gunmetal-coloured stream sweeping down towards a delta with
its creeks, lagoons and mud-bars. I drove to Ajena, a small
village now, but soon to be the site of an enormous barrage to
bay back the waters so as to form the biggest artificial lake in the
world, with an area nearly as large as Norfolk's. At Ajena also
will be the hydro-electric plant that will generate power to smelt
the bauxite from Ashanti, believed to hold the sources of the
largest aluminium supplies outside Canada. Down on the coast,
between the delta and Accra, a little fishing village called Tema
is already being swallowed by a new model port, through which
at least 200,000 tons of aluminium will be exported (if all goes
well) every year. New railways, irrigation, the supply of cheap
power to centres like Takoradi and Accra—these will be the
scheme's by-products. All this will take twenty years to accom-
plish and will cost at least £140,000,000.

It is a bold, imaginative scheme, this Volta River project, of a
size and scope to compare with the great dams and irrigation
works in India and Egypt. There will be a Volta River Authority which may do, on a smaller scale, for the Gold Coast what
the Tennessee Valley Authority has done for the Southern states
of America. But there is one big obstacle: how to reconcile the
investment of so large a sum of foreign capital with the coming
political independence of the Gold Coast.

Whatever the form of government, West Africa cannot develop
without foreign capital. Everyone recognizes that. But nationalists in power have a habit of seizing foreign investments. It has
happened in so many places—the Argentine, Indonesia, Burma,

Egypt, Palestine, China, Persia. Why should it not happen here? Behind the scheme's attractions looms the danger that another £140,000,000 of British and Canadian money will be expropriated when the project has become a paying concern.

Everyone hopes not, of course; officials have found a formula; politicians have given promises; both sides know they need the scheme. It would indeed display a breakdown in statesmanship were the bauxite to remain forever buried in rock because of mutual distrust. The scheme is to go ahead, financed as to two-thirds of the total by the British and Canadian aluminium companies and Governments, and as to one-third by the Gold Coast Treasury. No doubt, before it is completed, the Gold Coast will have full self-government. Then the test of statesmanship will come. Perhaps a strong national pride, and the determination to show the world that Africans can run their own affairs with sense and efficiency, will triumph over an inclination common to all humanity, to dig deep into any convenient honey-pot.

One practical difficulty will be to find enough labour to build so many things at once—railways, ports, dams, smelters, power lines. The country of the lower Volta is thickly populated, but too prosperous to supply thousands for manual work. The land's fertility, the people's industry are both reflected in the profusion of produce offered in the market at Assesewa, one of the richest in West Africa. You can buy almost anything here: beads, gold ear-rings, leather amulets, charms, "leprosy ointment", laxatives, fertility pills, home-grown tobacco, baskets, sandals, chamber-pots, spanners, huge straw hats. To one side are the letter-writers, who for a shilling will court a girl or dun for a debt in the most flowery and ornate prose. And cloths, of course, in every pattern under the sun.

The District Commissioner took one up and deftly wrapped it round his head, tucking in the ends. It was a turban, and there stood a fighting Indian from the hills, a Gurkha perhaps, or Nepalese, burly, copper-skinned, black-eyed like a hawk. It is curious how men will take the stamp of their profession, or even of the country that agrees with them best. The Indian Army has hallmarked Major Ferguson. Yet, in spite of his scout-like dash (one can almost see the Victoria Cross being affixed to his horse's empty saddle), he professes a strong distaste for the great out-

doors and a preference for the cities with their sophisticated
spivs and politicians on the make, their scabrous journalists,
their dance-halls and "high life" and gin bars. One of the most
revered West African traditions is that the hearts of all administrators are in the bush with the simple peasant, far from the files
and intrigues of the Secretariat. Many, in fact, greatly prefer the
comforts and cocktail parties of the capital, and it is refreshing
to hear one of them say so.

This eastern district, bordering Togoland, is at present rent
and diverted by a struggle between two members of the same
"royal" family: on the one hand the chief, the Konor of Manya
Krobo—a tall, good-looking man of middle age—and on the
other his cousin, an ex-police constable, an active supporter of
the CPP, and now Assemblyman for the division, who had just
arrived at Assesewa in a large American car and, clad in a pink
silk shirt, was preparing to hold a rally. The Konor, Nene Maté
Kolé, is generally conceded to be one of the country's most enlightened, progressive and honest chiefs—qualities which naturally exasperate the CPP, whose thesis it is that all chiefs are
reactionary and corrupt. I dined at his two-storeyed wooden
house in the centre of Odumasi, his capital. The food was wholly
European, the talk mainly of politics, our host genial; his daughter, an Achimota student, played the piano next door, but was
too shy to join the dinner-party, nor did any of the Konor's wives
appear.

Mr. Maté Johnson, a good-looking young man of eager eloquence, assured me that the CPP have 10,000 paying members
in his constituency. (The subscription is three shillings a year.)
Out of this they support a full-time secretary (£72 a year) and
treasurer (£60), and produce sporadically a small news-sheet.
He did not say what happens to the rest of the money, but no
doubt headquarters claim their share; accounts are not audited
or published. Holding rallies is the Party's main activity.

Here at Odumasi the doctor, in charge of a small hospital and
a large district, is an Edinburgh-trained African married to a
Scottish wife. One would think it a lonely life for an "expatriate"
woman, here in a gauze-enclosed bungalow (like a huge meat-
safe) perched high above the Volta, with her husband away on
tour much of the time, far from the hum of cities or the com-

panionship of other Europeans. But five children keep her occupied, and she gave an impression of contentment and cheerful domesticity.

Nearly all the mixed marriages I encountered in West Africa were between European women and African men. I do not know whether this was a coincidence or a fair sample. The majority are contracted by African students who come to Britain, with girls they meet on equal terms in universities and lodging-houses. Like all marriages, some succeed and some fail. Failure occurs most often when the girl pitches her hopes too high. Just as so few American soldiers prove, in the event, to own ranches, so do very few Africans turn out to be princes or landed gentlemen. A rather squalid little house (perhaps) in the crowded streets of Accra, plus the unexpected acquisition of an enormous number of aunts, stepmothers, sisters, cousins and sisters-in-law, can sometimes come as a shock to the more optimistic and less knowledgeable British brides.

Odumasi was my last stop before driving down from the hills and across the coastal plain to the flat, sprawling, ugly but alert capital. I was in time for a garden-party at Christiansborg Castle attended by, I think, 2,000 people, whose cars formed a line several miles long. Chiefs by the score were present, each in his rich silk and velvet robes, advancing under a huge umbrella held up by members of his retinue—resplendent enough, but how much less so than their fathers, whose great canopies were surmounted by images of gold, with all their bells and drums and flutes, their warriors and slaves and shaggy executioners.

Tall policemen from the Northern Territories in handsome tunics of hunters' green and red turbans, holding lances (a crib from India, but effective), stood in pairs on each side of the path leading to His Excellency, a noble and dignified figure in grey top hat and morning suit, and to his elegant wife. Amid a garden full of flowers and flowering trees, little tables bore ornamental little cakes created by Lady Quist, the Speaker's wife and Accra's leading confectioner. In a gloved and benevolent atmosphere we drank tea or lemonade while the Police band played Gilbert and Sullivan. It was a prim, decorous, English, curiously touching scene. On the stroke of six o'clock the band played God Save the Queen; as the drum-rolls faded, everyone started to file out to waiting cars. By six-fifteen the last guest had vanished.

That night, in the fishing village, there was much din and drumming. In one of the compounds there gathered a collection of men in nondescript clothes—tattered working shorts or trousers, old trilby hats, torn vests—who danced and stamped for hours on end, perhaps all night. A band of women shuffled up and down the street with bent knees, clapping and singing and swaying their behinds. The dancing struck me as rather slipshod and tatty, perhaps because the clothes were so incongruous—native dances should be done in native dress, with oiled and painted bodies leaping in the light of fires—but the rhythm was there, muttered out by the drums, the steady, never-missing rhythm that chimes in with the pulses and very slowly, very subtly quickens their beat until dancers leap like marionettes and all are keyed-up, expectant and submerged, the individual will surrendered to a mass compulsion of the muscles. Fires burned in the compound and meat was roasting on sticks; nearby squatted a row of fat, frothing calabashes of palm wine; in a corner sat the stiff-faced drummers, two of them, tirelessly rapping with open palms on the membranes of their drums. A chief had died, spectators told me; he would be mourned for a month. How long would the party last? A foolish question! People shrugged their shoulders and laughed. Until everyone was tired, until the wine was finished, until dawn broke, or until people decided to go to bed. The drums were still muttering when I went to sleep, and no doubt for long after. Two parties, two peoples, two ways: both old and obstinate, and neither having on their side all the vice or all the virtue.

NIGERIA

NIGERIA

POPULATION: About 31,500,000 (1953), of whom 17,000,000 live in the Northern Region. The main racial groups are: Hausa; Ibo and Yoruba (roughly equal); Fulani; Kanuri; Ibibio, Tiv and Edo (Benin). The Cameroons has a population of rather over a million.

CAPITAL: Lagos, whose estimated population (1952) of about 272,000 has doubled in twenty-five years. The birth-rate has risen from twenty-nine to forty-five per thousand.

AREA: 373,500 square miles, including the British-administered Cameroons. It is bounded by French territory to the north and west, and by the Gulf of Guinea, into which flow, through wide, swampy deltas, the Niger (2,600 miles long), Benue, Cross, Calabar and other great rivers. Parts of the Bauchi Plateau rise to 7,000 feet above sea-level, and the Cameroon Mountain to 13,350 feet.

TRADE: The leading exports are cocoa, palm kernels, palm oil and groundnuts, accounting in 1953 to over £85,000,000 out of the total of £125,000,000. These commodities, plus cotton, are handled by Produce Marketing Boards which stabilize prices, endow research, improve quality and provide funds for three Regional Production Boards. Imports, valued in 1953 at £108,000,000, consist mainly of cotton and rayon piece goods, clothing and footwear, foodstuffs, iron and steel manufactures, corrugated iron, road vehicles and cement.

HISTORY: A settled, if crude, form of government, based on Islamic law, has existed in the Hausa States of Northern Nigeria since the advent of the Muslim faith during and after the thirteenth century. Early in the nineteenth century a local sheikh, Uthman dan Fodio, raised the Fulani people in a *jehad* against the Hausa and established a militant Fulani rule over most of Northern Nigeria, except for Bornu. The Fulani were in turn conquered by the British under Lugard in 1898–1900. In the South, contacts with Europe began in 1472, when the Portuguese started to trade with the Beni and Yoruba peoples. For the next three centuries, the principal European nations contended along the Guinea Coast for the profits of the slave trade. The Act of Abolition, passed in 1807, obliged the British first to police the seas, and then (in 1861) to occupy Lagos, a nest of blockade-running slavers. Trade preceded the flag into the unhealthy interior. In 1879, Sir George Taubman Goldie amalgamated the principal trading firms into the United Africa Company, which so far consolidated British interests that a hitherto indifferent Government was able to claim a "sphere of influence" in this region at the Berlin Conference of 1885, and to establish the Oil Rivers Protectorate over the delta area. In 1886 the Royal Niger Company received its charter and pushed its agents into the interior, often in competition with the French. British influence was gradually extended, generally by treaty but occasionally (as, in 1897, over the state of Benin) by conquest until, in 1899, the Government revoked the Niger Company's charter and, on January 1st, 1900, declared a Colony and Protectorate in the South and a separate Protectorate in Northern Nigeria. The first two were amalgamated in 1906, and Northern Nigeria was incorporated into the Colony and Protectorate in 1914.

GOVERNMENT: The first of several drastic post-war changes took place in 1947, when non-official members assumed a majority in the Legislative Council, with jurisdiction over the whole country. Houses of Assembly, also, were set up in each of the three Regions. In 1951 this short-lived constitution was replaced by a new one establishing a Council of Ministers consisting of the Governor as President, six officials and twelve non-officials (four from each Region), and an elected central House of Representatives. Most of the twelve Ministers (all Nigerians) assumed control over one or other of the different Departments, and each of the three Regional Governments was provided with a Lieutenant-Governor, an Executive Council and an elected House of Assembly. The Northern and the Western Regions also had Houses of Chiefs. Friction between the Muslim Northern Region (with a majority of the population) and the Western and Eastern Regions, led to a breakdown of the constitution in 1953 and to its drastic revision. The new constitution of 1954 created a Federation of Nigeria, giving more autonomy to each Region, with the understanding that in 1956 any Region which so desired it would be granted full self-government, subject to safeguards to preserve the working of the Federation. Lagos, as the Federal capital, became Federal territory; the South Cameroons became quasi-federal territory with their own legislature and executive; the North Cameroons are administered as part of the Northern Region. The Lieutenant-Governors of each region became Governors, while Sir John MacPherson became the first Governor-General. Meanwhile, reforms in local government ranged from the abolition of Native Authorities (i.e. traditional chiefs and elders) in the East, and their substitution by elected County Councils, to the setting up of local councils in the North and West, with a greater or lesser proportion of commoners to advise the chiefs.

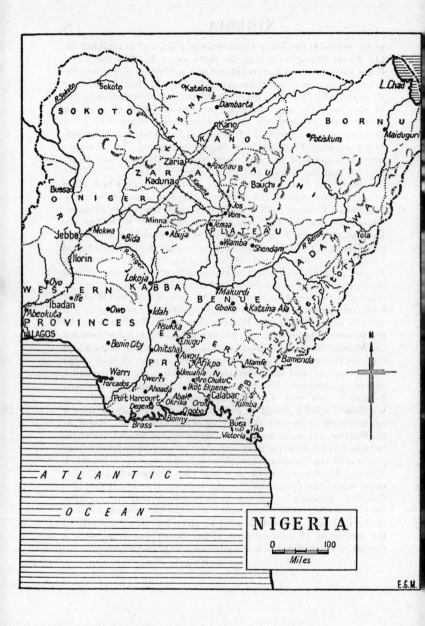

NIGERIA

0   100
Miles

E.G.M.

NIGERIA

The West

LAGOS assaults you with its squalor and vitality. The narrow
streets, the houses—hovels, mainly—made of mud or old
tin and packed as close as playing-cards, the stinking open
drains, the noise, the traffic, the jostling throngs—Lagos is Eastern in its feeling that sheer naked human life, mere existence,
bubbles and pullulates with the frightening fecundity of bacteria.
The town is on an island surrounded by a lagoon into which all
the drains empty, and a sour and sulphurous smell frequently
envelops the Marina, Lagos' nearest approach to a Chelsea
Embankment or Riverside Drive.

Most Lagosians are in origin Yoruba, although every one of
the multitudinous races of West Africa must be represented here.
Yoruba women wear big, gay head-ties done in a knot at the
back with the ends protruding, like brilliant giant butterflies.
These women would sell their mothers' milk at a profit. In
Lagos market they are packed as close as hens in a battery, each
with her pile of wares. I was drawn to the herbalists' and witch-
doctors' stalls, loaded with all sorts of leaves, pods and lumps of
clay or chalk having medicinal properties and with juju objects
of many kinds, most of which defy recognition, though you can
identify the tiny skulls of monkeys, the wings of bats and small
crows, the antlers of baby deer, dogs' paws, bundles of feathers,
all exactly like the witches' brew in *Macbeth*. Odd, how all the
world over "eye of newt and toe of frog, wool of bat and tongue
of dog, adder's fork and blindworm's sting" are the stock-in-
trade of magicians.

I tried to ascertain the use of some of these remedies. A
wizen-faced elder explained that if you burnt a bunch of
feathers and mixed the ash with scrapings off a monkey's skull
and some dried bats-wing, and swallowed the resulting powder,
you would vomit out a sickness of the stomach. Several were
remedies for syphilis. Those—the majority, I expect—used for

curses and charms were not explained. Cursing and poisoning are popular pastimes; a man was caught the other day putting pus from smallpox sores into an enemy's food. Probably he was a follower of Shopano, the Yoruba god of smallpox, whose priests by custom inherit the property of victims of the disease. Little wonder that, in bygone days, smallpox outbreaks were many and devastating.

The town is growing fast and sprawls across more and more of the island. But there are still unspoilt beaches, with long Atlantic rollers breaking on the hot white sand. Nothing is pleasanter than to walk there in the evening, away from the heat and noise of the town. The sea is quiet and colourless and the sun sinks flatly into it, without effulgence, red as a Dutch cheese. Outlines are not exactly blurred, but lack sharpness, because of the harmattan that blows over the desert a thousand miles away and yet dims this bright Atlantic air.

I came to a casuarina grove, melancholy as all firs are, with tiny cones lying on the beach and drooping, olive-tinted leaves. Two small candles burnt at the foot of a tree. Nearby, a squad of kneeling men and women dressed in white robes and red sashes faced the sea. Out in front a bearded priest intoned hymns—sad hymns with strange tunes. At his command, his followers bowed their foreheads to the sand and remained there in that odd, hunched posture, rumps to the sky. All around them, empty bottles lay. I asked what these had contained.

"Palm wine!"

The members of a group a little farther on flung themselves face downwards. A third batch, kneeling and singing, started to sway from side to side; a man rolled slowly over and over in the sand. Some pigs appeared, thrusting their long, nozzle-like snouts, resembling the proboscis of an insect, among bicycles that leant against the casuarinas; black, woolly sheep with long tails nibbled at discarded banana skins. The sun vanished, leaving the singing rollers more than ever lonely on the tenebrous shore. The service would end, perhaps, with all the congregation rushing into the sea. I waited for this climax, but darkness spread in from the ocean, and they were still chanting, swaying, now and then taking a swig; and so I left them there. Several more candles had by then been lit under the casuarinas; they looked like the glinting eyes of small wild beasts.

No one ever throws away an old bottle; they are treasured here. Every palm tree you pass has one at least tied to the crown, like queer fruit, collecting sap. In two days the fermented sap is ready for enjoyment—frothy, yeasty, strong as the cider of Normandy. And no tax.

✧ 2 ✧

Lagos was packed with politicians, for my visit coincided with the opening of the first session of the House of Representatives. Like the Gold Coast, Nigeria has a new constitution which gives local politicians a large measure of self-government.

The process begins simply enough, with miniature elections in many thousand districts and villages. (No need to write: you put your cross opposite a picture of a lion or an elephant.) This is as democratic as can be, but not always understood. There is a story going the rounds about a remote country district which sent in no return. An enquiry went forth to ask why the name of the successful candidate had not been registered. "Sir," came back the clerk's reply, "we regret that in this district it is impossible to hold elections, as there are two people who wish to be our representative."

Success in his local contest will carry a man first to his district, then to his county council and further still, if he is lucky, by a sort of leap-frog process, into one of the three regional Houses of Assembly. Finally, from each of these three Houses men are chosen for the central House of Representatives. Half its members come from the North, which holds half the country's population. The other moiety is equally divided between men from the Eastern and from the Western Regions. (Men specifically: there are no women members.)

It is the Northerners who, in point of looks, give the House its character. From the strangers' gallery of the new building (Festival of Britain crossed with a Beau Geste fort) you look down on rows of opulent turbans and majestic figures swathed in robes, either of pure white, fresh as a snowdrop, or of powder blue. Turbans and robes alike shine with a sort of lustre and stand out as if well starched, and these tall Mallams and Emirs walk with a swish and rustle that enhances their already formidable dignity. The starchy, shimmering look of the material comes not from laundering but from beating it with clubs. I saw this process later, in Kano. Five or six men armed with clubs sit cross-legged in a dark hut and, in unison, whack the cloth spread on the ground, using a fascinating rhythm, singing as they beat. Close your eyes and it is like a dance, with men stamping their feet. They keep this up for hours, perhaps days, and the cloth emerges as if glazed, fit for the turban of a potentate.

The Emirs are heavily scented and wear jewelled rings. Each brings with him a selection of wives. When the House assembles, the road from the North is full of cavalcades: first a car with a long stave or wand projecting from the window—part of the royal insignia—and a figure in the back muffled by robes, then two or three closed cars in which one can catch glimpses, as they speed by, of packed and swathed femininity concealed behind veils. A car for luggage and attendants brings up the rear. The Government has built for Members flats which are convenient only for monogamists. Most of the Emirs hire houses from rich Africans and instal their *entourage*.

In the House of Representatives, members of the two main parties face each other in mutual enmity. The National Council for Nigeria and the Cameroons is an Ibo party, founded by the Ibo leader Dr. Nnamdi Azikiwe and therefore mistrusted by most non-Ibos. The Action Group was founded by Mr. Obafemi Awolowo, a barrister from Ibadan, largely as a *riposte* to the NCNC, and is confined mainly to the Yoruba-speaking West. Both parties hope for national followings.

In the Regions, the Western House of Assembly is wholly dominated by the Action Group, the Eastern House by the NCNC. As it is one of the functions of these two Houses to elect men to the central House in Lagos, all the Western representatives are Action Groupers and all their Eastern colleagues are members of the NCNC. Most controversially, Lagos forms part of the Western Region and elects its men to the Western House in Ibadan. Here in Lagos the first contest was incandescent in its fervour. The NCNC emerged triumphant and sent Dr.

Azikiwe—"Zik"—with four henchmen into the stronghold of the Action Group in Ibadan.

A national figure such as Zik should by rights become a member of the national parliament. But in Ibadan Zik stuck, because the Western House is controlled by the Action Group, and the Action Group would not send its hated NCNC rival to the central House in Lagos.

The full story was far more complicated than this brief outline suggests, and also a great deal more infamous. Bribes and counter-bribes changed hands, the Press hurled charges of the most lurid nature and one individual was believed to have accepted cheques amounting to £7,000 first for resigning in Zik's favour and then for cancelling his resignation. Zik is still outside the central House.

The whole of literate Lagos takes an intense interest in such rivalries, which the Press chronicles round by round. They are, I suppose, the only substitute (a pale one, indeed) for the tribal battles of former days, and are to the African as bull-fighting to the Spaniard or grasshopper duels to the peaceful Balinese. Europeans deplore the invective used, the mud-slinging and general bribery. But when you consider the newness of it all, the rawness of society, you can but be amazed at the restraint. So far, there have been no assassinations. Of course, it is early days yet.

Dr. Azikiwe rose to fame as an editor, and there is no doubt that he is a journalist of grand adroitness, if you do not set too much store by the standards of, say, the *Manchester Guardian*. He owns and edits the *West African Pilot* in Lagos and owns four or five newspapers elsewhere. There is no more fascinating part of the Nigerian scene than these electric, uninhibited sheets. It is a great temptation to any visitor to quote from them continually; here are two examples, taken at random from the first two or three papers I read; these are no gems, merely the beads of everyday:

I am writing to save the public from the Zikist hireling Mr. X., who is not satisfied with prostituting his own intelligence and selling his manhood, but who with his malicious wits and uncharitable temper is besmearing honest fellow citizens with mud.

I discover that the majority of the Lagos electorate is still suffering from invincible ignorance of the unholy alliance of the top-ranking leaders of the NCNC with the arch-hypocrite, the arch-political gamester Dr. Y. as the pivot whose dexterity and Machiavellianism is still a problem to his associates. . . . Most of the supporters of the NCNC are mere ideopraxites who unmindful of the suicidal result voted for a planless political party. . . . But thanks to Father Niger about 40% of the electorate are now alive to the ultimate danger of backing the ego-centric, mob-deluding, planless, irreconcilable, irremedial dictatorial leaders of the NCNC.

Disgusted, as one may suppose, at being shouldered out politically, Zik is building himself a large and ugly country house near the airport five storeys high and ringed with balconies, and states that he is going in for poultry-farming. His newspapers, and the harvest of popularity, have made him a rich man; but, like Nkrumah, he is said to be abstemious, simple in tastes and reserved; and, like him again, went to college in the United States. Still under fifty, in appearance lanky, bespectacled and intellectual, he shares Nkrumah's gift of spell-binding oratory, his capacity for work, his nationalist fanaticism and his biting ambition. "Self-government Now" has for many years been his creed and catch-cry, and it is ironical that when it is more than half-way towards achievement, he should hold no office and have no say. He is not even a Regional Minister. As a national leader he is threatened from the West, and by one of the despised Yorubas. The nationalist fervour of both parties is equal; and both are faced with the same necessity to win nation-wide support. Whether this can be done touches upon Nigeria's fundamental political weakness. There is no unity. Nigeria is less a country than a geographical accident resulting from historical caprice: for instance, from Franco-British rivalry and explorers' whims.

⋙ 3 ⋘

Geographically, racially, and now politically, Nigeria is divided into three Regions. So stultifying is this to nationalists burning for immediate independence that they accuse the British of inventing these divisions the better to "divide and rule", despite the fact that the British have thrown over these chasms the only existing bridges, and that the object of the new arrangement is not to rule, but to prepare the way to cease from ruling. Moreover, many of the Muslims of the North, and of Yoruba, would like to break away altogether to join their own separate nations. The attitude of extreme nationalists towards the facts of Nigeria's history and structure has been somewhat like that of the child confronted with the giraffe—"there ain't no such animal".

Under the present set-up—the "Macpherson constitution" which, after three years' life, must soon be altered—each of the three Regions has its own parliament, cabinet and government, federated at the centre under a House of Representatives and a Council of twelve African and six European Ministers presided over by the Governor and main architect of the plan, Sir John Macpherson, a restless, bright-eyed, eloquent Scot who reminds me a little in his energy, inventiveness and lack of all pomposity, as well as in his lean and hungry look, of John Buchan. His is the creative and nerve-straining task of breathing life into the bones of a plan excellent on paper, but jeopardized continually by feuds, fears and enmities between different races and religions no more ready for a true merger—much less so, in fact—than the peoples of Europe. He drives himself so hard, and gives out such currents of nervous energy, that everyone gloomily prophesies the nervous breakdown his resilience continually repels.

His task is formidable. Nigeria is a vast, sprawling country four times the size of Britain with a population, mostly primitive and illiterate, probably in the region of 30,000,000, speaking several hundred different languages. Unity is neither surging up from the people, nor being forced upon their leaders by circumstance. It is being imposed by an alien Power, the British, who have renounced the use of force and already proclaimed their own abdication. Nigerians may accept it temporarily as the price of complete independence, but such a spurious form of unity is unlikely to survive the British withdrawal, even if it lasts as long as that.[1]

❦ 4 ❦

Ministers and other of the Lagos intelligentsia and upper class are often to be seen off-duty at the Island Club, where inter-racial *bonhomie* is engendered. I was taken to a dance there and much enjoyed the friendly atmosphere, the lack of racial bar-riers, the "high life" dancing (a sort of jitterbugging) and a lawn lit by fairy lights where one could sit under the stars, at the tem-perature of a steam-heated American living-room, sipping a cold drink and watching the rank and fashion of Lagos. Some of its leaders were pointed out: a tall, thin Olympic sprinter and self-styled Prince, glossy in his white tie and tails, with a lovely Creole wife from Freetown in green and gold brocade; Ernest Ikoli, the burly, senatorial, jovial correspondent of *The Times*; a Western chief with the physique of a boxer, now a Minister, and his even heftier young partner in a firm of able barristers; several loquacious editors; a quiet young artist with a beard; and so many others, young and old, friendly, fluent and not a little inscrutable, that one soon grew dazed. On such big occasions, many are in evening dress and "high life" dances are restrained; everyone has become a dark-skinned, middle-class European. I had the feeling that I was watching some huge, rather solemn charade, much enjoyed at the time by the participants, but fugi-tive; and wondered why the naturally ebullient people of this lagoon-enfolded tropic island should strive so closely to imitate the not especially joyful *bourgeoisie* of Cambridge or Surrey.

Inter-racially, the Island Club is a great success, and its only flaw from a visitor's point of view—a flaw (if it is one) by no means confined to the Club's membership but common to the whole West African intelligentsia—is a tendency to talk about

[1] Since this was written, the Action Group precipitated a crisis by withdraw-ing its Ministers from the central Council, and the constitution in its present form was acknowledged to be unworkable. A new one, allowing much greater local autonomy to the Regions, was introduced in 1954, to lead on to self-government for those Regions who desire it in 1956.

nothing but politics. This is natural enough, of course, in countries passing through a revolution, where new constitutions spring up, bear fruit and are cut down as fast as plantain trees; but, like the harmattan, the empty skies and the level bush, it can become a trifle monotonous.

Some Africans feel this too. The bearded artist, a slight figure with a clever, alert, slightly Mephistophelian face, observed:

"My contemporaries talk of only two things—politics and money. Because neither interest me, they think I'm a fool. They judge a man by his position; a big man is a man with a big car and servants and grovelling office boys. When I visit my home, my family asks only one thing—how much money have you brought? I bring very little, and so my people despise me. There is no one interested in music and art, no one I can talk to here, except a few Europeans."

It is the old story of the misfit in the provincial city. This lone artist has lived in Paris and London, and hankers to return, yet Nigeria holds him, not only for economic reasons; the sources of his art lie here.

There is no world of art in Lagos, or indeed anywhere in West Africa that I could discover; not even the smallest band of votaries, let alone a ferment of creators; seldom can there have been a more whole-heartedly materialist community. The creative impulses in African society seem to have been flattened out of existence, for the time being, by the Western steam-roller. Perhaps this is not surprising, for the art of Africans was always limited and patchy; that is to say, it cropped up in any force only among certain peoples (in West Africa, mainly the Ashanti, the Yoruba and one or two Cameroonian tribes) and was virtually confined to dancing and sculpture. Painting and architecture were almost unknown; poetry had its folk-tales and legends, but no technique for recording them.

Dancing and sculpture were so closely bound to religion that perhaps they must needs die with the beliefs which they expressed and adorned. Yet it is odd that so highly developed a technique should not have been turned to the expression of new emotions, beliefs and fears. Nearly all modern African sculpture is unworthy of respect.

As to literature, there are plenty of young men writing books, but all in imitation of the European tradition, and with results that are either ludicrous (I was once lent the manuscript of a novel called *Under the Palm Trees with Fatima*) or jejune and flat. But now a lone harbinger of West African literature, Amos Tuteola (a junior civil servant in Lagos), has had the perception to go back to the true source of new literature, the traditions and myths of his race. *The Palm Wine Drinkard* is a folk-tale, full of the queer, distorted poetry, the deep and dreadful fears, the cruelty, the obsession with death and spirits, the macabre humour, the grotesque imagery of the African mind. It is the only piece of original, not imitative, African writing I have yet seen.

African art, if it is genuine, is never comfortable, noble or serene; perhaps for that reason it may never reach the heights—rather will it explore the depths of fear and torment and intimidation, with a relish of humour. It is possessed by spirits, and the spirits are malign.

◈ 5 ◈

We paddled slowly up a creek through water still and colourless as mica, among a silent waste of reeds. Or not a waste, perhaps; a great, dull expanse; but here and there small parties of women were cutting reeds and spreading them to dry. So wet is all this country round Lagos—so full of creeks and marshes—so flat and reedy—that there is little land to cultivate, and people gain their living by selling fish and mats.

We beached the boat in a village which sprawled to the water's edge, and jumped ashore to find ourselves serenaded by the school band. The children were all tiny, and carried enormous drums; they sang the National Anthem in Yoruba. The village chief came forward: an old, pock-marked, hook-nosed, turbaned man in flowing robes, Northern in feature, although in race a Yoruba; a Moslem, and with an air of dignity and welcome. We had not come fifteen miles from Lagos, and in this sad and silent landscape, among these gentle, sleepy-seeming people, might have been a thousand miles and several centuries away.

I was taken with pride to see the new mosque. One very handsome wall was built, in brick, the gift of a merchant; two other less splendid walls were half-built but already falling down; the

fourth wall had not been started. Meanwhile the *imam*, who saw
with affection its future glories, made do with an old mud
mosque indistinguishable from an ordinary house. The children,
he said, go to the C.M.S. school, which has a teacher; and their
fathers, Muslim and Christian alike, belong to the Ogboni
society, a pagan institution, which meets once a month by moon-
light to sacrifice a goat to tribal ancestors. This village sets an
example of religious toleration that prouder places might do well
to follow.

The show-place is the school, built on high stilts and with a
floor of reed matting made for bare feet; in shoes, one slithers
awkwardly. Roofs, walls, all are of reeds, and pencils of sunlight
slant through the interstices. It is like a huge birdcage, and
packed with children: fifty-six in all, I was told, but the village
holds at least another hundred who do not attend, and so grow
up, within a few hours' walk of the capital, as ignorant of letters
as their grandfathers were.

Did they, I wondered, find the listless fishing of the creek too
attractive? Or did their parents object to new-fangled ways?
The hook-nosed headman beckoned to a youth dressed in a yellow polka-dot shirt who was idling by and asked him, in Yoruba,
if he had been to school. Yes, the boy replied; in fact he had
been away to a better school than this and had reached the
heights of Standard VI; he was exceptionally well-educated.

"What do you do now?" I asked.

"Nothing."

"Why not?"

"I don't know anything to do."

There you have it, the headman explained, rather more
ornately. The boy is too grand to fish, and there is nothing else
for him in the village; he might go away, but his parents distrust
the town; they fear he would be dead to them and never sacrifice
to his father's spirit. And there is the future malcontent.

Coloured reeds lay drying in the sun; the women dye them to
make the gay mats they carry in to Lagos and sell to market
women. This gives them cash to buy food. Behind the half-built
mosque was a mud-and-corrugated-iron lean-to shed with some
drums stacked in a corner, and the ashes of fires. The Ogboni
temple, said the headman, rather grandly. A path led back into

the bush, and when I tried to follow it I was politely headed off.

"To the juju shrine," the headman explained. "They do not like strangers there."

"Too many human sacrifices, perhaps," I suggested facetiously.

"Oh no, not *here*," said the headman gravely. "Those are in Benin and Abeokuta."

Or in Lagos, possibly? Only the other day the body of a boy with feet and hands missing was dug from a beach, and several of the bodies often fished out of the lagoon are incomplete, the missing parts those often used for witchcraft or sacrifice. A cult of witch-smellers from Dahomey, the Itiukas, did such good business in Lagos hunting out witches and wizards, several of whom were killed out of hand, that the Government was forced to ban their visits.

On the way home we passed a roadside barber's shop where the young proprietor was shaving heads under a little shelter of leaves and branches. Laid out beside him, in a neat row, were eight pairs of clippers. I asked why he had so many.

"A different one is for each part of the head," he answered. This seemed to me the highest refinement of barbery.

In half an hour we were back in the capital, through the hideous sprawling suburbs, at the time of the "Lagos snow-storm", as it was named by my companion, Major Allen, then second-in-command of that small area round Lagos known as the Colony. This is the hour when school doors open and suddenly the streets are white with black-faced schoolboys, thousands and thousands of them. You can *see* the birthrate rising in Africa, as sometimes you can see flowers opening in the sun. We passed also a large, square, gleaming edifice behind a wall.

"The White College, they call it," Major Allen said. "A term in there is better than a degree from the university, if you want to get on in politics." It was the jail.

All the same, people are not always anxious to go there. The Police Commissioner told me of a case against two men—a fairly simple one of larceny—which had been adjourned no less than eighty-seven times. On each adjournment, the defending lawyer received a fee. The accused had been on bail for nearly two years, living meanwhile on the proceeds of other larcenies.

A splendid plan has been prepared to clear these stinking Lagos stews with their packed humanity, their foul open drains, their shacks of rusty tin, their heaps of rubbish, their squalor and poverty. It is to cost £20,000,000 for the first ten years. The initial stage is to build 5,000 houses on the mainland into which to move the occupants of the first block to be purged. Then the vacated site will be bulldozed and levelled. Authority will instal piped water and drains and then allow the landlords to rebuild their houses to approved plans. Experts from Britain have drawn these plans; the houses are to be built at a density of sixteen to the acre and to be several storeys high. As each block is completed, the next will be tackled, until the whole seventy acres will be rebuilt.

It is a good plan, and work has begun on the first 5,000 new houses. Lagos is now under the management of an elected and self-governing Town Council. The Mayor is an active politician —one of Dr. Azikiwe's most serious rivals, in fact, for Nigerian leadership. Possibly the Lagos Town Council is full of civic pride and anxious to see the slums replaced by model dwellings; but the fact remains that the members are elected and most of their electors lack all enthusiasm for the scheme. Some are landlords who do not wish to see their profitable town houses bulldozed down, and all will have to face higher rates to help pay interest on the loans. The demand for slum-clearance has not come from the Lagosians; it has come from the British, who live in comfort and feel ashamed. It is their plan; but before they can execute it, the power has been taken out of their hands. Will the ten-year plan ever be completed? Everyone hopes so, including all socially-conscious Africans; but no one would care to back their hopes with a year's salary.

"The Town Council has been in being for thirteen months," an observer told me. "They have spent most of the time wrangling over jobs for their friends and each others' salaries, half the committees do no business because they can't get a quorum, and as regards the welfare of Lagos—well, in that time they have taken absolutely no decisions at all." [1]

[1] Since my visit, a Commission of Enquiry into the affairs of the Town Council, conducted by the Town Clerk of Norwich, reported that it had failed in ten specified respects to fulfil its functions, and indicted its members for

G

✤ 6 ✤

The road to Ibadan is red, excellent and dangerous, by reason
of the terrifying speed enjoyed by all African drivers. Mine was
a Yoruba, a charming individual with a long, thin face, long,
thin limbs and a rather mournful expression. I do not think he
was mournful by nature, however; he had two wives, both out
trading and bringing home plenty of profit; he wished to start
a business of his own and needed a connection with a British
firm who would send him goods on credit. As a driver, he seemed
possessed by demons. We hurled ourselves past crowded lorries
which were themselves racing forward as if pursued by wolves.
All cyclists were compelled—or at any rate well advised—to fling
themselves and their machines bodily into the bush at frequent
intervals in order to escape the juggernauts that thundered by.

It is all forest in the West—forest honeycombed with little
farms and cocoa plantations; but a strip is left untouched beside
the road, and one's view is thus confined to tall trees and creepers
filmed with red dust. This grows monotonous. The towns are
ugly, all rusty red with their unpainted corrugated-iron roofs,
red clay houses behind red clay walls, roads thick with red dust.
Here, one longs for trees, but there is complete *apartheid*: trees in
their place, in the forest, men in theirs, the red clay towns.

In no time we had covered 112 miles to Ibadan, the largest
African town in Africa—the largest created by and for Africans,
that is, without the intervention of Europeans. Most cities are
European in origin, even though Africans by the hundred thousand now occupy them; before their rise, the people lived in
scattered villages or homesteads in the bush. But these Yoruba
towns are African in origin, in style, in architecture, in government. Ibadan has a population probably not much below half
a million souls.

It looks its best at night. By the door of every close-packed
dwelling, at every booth lining the streets, glows a candle or
home-made oil lamp, each throwing its little nimbus of light

financial malpractices. The Council has been dissolved by the Western
Regional Government and an interim committee set up to manage Lagos'
affairs, under the chairmanship of Sir Kofo Abayomi, pending new elections.

into the warm air. The whole centre of the town is a-glow, as if
the Milky Way had floated down to earth. All ugliness and dirt
are hidden. A gentle light flickers on bronze cheek-bones,
shadowed eyes, on slim wrists and fingers. The women's heads
are swathed in folds of cloth and they sit beside their stalls like
crowned princesses waiting for suitors. Noon or midnight, every
woman trades; as surely as her lungs need air, her spirit needs
commerce. In the dark, soft streets—there is no paving—the
men pad quietly to and fro in their native dress of baggy trousers
and full tunic, greeting, smoking, gossiping. Far into the night—
all night, perhaps—lamps burn, footsteps shuffle, tongues wag.
Trade and talk, talk and trade, night and day, late and early—
that is Ibadan.

By day, the city is all rust red and ink blue. The women wear
blue robes, different shades of blue, all dyed with indigo. They
are handsome, the women, with small features, thin bones and
fairly light skins, but not so the men; there is something ungainly
about many of them and little that inspires trust. They do not
smile so readily as many Africans. But Africa's hospitality and
courtesy are here.

My driver has relatives in Ibadan, the grandest of them a sort
of chief: the president of the Native Court. A rich man and
cocoa-plantation owner, he lives in a gaily painted wooden
house with two storeys. Entering through a baroque sort of front
door, we climbed to a parlour whose walls are painted bilious
green with yellow-ochre and chocolate-brown fluted pillars and
shutters. The window-sills are picked out in mustard yellow.
On the wall hang the covers of many china vegetable dishes of
exuberant but hideous design. Doe-eyed maidens, their heads
peppered with little plaits, clustered in doorways, and a radio on
the wall interjected into our conversation a summary of English
football results. The portly chief, immersed in yards of robe,
swamped an upright chair, giving me the seat of honour on a
horse-hair settee. The interview ran on these lines:

"It is kind of you to invite us to your house."

"Bristol Rovers five, Swindon Town nil; Colchester three,
Watford one; Coventry four . . ."

"I hope you will enjoy your stay in Ibadan."

"Thank you. Have you lived long in this house?"

"Crystal Palace three, Reading three; Queen's Park Rangers one . . ."

"I built this house fifteen years ago, but before that there was another house which burnt down."

"Bradford City four, Scunthorpe two. . . ."

A man came in and put two live cockerels into my hand—the chief's dash. I wondered what to do: to refuse, or to take them and offer him something—but what?—in return. The chief led me across a sort of wooden bridge and down a flight of steps to the women's quarters, which looked like four loose-boxes with four stable doors, a radio in each. The narrow balcony on to which they opened was full of babies and children of every size. All around stretched a sea of similar houses, only some less grand, each with its walled compound where the women's quarters lay. The houses were so close they almost touched each other, with narrow alley-ways between, and shallow open drains. In one such alley-way I saw a flock of small, fluffy chickens—all blue. Astonished, I watched them scurry through a hole in the wall. They were gone, and I stood wondering—perhaps a touch of the sun? The driver reassured me. They had been dipped in indigo, he said, to discourage hawks. In the street, a man wearing pink trousers and a gown with broad black and white stripes flew past on a bicycle.

As the driver's family unfolded, it transpired that some of his children lived here with a brother, in order to attend school. A charming teen-ager joined us, dressed all in white, like a confirmation candidate, a white scarf over her ringlets.

"My firstborn," he said proudly. "She is at Ibadan Grammar school. Next year she will go to college if she passes the exam; it will cost me £36 a year."

"Perhaps your wives will contribute, with their trading?"

"Oh, no, that could not be," the driver said, surprised. "But my brother is a first-class clerk; he will help me."

"And after that?"

"She is to go to England to study medicine."

And very likely she will.

To end our tour, her father showed me some of the proper tourist's sights—a sacred crocodile, and the temple of the thunder-god Shango. The crocodile was confined in a mud compound about six feet square, not long enough for it to stretch its full length, with a puddle of water insufficient for a frog. The sun beat down on it and there was no shade. Round it lay the decayed remains of dead chickens. Crocodiles do not normally inspire sympathy, but the plight of this one was depressing. Small boys crowded round holding chickens which they wished me to buy and toss, alive, to the reptile. When I declined, they followed me down the narrow street screaming abuse and hopping with rage.

To reach the temple of the thunder-god you pass through a small court into a mud-walled inner room where a toothless old man guards the fetish. All you can see of it consists of several lumps of black metal, said to be thunderbolts, and various objects suspended from the roof: several calabashes, some beads, bunches of feathers, cowrie shells, knobbly roots, leather thongs and various strips of cloth. Like every sacred object that I have seen in Africa, they lack all apparent purpose, but to their worshippers are charged with necromantic currents as potent as electricity.

This old temple and its meteorites have a seedy, half-neglected air. The ancient faith of the Yorubas is in decline. Yet (as is so often the case) many customs survive, half believed-in and half meaningless. Sometimes Egungun "spirits" parade through the streets masked and covered so completely that no part of their body can be seen, for in olden days the least glimpse of the man beneath meant instant death for any woman, and every female bolted indoors when the eerie moaning of their "bull-roarers" (wooden laths which they whirled round and round at rapid speed), and their own deep "spirit" voices, sounded through the streets.

That is a relic of old Ibadan. The new sprawls round the perimeter, where rich evolués build in imitation of English suburban villas. The driver took me slowly along a row of them, describing their owners. This belongs to a trader, that to a lawyer, this stream-lined modern one, all balconies and flat roofs and horizontal lines, to a building contractor. All are of concrete blocks, unpainted—a clammy grey—and stand on a bare soil without gardens.

We halted opposite the grandest house of all. It had four

storeys, with a double flight of steps rising to the front door and a roof so pitched as to give it a baronial air. The driver spoke of it with the reverence due to the most expensive house in town.

"Whom does it belong to?"

"The Treasurer of the Native Authority," he said.

We came to a level crossing, and I was surprised to see a hurrying train: surprised, because a "go-slow" railway strike had been in progress for ten days. Trains were taking three days from Lagos, and a favourite gambit of their drivers was to pull up at a level crossing, so as to block the road. Strikes here are often complicated by magic; a curse is laid upon the locomotive to bring sickness to anyone who touches its controls. An official who negotiates with Trade Unions told me:

"If there's any trouble, and I want to find the Trade Union secretary, I always go to the cemetery. Sooner or later he turns up there with his lieutenants to unearth a corpse and use bits of it for medicine to keep the strike going."

I was therefore surprised to see a hurrying train, and asked the driver to explain. He glanced into the cab of the locomotive as it puffed by.

"That is Mr. Kosoko, who has won a scholarship to England," he said. "He does not like to go slow in case they take it away."

∾ 7 ∾

Ibadan is an old town, but its name has taken on a new significance, for the University has been established here.

A site of untouched bush, forest and farmland was given to the architects, Maxwell Fry and Jane Drew, to create upon it, starting from scratch, an entire university. Such a chance comes to few nowadays. Moreover, it was a chance even more than usually untrammelled, for Nigeria has no style or tradition either to inspire or to constrain. The architects had a true *carte blanche*.

Their scheme was, when I saw it, still unfinished, and therefore hard to judge; only when the buildings can be seen as a group in their setting of lawns and trees and distant forest will a verdict be possible. They are spacious and have unity. The large flat surfaces, the sweeping horizontal lines characteristic of modern architecture are there, but the walls have been imaginatively treated not by an added decoration but by patterns punched into the concrete: patterns of crosses, squares and petal shapes repeated over whole sides of buildings, most arresting to the eye.

This *broderie anglaise* treatment breaks the light that floods against the walls into a thousand shafts and circles, and so creates a shadow-pattern on the wide floors, a trellis-work of light and shade. It is a clever trapping of the ever-present sun. The use of balconies is another *coup d'œil*. The dormitories, roughcast in light grey, rise in three tiers, each with its fretted balcony, colour-washed in cerulean blue and light maroon, running the full length of the building. These colour effects are striking and, I thought, most successful. Modern Brazilian architecture has perhaps influenced the two partners. This follows tradition, for the notion of patterned balconies, which adorn most of the larger, concrete-block African houses, is said to have come from Brazil with repatriated ex-slaves.

The designers of the university, while planning for an immediate enrolment of 600, have looked forward to the time when at least a thousand students will be in residence, and what today looks vast and new and empty may all too easily seem cramped tomorrow. And so, also, may the Brazilian patterns, today so fresh and sharp in the light, gay buildings, grow with age and erosion a little shabby, choked with owls' nests and vagrant vegetation; or else cost a lot to clean.

All the same, Nigeria already has a university to be proud of. The library musters 70,000 books, and more arrive by every mail. Yet the day may come when books will be anachronisms in a library. Already Ibadan has a big stock of microfilms and three or four reading machines, and a stock also of those near-miraculous "microcards" which compress the contents of an entire book on to a postcard. The saving of money and space which new libraries can effect through these techniques is remarkable, the implications for the writer sinister. Even more depressing, I thought, was the skilful photography on to microfilm, for posterity's benefit, of every page of every newspaper published in Nigeria. One's thoughts baulk at a computation of the tons of nonsense posterity will inherit. How historians of the future will yearn for the simplicity of a few sherds and axe-heads!

Little more than half the full complement of 600 students is, as yet, enrolled at the University College, which took its first freshman only in 1948. Its academic staff numbers nearly a hundred and is mainly British. At their head, during my visit (his term of office has since ended), was Dr. Kenneth Mellanby, an eminent authority on parasites. A small, slight, wiry man with a lively sense of humour, a sometimes caustic tongue and a great deal of energy, his has been the hard task of making the University College literally from nothing: no buildings, no students, no professors, no books, no syllabus. What has been done in less than five years, in temporary hutments and make-shift buildings and with a new, uneven staff and raw students, is remarkable. Towards the new buildings the British taxpayer gave £1,500,000 and the Cocoa Marketing Board another million. The Nigerian taxpayer produces about a quarter of a million annually for upkeep, costs which will certainly rise. At present, for instance, there is no hospital where medical students can take the clinical part of their course, and they must go to Britain for two or three years. London University has refused to recognize for teaching purposes any hospital in Nigeria, so the University College is to build one in Ibadan at a cost of £2,500,000. Some think this out of proportion in a country where whole districts are without the simplest kind of bush hospital or clinic, and where the greatest need is to control the obvious diseases rather than to treat a few people very expensively.

That all students are ardent nationalists scarcely needs to be said. So are many of their mentors: and especially a brilliant young Ibo lecturer I met one evening. Thin, tall, young-looking, he had that lean and hungry look we are so aptly warned against, and spoke with a naïvety that would have been incredible were it not that scientists so often lack all grip on the slippery and imprecise vagaries of human nature.

"The British could leave Nigeria tomorrow without the least disturbance to the country's progress," he averred. "We should keep those we want on contract." (So many Africans seem to regard the British like company's water; when the need arises you turn on the tap and help gushes forth; when the need is over, you turn it off.)

"Our lack of unity?" he continued. "Totally artificial! Trumped up and exaggerated by the British! Give us our freedom, and we Nigerians will come together as one family and work twice as hard because we are free. We shall forget our petty differences in labour for the common cause. We are not like India! There'll be no quarrels *here*! But Britain is determined at all costs to crush and trample on the African."

What about all the effort and money Britain was pouring in— for instance the £1,500,000 to build the University?

"Eyewash! Sheer hypocrisy! What is a paltry sum like that compared with the vast profits made by the UAC?"

And then, back again to freedom.

"Czechoslovakia is a hundred times more free than Nigeria! We would support any enemy of Britain's—first Hitler if it had been necessary, and now Russia—who'd help us in our struggle. Have we enough trained men? Of course we have. That is Britain's latest excuse to cheat us. The need is greatly exaggerated. If necessary, I could be Prime Minister tomorrow, and so could several of my friends. It is not difficult. Oh, yes, we have the right men!"

Yet this fiery person, who had been at Cambridge, cherished a loyalty only a shade less warm for his old college—"my college". "I should have stayed in Cambridge," he said, "if Nigeria had been free."

Here was a man, one felt, who though burnt up with passion might yet be happy, for he had a faith, a fixed centre of loyalty. Shango the thunder-god is dead, his temple empty, but a new god from the West has come to replace him, the god of nationalism; and if he, like Shango, demands human sacrifices, that is only to be expected of a virile deity.

Nationalism—more accurately described as racialism here— can be regarded as a disease or as a religion. A Western exotic, it is now rampant, as exotics often are when taken to a new environment away from the factors which kept them in order at home. (One thinks of rabbits in Australia, or the prickly pear; brambles in New Zealand, tuberculosis in the South Seas, sparrows in America, many other instances.) Racialism could,

G*

perhaps, bind together these new countries full of unco-ordinated peoples and creeds. But it has also, and in full measure, that jealous, destructive element of hatred that has caused such havoc in the West, and may do the same in hatred-ridden Africa.

Politics are in the air at Ibadan, for it has become the capital of the Western Region which has a House of Assembly, a House of Chiefs, a Cabinet, a *de facto* Prime Minister and a Lieutenant-Governor of its own. It is, in fact, almost a miniature state—and not so miniature at that, having a population of between 6,000,000 and 7,000,000, nearly all members of the great Yoruba-speaking group, comprising a number of slightly different but closely related tribes.

"Some constitutions were written on parchment and some on paper, and some dwell like the Holy Ghost among books of law; but I believe this to be the only one in the world to have been put together on the telephone." This was said by a Secretariat official introduced to me as the only man in Nigeria who understood the Western constitution. The British passion to be fair to everyone, somewhat over-indulged, has led to fantastic ramifications and proliferations of the various democratic devices, and all for an illiterate peasant people, quite new to the practice of democracy and destined soon to take charge of the machine.

To start the ball rolling, 1,500 primary elections were held to pick candidates for 240 "intermediate electoral colleges". This took four months, and no wonder; most of the voters were illiterate, and only about 25 per cent could be enticed to the polls. It was laid down that all the members of the Native Authority Councils (the unit of local government) should go forward to these "colleges", plus a bevy of directly elected persons who must outnumber them. Some of the Native Authority Councils are very large. Benin's has 238 members, so another 239 persons had to be elected and the whole 477 proceed to the next stage. Then all the 240 "intermediate colleges" met in order to elect some of their number to twenty-four "final electoral colleges". And then the twenty-four "final electoral colleges" met to elect eighty members to the Western House of Assembly. And then the House of Assembly met and elected thirty-one members to the House of Representatives in Lagos. After that, everyone must have needed a month's holiday.

Mr. Awolowo's Action Group dominates the Western political scene. His dream, I think, and the dream of all his followers, is an independent and exclusive Yoruba state. They want Yorubaland for the Yorubas and a revival of ancient glories in an independent Nigeria, with the Ibos kept in their place. It is significant that Mr. Awolowo has declined office in the central government but preferred to stay in Ibadan as Minister of Local Government in a council of nine Ministers, including two chiefs.

The institution of chieftainship is strong amongst the Yoruba, and the Western Region (unlike the Eastern) has a House of Chiefs. Some are great potentates with large kingdoms, their prestige still undimmed by the education of their subjects, who prostrate themselves in the dust when their rulers walk forth under their great umbrellas.

∾ 8 ∾

I met two such chiefs, the Alafin of Oyo and the Oni of Ife, who is the spiritual head of the Yoruba nation. To Europeans, Ife is famous for its astonishing bronze and terra-cotta heads whose origin is still a mystery. Even the date of their creation cannot be settled, though it seems most likely to lie between the fourteenth and sixteenth centuries. Most remarkable of all, this style of art, which reached the highest levels of achievement, seems to have arisen unparented and died without offspring, save for the more baroque art of Benin. Suddenly, achievement flowered; it ceased, and left behind no tradition, no myth, little but the ancient technique of *ciré-perdue* casting.

Ife is like all other towns in Western Nigeria, flat, low, red and corrugated. In the middle sprawls the Oni's palace, a rump of its past grandeur. We arrived to find some of the Oni's loyal subjects flat on their faces on the gravel outside, doing homage. The Oni, a bulky figure swathed in handsome robes of faded pink brocade and wearing ornamental sandals, stood in the veranda, flanked by his attendants. I felt that we had perhaps arrived inopportunely, but the Oni breasted a way through obeisant figures to greet us, almost out-distancing his umbrella-holders. This, he explained, was the Oduduwa ceremony, held in honour of the founder of the Yoruba nation. It would last seven days; chiefs and headmen came in from far and wide to demonstrate their loyalty; many sacrifices would be made— nowadays, only dogs, goats and fowls. He was not supposed to leave the palace during the ceremony, he said, but did not seem to mind making an exception in our honour.

He took us straight to his museum, a handsome new white building which was quite empty except for some showcases (all but one of those was empty too) and packing-cases. These last contained nearly all the famous heads, back from an exhibition in London.

"Why have these not been unpacked?" the Oni demanded.

No one knew, and the clerk to the Native Authority was sent for.

"Are they all here?" the Oni asked, and no one knew that either; the Oni thought not; a discussion ensued, and it was decided to telegraph to the Surveyor of Antiquities to find out.

Interest in these Ife treasures has always been more European than African. Rumours of their existence got about during the early days of British administration, and one or two percipient travellers took away a few specimens; but it was Leo Frobenius, leader of the German expedition of 1910–11, who made the world acquainted with this *cache* of art. Some of the sculptures were buried, others lay disregarded in old compounds, many of the terra-cottas had been smashed and thrown into the bush.

Frobenius' expedition quickly aroused feelings of nationalism, less, it appeared, among the Yoruba than among the British, who decided, rather abruptly, that such valuable art treasures ought not to go to Berlin. As a result, according to him, of intrigues by the Yoruba, whom he regarded as the "slyest and most subtle people of West Africa" as well as the cleverest and most talented, he was accused of bullying and bribing the people to part with specimens against their will—his own story being that they had parted with them well satisfied to be paid for something they had looked on as junk. An enquiry was held. African officials forcibly seized Frobenius' baggage and invited the vendors to reclaim anything in it that they wished to recover. The main part of his collection was thus re-absorbed into bush and compound, to the great satisfaction of the men of Ife, who were left in possession both of the money and the *objets d'art*.

Frobenius had paid £6 and a bottle of whisky for the now-famous head of the Sea-god Olokun, which he had dug up in a sacred grove.

He went on his way disgruntled, but having managed, with cunning superior even to the Yoruba's, to retain a few terra-cotta heads. These, when shown in Europe with sketches of all that he had lost, aroused the greatest excitement in the art world. They were so completely unlike anything found before in Negro Africa—so European, so classical in form, that all sorts of specu-lations were set loose as to forgotten civilizations and links with the antique world. Frobenius himself, a trained archæologist, identified Yorubaland with lost Atlantis, "where all tropical plants flourish and elephants gambol, where brass is smelted and the houses are strange", and which Pseidon won, by casting lots, as his share of the universe; and he linked it also with Etruria, suggesting that in remote antiquity the Phœnicians had planted a colony on these shores.[1] Hence the worship of Olokun the sea-god—Poseidon in another guise; hence Yoruba art; and hence, above all, Yoruba religion, which Frobenius considered to be "purer and more original, more consistent and more unbroken than any other cult of the classical ages known to us". The Yorubas (he said) are, "above all nations, saturated with the spirit of religious thought"; adherents of beliefs "spacious, broad, lofty and profound, however unsympathetic, even to repulsive-ness, may be their character".[2] (Frobenius never forgave the Yorubas for their sharp practice in regard to his collection.)

As a result of Frobenius' expedition, a law was passed for-bidding the export of any work of art without a licence, and this has undoubtedly saved much good material for Nigeria: even if the Nigerians themselves have, hitherto, displayed little interest.

After Frobenius' discovery in 1910 of the single Olokun bronze head, it was twenty-eight years before some more were accident-ally unearthed near the Oni's palace when foundations were

[1] For these and other details of Yoruba religion and art see *The Voice of Africa* by Leo Frobenius. Hutchinson, 1913.

[2] Compare with the observations of a later writer, the missionary Mr. Farrow, in *Faith, Fancies and Fetish* (S.P.C.K., 1926): "Religion is intimately associated with every detail of the life of the West African negro. From birth to burial, and even beyond, his whole personal experience is regulated and controlled by his religion. The system of government is likewise entirely religious."

being dug for a new house. No one had suspected their existence. This does not suggest either a lively tradition among the Ife people, or great enthusiasm among the British.

It is not only in the museum that Ife art is to be seen; there is plenty of it *in situ*. Conducted by a clerk, we drove a few miles into the forest and followed a shady footpath to a shrine. Three stone figures, each perhaps eighteen inches high, forlornly stood among the undergrowth. Queer little figures, they were: dumpy, fat-thighed, brooding, full of character, and showing no obvious affinity with other African styles of art. They were copies, I should imagine; weathered, but not very old. This was the shrine of Ore, a mythical hunter turned demi-god, his wife Rere and their gate-keeper Olofefunra; but Ore himself was missing. He had disappeared about ten years ago, the clerk said—stolen, or hidden by the followers of his cult to keep him out of the museum. People still bring sacrifices once a year to the shrine and kill cocks over the statues, but the worshippers are dwindling year by year, the clerk said.

In another part of the forest we visited a shrine sacred to a woman called Eshu Obasin who, in her husband's absence, had defended Ife against invading tribes. She was in terra-cotta, and in a poor way. Kind friends had built a shelter over her head, but the corrugated iron had been stolen, leaving her defenceless clay exposed to storms and imminently menaced by a rotting beam just over her head. Sooner or later a tempest seems certain to send the beam crashing down to finish Eshu Obasin for good. They are sad, these statues, though I suppose in their day hungry for blood. A whole pantheon of gods and goddesses, heroes and demons, is dying in these high forests, just as goat-footed Pan and lecherous Silenus perished, in their day, with all the host of satyrs, dryads and naïads on the olive-speckled mountains and in the sun-trapped valleys of Greece. And yet, perhaps, the dead die not, but circle round in time; and their ghosts may haunt these dark and steaming places forever, as the Attic landscape still faintly echoes with the naïad's murmur and the satyr's hoof.

Evidence of art's degeneracy and the decay of Yoruba religion —the two are joined—offers on all sides. We passed a temple sacred to a Mercury called Oluorogbo who went to heaven once a year and brought back divine messages which he wrote in symbols on the wall of his shrine: a seedy, open-fronted, thatched shed whose back wall was covered with scratches and scrawls. The key to their meaning has been lost and no one can now interpret them. An old, toothless, scrawny woman appeared from a hut and started to beg for money in a high-pitched whine: the priestess, who now lives, or just exists, on the charity of pilgrims who never come and on the sacrifices which are still brought once a year. And once a year she adds to the wall's doodles without knowledge of what she scrawls.

Ife is as full of holy relics as Rome. Each grove and shrine is sacred to an *orisha* or demi-god, who is not merely the guardian and patron but the progenitor of a clan. For once upon a time the gods lived on earth, and there is no Yoruba who cannot trace his ancestry back to one of them. Thus there is godhead in every man. The clans are known by tattoo marks and also by food tabus, observed to this day. And it is common, too, for a man in doubt or trouble to consult the Ifa, the oracle, whose priests divine its intentions by casting sixteen palm kernels on a board, reading off the permutations and then reciting one of 1,680 stories or couplets appropriate to each fall of the nuts.[1] No wonder that it took an Ifa priest five or six years to train for his task. The carved cups and trays used for divination are among the finest specimens of Yoruba art, but their making is a lost craft today.

Not merely the Yoruba nation but the world itself came to birth at Ife. At first there was only Olorun, the Creator, god of the sky, and Olokun the sea-god; there was no dry land. Olorun had two sons. He gave the elder son a hen with five claws and a ball of sand, and told him to go down and make an earth upon the face of the waters. On his way down this young man encountered some palm wine, which he drank, and then fell asleep. So Olorun sent for his second son, Oduduwa, who laid the sand on the surface of the sea. The hen began to scratch, spreading the sand and driving back the water, until the earth was formed with Ife at its hub and Oduduwa as its first king. After a while

---

[1] This is the number given by Farrow (*Faith, Fancies and Fetish*), who adds that Ifa priests or diviners are "the shrewdest and most intellectual of their race, profound thinkers, and of great subtlety and knowledge. They are preeminently responsible for the cruelties and evil deeds."

both the sky-god's sons disappeared into the centre of the earth at Ife, and so it is here that Oduduwa must be worshipped every year.

Oduduwa had a number of sons, all heroes, and now *orishas*. One of them is commemorated by a stone column marked with a pattern of metal studs which stands opposite the warehouse of the Cocoa Co-operative Union. This is the staff of Oranyan, who left Ife to march southwards, conquering everyone as he went; but he left a promise with his people that, should they ever need him, he would return. Years went by; Ife was threatened; the people gathered together and shouted many times. Oranyan heard and came striding back, still laying about him with his sword. Suddenly, looking down at a dead warrior, he recognized a friend and knew that he had come among his own people. Dismayed, he thrust his staff into the ground, where it petrified, strode on into the forest and disappeared. What the metal studs represent, no one knows. Our guide suggested that they were the bullets fired at him—an anachronism, clearly; or perhaps the number of his years on earth.

It was at Ife, also, that Yemaya, the goddess of moisture, gave birth simultaneously to sixteen divinities, including the mighty Shango, god of thunder. "When Shango rides across the heavens in a storm," an old man of Ibadan told Frobenius, "he stands upon the backs of goats, and his favourite food is a ram." In nearby Oyo, Shango's effigy is a ram's mask. From these and other signs, Frobenius deduced a link between this deity and Ammon, the ram-headed god of Egypt, who might, at so early a date, have made his way across the Sudan. Certainly there seems in this nothing improbable, since Yorubaland was always in touch with the Hausa states, and links of trade have joined those states, since time immemorial, across the desert to the Mediterranean world.

As for Etruria, the link there is the number sixteen. The old town (which was rebuilt in 1882) was divided into seventeen wards or quarters—sixteen for the clans descending from the sixteen gods born there of Yemaya, and a seventeenth for the Oni's palace, the hub of the world. The Etruscans, too, built their temples in sixteen different quarters, and divided the horizon into sixteen parts for the practice of divination. The sixteen palm kernels used by the Yoruba for the same purpose were brought to the world by Edju, the god of mischief, who got them from monkeys, and was told to go round the world to ask their meaning in sixteen different places—which he did, and got sixteen different answers, just as he might today.

Perhaps all this is strained, and it is certainly conjectural; but one's interest in this outwardly drab and even squalid town is piqued by the notion that history may link it with the great monuments at Karnak, with Tarquin's warriors and with the dark-eyed, distant-ranging sailors of Tyre.

∾· 9 ·∾

Our clerk led us through rows of prostrate homage-payers up some steps to a veranda and into a two-storeyed wooden wing of the Oni's rambling palace. The Oni greeted us genially from a plush-upholstered armchair. On the sideboard stood a large ornamental fish in many-coloured glass and a modern carved lion. Photographs of previous Onis lined the walls. Champagne and sandwiches were served, and the Oni, Sir Adesoji Aderemi, K.B.E., C.M.G., talked with fluency and vigour. Now in his early sixties, he started life as a railway clerk and then became a most astute and successful produce trader before succeeding to Onihood, which has led on to the rank of Cabinet Minister (without portfolio) in the Central Government. The African system of succession most ingeniously combines the advantages of heredity with those of election. A new ruler must come from the royal house, but he may be one of many sons, and it is the task of the council of elders to choose the most suitable. Meanwhile the royal sprigs must earn their living in the ordinary work of the world, knowing that a great prize awaits the worthy. (The attractions of the prize might seem to some dubious; two years was said to be the average term of office of lesser chiefs in Yorubaland, after which they were generally poisoned.) The brightest of the present Oni's many sons are all in training for some useful work. One is studying medicine in Edinburgh, one is to become an engineer, one a teacher, one an economist and one a barrister. A sixth is expected to take up agriculture.

Politically, the clipping of the Oni's wings has started, with the introduction of elections to the Native Authority council. Half its members are now voted in and the other half selected by traditional methods. No doubt, before long, he and these other Nigerian potentates will go the way of their Gold Coast fellows, transformed into figure-heads by the wand of democracy. But the present Oni surely has too much personality, vigour and prestige to go quietly.

While he is the religious head of the Yoruba nation, his colleague the Alafin of the neighbouring state of Oyo is, by tradition, the secular senior. This position he owes to his direct descent from Shango the thunder-god who once ruled in Oyo. It is said that he was so war-like and bloodthirsty that even the Oyos expressed their wish for a being who would give them meat, not slaves. Shango, in royal dudgeon, took a rope and hanged himself from a tree. Two chains sprang up from it, and by these he climbed to heaven; and his wife turned herself into the River Niger.

Enshrined in this legend is an ancient principle of Yoruba politics: that the chief, mighty and sacred as he is, rules only with the consent of the people. He can go too far, and that is the end of him. If the Alafin (or any of the other rulers) grows too tyrannical or corrupt, a council of seven elders sends him the *igbava*, a covered cup containing parrots' eggs. This is a hint that he must go into the bush and commit suicide. Should he ignore it, the council of seven is then entitled to have him strangled (for royal blood must not be shed) and elect a successor from among his sons.

The ritual of succession is elaborate, and in former times bloody. The dead Alafin's head was cut off and his heir drank a potion from the skull and ate the heart or tongue. The royal corpse was buried in the bush with eight living companions, and his horse killed on the mound above, to follow his master. After many rites performed at the shrines of Shango and other *orishas*, the new Alafin kissed the sword of justice, kept at Ife, and entered the palace for the first time by a new gate sanctified by the blood of a man, a woman and various animals. His person was so sacred that he appeared in public only thrice a year. Nowadays he travels freely in his car and is an active member of the Cocoa Marketing Board and the Regional Council of Ministers;

the Divisional Council over which he presides has a majority of
elected commoners; but he still eats in seclusion from his own
people.

·◇· 10 ·◇·

On the road between Ibadan and Oyo lies a small village
called Asijire. There is nothing special about it, to the eye: a
river close by, a lot of forest; clearings with cassava in them, and
yams; oil palms rearing above the bush and cocoa here and
there among the trees. But cocoa is on the wane, for all this
region is badly hit by swollen shoot disease, and round Ibadan
production is virtually ceasing.

If palm oil could replace cocoa, the region's economic foundation would be secured. The tree grows well enough, but methods of
extracting the oil are so crude that about half of it is thrown away
with the husk. After the war, the Department of Commerce and
Industries built eleven oil-extracting mills in the Oyo division.
They quickly lost money. Growers refused to bring in their nuts
and several mills were attacked by women, furious that their
source of income from the oil extracted from the kernels (tradi-
tionally their pin-money, so to say) was threatened.

Meanwhile, three Regional Production Development Boards
had been created in 1949. The Western Board took over these
mills and set up others, to the present total of forty. Asijire fell
into the orbit of a Welsh crusader, who with all the fervour, eloquence and fanaticism of his race has embraced the cause of
co-operative societies. Largely at his instigation, the cocoa-
growers have already been organized into thirteen Co-operative
Marketing Unions, which between them produced 180,000 bags
of cocoa last year; and, under these, into a large number of
Cocoa Marketing Societies which muster 20,000 members. Now
it is the turn of palm oil.

The task, as Mr. Price sees it, is not merely to introduce better
methods of extraction but to organize supplies. This sounds
simple; in actual fact it means changing the whole system of
farming, of land tenure, of life. It means, in effect, persuading
(not coercing) peasant farmers to adopt plantation methods of
palm-oil production. A tremendous, a Himalayan task. But

co-operators are not daunted by it, and here at Asijire is a working model.

First, Mr. Price and his team tried to persuade the local farmers to pool their land, which was hopelessly fragmented, worked in discontiguous pockets and quite impossible to plan. The farmers were full of suspicion, and all sorts of rumours went round: that the British were selling out to the Americans (curiously widespread, that rumour, cropping up all over the place) or seizing the land to make forest reserves. At last, by a miracle of persuasion, Mr. Price secured the pooling of about sixty acres in three blocks, involving fifteen individuals. The land was cleared, ploughed communally, and planted with seedlings from the Palm Oil Research Station at Benin capable of yielding six to seven times as much oil as the ordinary tree. Mr. Price believes that when the fifteen pioneers are seen to be growing rich, and provided that no disaster overtakes them, the demand for better seedlings will become torrential. The whole project has been put under a management committee consisting of one representative each of the Development Board, the Agricultural Department, the Registrar of Co-operatives and the farmers.

At the same time, Mr. Price and his colleagues have founded Supply Societies whose members pledge themselves to bring their nuts to the mill. The oil is sold through a Co-operative Marketing Union covering the whole of Nigeria. Now that people can see their money coming back, enthusiasm has kindled and Mr. Price believes that co-operatives have taken hold. Next year he hopes to have 300 acres of oil palms planted, and three more extraction plants in use.

The main threat to co-operation in Africa lies, as always, in the moral standards of the members. Most Africans trust no one and, even more than Europeans, look on public funds merely as hives from which every sensible man should extract honey. Co-operatives offer great opportunities to the sweet-toothed, and every one of the officials had to be dismissed for peculation within the first two years. Continual scrutiny is needed. This can be managed, when the men at the top are disinterested; but what will happen when they are not?

I was given this instance of the difficulties met with in getting co-operation established. A well-trained African official secured from each local branch a payment in advance for some promised improvement—here £10 for a weighing machine, there £70 for a shed. Time passed, but no improvements came. Nor did the swindled societies—and this is a peculiarly African feature—lodge any complaints. A senior British official investigated, and at last collected enough evidence for a prosecution. An African police officer delayed execution of the warrant for long enough to enable the accused man to square the principal witnesses, all of whom recanted their evidence, and so the case fell to the ground. (For this reason the various enquiries made from time to time into allegations of bribery and corruption are almost useless; the fangs of all potential witnesses are drawn by a combination of intimidation and bribery.) The offender was subsequently dismissed, but with the right to draw one-third of his full pension from a grateful Government for the rest of his life.

"They will learn," say optimists, and point out how very recent is the notion of incorrupt officialdom in Europe, and how precarious its tenure. From this they argue that in a very short space of time Africans, also, will create a tradition of disinterested honesty and high resistance to bribes.

This may be so; everyone hopes it will. It may also be that Africans have themselves no great wish to create this sort of tradition. It is not *their* idea; it is wholly alien, and may seem to them not only stupid, but disloyal. It is irritating to be swindled by a relative, but not a matter for the police. Perhaps he needed the money; perhaps he can be made to give it back; and if outsiders are brought into it, who knows what gods and spirits may not be angered—or what vengeance exacted? A man who robs no relative, but only an unfeeling, impersonal fund, a rich abstraction like Government or Company, commits no offence against gods or men; he seems to most merely a sensible and lucky fellow.

The Western Regional Production Development Board, which finances these co-operative oil mills and other experiments—for instance, the cultivation of citrus, and a survey of cocoa soils—draws its funds from profits made by the four Produce Marketing Boards which buy all Nigeria's main products (cocoa, palm oil, groundnuts, cotton) from the growers and sell them again in world markets. These profits have now grown very large—

£150,000,000 for the whole of West Africa—and the Marketing Boards have been attacked on the ground that all this money should go direct to the producers in higher prices for their produce. The Government believes that more good can be done to more people if it is spent on useful works by Production Boards in each Region.

Here in the West, the Production Board's plan has four main objects. First, in the forest belt, to start co-operative plantations run by the native people, instead of (as in the Belgian Congo) by alien companies, with high-yielding oil palms and up-to-date machinery, the trees being interplanted with food crops. Second, in the savannah belt farther north, greatly to increase food-production, perhaps by large co-operative and semi-mechanized farms. Third, to improve communications; the Board is spending a million pounds on roads, mostly with tarmac surfaces. Fourth, to start new industries; for instance, £100,000 has been authorized for a rubber factory and about £300,000 spent on loans to African business men who have started, respectively, a bus company, a tyre re-treading factory, a small fleet of launches on the creeks, a rice mill, and so on. (The bus company has coined money; the future of the other schemes is dark.)   In all directions, development officers are at work, soil surveys are in progress, and at last British technique and skill are being (so belatedly) injected into this region of potential fruitfulness. No doubt on theoretical grounds Production Boards can be criticized, but their work seems to me to justify them several times over.

◇ II ◇

"Benin has an extraordinary fascination for me which I cannot explain," wrote a traveller who knew it before the destruction of the old city in 1897.[1] "All the rest of West Africa that I know is squalid. Benin in the old days was more than squalid, it was gruesome. . . . No one who went there came away without being impressed."

You can still feel this fascination. It is in the history, I sup-

[1] Mr. Cyril Punch, quoted in the Preface to H. Ling Roth's *Great Benin*, 1903.

pose. You think of the bloodstained altars, the pits full of dead bodies, the crucifixion trees—of all that so justly earned it the name "City of Blood". (The people's own name for it, Ile-Ibenu, means Country of Hatred.) That sinister jingle rings in the ears:

> *Beware and take care of the Bight of Benin*
> *Where few come out, though many go in.*

Perhaps, if one had never read of all the goings-on before the punitive expedition of 1897 put an end (at least for the time being) to the orgies of human sacrifice in which its inhabitants indulged, Benin would seem like any other West African town. The walls, the gates have gone, and there is nothing but an over-grown ditch to mark the limits of the modern city. I walked the streets alone as safely as in Salisbury, receiving open smiles and friendly greetings; I passed a children's clinic founded and run by an African woman doctor; nearly opposite stands the Moon-light Gardens Club, an open-air dance-place for "high-life" addicts, owned by the wife of the Prime Minister, himself an Oxford graduate and C.B.E.; the Town Clerk had but recently returned from a period of training under the Clerk to the County Council of Wiltshire. On Sunday morning a dozen churches, from Roman to Methodist, were packed with white-clad school-children; all the women were clean and gay in their best; an air of benevolent leisure hung about the town; and, just beyond the golf-course, in a new detached suburban villa, the Oba, in a plain tussore robe, took Sunday luncheon with the District Officer.

And yet, and yet . . . I suppose it is only the history, and yet inside the Oba's rambling, darkened palace there surely creeps a little breeze of death, there lingers just a faint odour of decay. If ever ghosts had cause to walk it is here, where the king could scarcely spit or swallow without a slave's head falling, and the altars were so caked with human blood that when they were touched, crusts of it fell away.

I met the Oba at luncheon: a tall, slim, clever-looking man, spectacled and rather grave, plainly dressed in a high-necked cream robe and cap, reserved and dignified. With him was his

Prime Minister, the Iyase, the Hon. Gaius Obaseki, chairman of the Native Authority and a member of the House of Representatives in Lagos. The Oba kindly invited me to see his palace and greeted me there with one hand on the neck of a boy of eleven or twelve who held erect an execution sword with a carved blade, part of the old insignia. This boy used to be naked, but now wears a black swim-suit. In older times, attendants would have held the Oba's arms out in a horizontal position to support the great weight of coral beads and brass armlets.

The palace rooms are windowless and gloomy. An aperture in the roof lets in light and also, in wet weather, rain, for the roofs are pitched downwards, as it were, in the centre, so as to lead the water into a shallow open tank or reservoir in the floor, whence it is drained away through underground channels cleverly made by laying paw-paw stems in each gutter and then stamping down the clay. In a few weeks the paw-paw stems wither, leaving a clear drain.

Recesses in the clay walls form alcoves round each room for people to sit or lie in. There is no furniture except an altar, festooned in the usual baffling symbols of idolatry. Over the first, a cluster of coconut shells stuck with feathers hangs from the roof; above the second dangles an oval, about the size of an ostrich egg, wrapped in cloth and bound with string. A third altar bears queer contorted iron stands, rather like sculptures by Reg Butler, and yet another is decorated with a curious bas-relief of a bat-like creature having a lion emerging from its mouth; on top rests an elephant's tusk carved with an intricate, rather Celtic-looking dragon. This, said the Oba, is "the altar of the left hand" reserved for rich men. The roof is supported on splendid rafters carved in endless, flowing designs; these are of *iroko*, a royal timber that, in Benin, could be used only by the king.

I had thought that all these altars would have fallen into desuetude; but that is not so. Goats, sheep and fowls are regularly sacrificed. On his last visit the District Officer found several goats hanging from the rafters and the floor greasy with blood. Curiously enough, he had come to supervise democratic elections to one of the "electoral colleges".

The doors are thick and heavy as portcullises, and clumped behind us as the Oba led our little party through. I could not help thinking of the countless victims in whose ears that heavy noise had sounded like the thud of agonizing doom. The Oba walked slowly, his face impassive, his hand on the neck of the boy with the naked blade. As a door before us opened, the sound of chanting came to our ears: slow, rhythmic, melancholy. We entered another dark-red room, and in the shallow well a dozen men were stamping their feet and striking palms into fists. Cloths tucked round their waists fell to their ankles and hid their churning knees. Their tops were bare, and each man's neck was circled by a coral chain, the symbol of nobility. In the time of the Oba's grandfather, any man who lost his chain, even if it were broken in battle, was invariably executed.

"They are singing the praises of the Oba," I was told. They stamped, swayed, rubbed their palms together and then raised the right hand with clenched fist. Not Communists, however, but members of one of five Palace Societies. Each is a kind of guild, whether of cooks, women's guards or wardrobe-masters, whose membership is hereditary. How strange it was to see these elderly, bare-chested men in necklaces of coral stamping out their praise in words that may have come down unchanged for ten centuries! For the kingdom of Benin is so old that no one can tell its origins or date its dynasties. The first European contact was in 1472, and Benin was not then a new kingdom. *Plus ça change*—that hackneyed tag seems very true here. Even the design of the buildings has not altered, and is peculiar to Benin. Peculiar, that is, in West Africa. "We find in every house a perfect Tuscan atrium," Richard Burton wrote,[1] "with a gangway running round the rectangular impluvium, and the tank or piscine which catches the rain and drippings falling through the compluvium or central opening in the roof." The tornadoes, harmattans and violent rainstorms of Benin do not render this type of architecture a suitable response to climatic conditions, and Burton concluded that the Beni people must have derived it, in bygone ages, from the Romans, by way of North Africa. Dr. Ling Roth considers this hypothesis "remote", and suggests that the Benin style arose from a modification of the Gold Coast compound, where several open-fronted houses were often joined

[1] Quoted by Roth (*Great Benin*) from articles by Burton in *Fraser's Magazine*, 1863.

together with their verandas facing the courtyard. "A fourth house and the drainage of the centre brings us to the Benin house," he says. But it is just the shallow well, its underground drains and the surrounding gangway with its alcoves that distinguishes the Benin house from any others in Africa and reminds every visitor of Pompeii. The rigid persistence of Benin customs is such that lessons taught by some ancient colonizer from Cyrenaica or Tripoli, or even Carthage, may have been assimilated and carried on to this day.

This persistence in Benin tradition is very marked in art no less than (problematically) in architecture. The famous Benin bronzes—masks, plaques and small statues—display an influence so strongly Portuguese that for a long time it was thought that the whole art and process had been introduced from Portugal in the fifteenth or sixteenth century. Now most experts think that many of the bronzes date from long before the coming of the Portuguese, although, for four centuries after it, Benin artists incorporated into their work Portuguese subjects and *motifs* which became traditional.

The process by which these bronzes (like the Ife heads) are cast, known as *ciré-perdue*,[1] was most likely learnt from the ancient Egyptians via the Yorubas. Beni artists are said to have gone to Ife to learn, but while they adopted the technique, they left the classical style to their neighbours, and themselves developed a

---

[1] A very ancient process, which varies somewhat in detail. Here are two brief accounts. "On a core of hardened sand is moulded a wax model, which is then carefully coated with clay; the wax is melted out and the molten metal is made to take its place; when cooled and the clay removed the rough casting is the result. This is then finished by tooling, punching, etc. . . The ancient Etruscans and Greeks made their castings solid, without any sand core, while the Bini were evidently adepts in the superior method practised by the ancient Egyptians." Roth, *Great Benin.*
"A model is made in wax, usually about a quarter of an inch thick. The model is then tilted to the most convenient angle for casting, and at its highest point several sticks of wax are attached to it in such a manner as to lead downwards from a wax pouring cup. The sticks of wax leading from the highest points are to become a number of channels, termed runners and vents, which serve to conduct the molten metal in an even flow over the whole area. . . . The wax is now invested, outside and in, with wet plastic fire-clay. . . . When the whole mass investing the wax has set and become air-dried, heat is used to melt and burn out the wax model, leaving a clear space in the previous place of the wax. . . . When the metal has cooled the investment is broken away and the system of runners, vents and cup in bronze removed." Leon Underwood, *Bronzes of West Africa,* 1949.

purely African art, not naturalistic and graceful, but romantic and symbolic, full of formalized designs of serpents, lizards, lions and fish, and one which arrived at a standard treatment of the human form as conventional as that of any medieval artist. There is no African art more typical, more bold, more pure than this of old Benin, now, alas, extinct, and scattered about the museums of the world.

It is a style hard for the European to enjoy until he grasps the fact that the whole classical concept of proportion and geometry on which our art is grounded has never existed in Africa. Look around you, at the sculptures and decorations, the houses, tools, dress, farms, towns, the very features of the people, and you will see that the straight line is unknown. The shortest distance between two points—that great principle is not only undiscovered, it is a matter of indifference, perhaps even of dislike. No path in Africa is ever straight, no field rectangular. Proportion is replaced by rhythm, the ideal by the grotesque. Here is a different vision, and one that we can perhaps never fully enter into, for it derives from different beliefs and modes of thought. Those demons and spirits which share, in Africa, the living world, the *orishas* of thunder, storm and war, spill over into art, drawing with them the symbols of terror and revenge. Fra Angelico depicted devils and the damned, but what a world of philosophy lies between those instruments and victims of God's retribution and the heartless, proud and ferocious masks of kings, warriors and gods! But how magnificent the freedom, the strength, boldness and control of these intricate and whirling designs! No artists in Africa since the days of ancient Egypt—unless it be those of Dahomey—wrought more copious and vital work than these nameless bronze-casters and ivory-carvers of Benin.

I used the word "pure" of Benin art, meaning that here, in these steamy forests, where only armies could travel without the certainty of capture as slaves, the kingdom of Benin developed, or perhaps just continued in its tradition-fettered way, through the centuries with very little interference from outside, until in 1897 the world broke through, and in an instant, like a mummy when the sarcophagus is ripped open and air rushes in, it simply crumbled away. Yet in another sense art is never pure, but always to some extent derivative; and Africa provides no exception. There is no doubt that the influence of ancient Egypt is strong. Among the treasures found in the sacked city was a beautifully carved ivory sistrum; and the sistrum had its origin in the worship of Isis. Dr. Roth illustrates a carved staff-head in which a leopard supports on his back a column, a *motif* common in Assyrian architecture, and a brass casket, elaborately chased and ornamented with snakes, lizards and queer faces, whose design he thinks may be Assyrian or Phœnician. After perhaps the most thorough study of Benin art ever made, he finds designs in wood-carving common among the Hittites, a ring of Græco-Roman pattern and another that looks like Saxon work, designs on bracelets resembling the Celtic and a squeezed-up lizard that might be Scandinavian, and concludes that the mixture of designs is as great as that of the population of Babylonia.

These influences are too various and widespread to be fortuitous, and surely explode the theory, advanced from time to time, that Africa is backward because it was for so long cut off from the rest of the world. The fact is that the continent was never cut off completely, and much of it was subject to a series of invasions, trade connections and what are now called culture-contacts at least as continuous and strong as those affecting, let us say, China, India and Japan. Phœnicians, Greeks and later Portuguese sailed down the coasts, established embassies, explored inland; the empires of Songhai and Melle linked the southern Negroes, by the caravan routes of the Sahara, with the Mediterranean world; the arts and customs of ancient Egypt worked their way westwards through the Hausa states; for the last four centuries, West Africa has been trading with Europe; there scarcely seems to have been a time in history when the Guinea Coast and its hinterland was not in touch with other peoples and lands.

And so the isolation theory seems to me hollow. Perhaps we have sought the reasons for African backwardness too much in the environment and too little in the will of the people themselves. The simplest explanation is the one most often overlooked: that Africans have stuck to their own ways because, on the whole, they have preferred them, primitive though they seem to us to be.

But are they primitive? In the sense that they are crude, certainly. But the primary meaning of primitive is not crude; it is first, early, pertaining to the infancy of man. This is in line with the notion that Africans are children ready and anxious to be taught. But I doubt if this is true. Africa is very old—the oldest continent in the world, so old that the rocks have no fossils; they were laid down before ever life began. Some now say that human life itself was born here, in this torpid Eden, many million years ago. Throughout the ages, wave after wave of human life has poured in from the north and east, working its way down from India and Arabia and Persia, from the home of Berber and Turk and Syrian, of Hamite, Negro and Jew. These many races and peoples have brought their artifacts and skills, their legends and beliefs, their blood and vigour, all to be blended and attenuated and at last obliterated, like a river that flows into desert and never reaches the sea. Here and there traces remain —designs, plants, beasts, weapons—but only traces; the rest has worn away. Africa is like a crocodile that swallows people, cultures, ideas, and then breaks down, digests, disperses, builds their substance into its own; and in the end there is just the crocodile, with its cold unwinking eye. Perhaps it is all because this great continent has never known the benison of Athens or the rule of Rome, or perhaps it is the northern winter that is lacking, and the challenge of life has been too feeble to provoke a resourceful response. Whatever the reason, the result, I think, is simply this: that Africa is not primitive, it is decadent.

If this is so, the question then becomes: will the crocodile swallow, too, this latest European invasion? No one can say; but we shall at least afford the most indigestible meal the creature has had for some time. For one thing, we resist assimilation; for another, with great subtlety we have gone to work less on kings and elders, the ruling few, than on the children, so much more susceptible and defenceless. General education is the most revolutionary force since the introduction of iron. It teaches children to destroy. With their sharp tongues and quick minds they are pulling apart the whole fabric of African society, laying in ruins the whole system of African rule.

The next stage is the building-up and that is where the test comes. Will the meal transform the crocodile, or the crocodile absorb the meal? Can decay be reversed, effort engendered, the will of Africa changed? Those are questions for the future, to be answered in another two or three hundred years.

❧ 12 ❧

We left the members of one of the Palace Societies stamping their feet in a dark-red well and chanting the Oba's praises. They would not mind, I expect; their dance seemed timeless, and I daresay they are still singing, and will be in a hundred years, their coral necklaces about their dusky necks. One of them desisted from his stamping long enough to give us an eye-witness account of the fall of Benin.

He had been a married man with children when it happened, and all his youth had been spent in a kingdom untouched by European influence, absolutely unchanged. Then, in the flick of a chameleon's tongue, the armies of Great Benin were routed, the Oba fled and new rulers came with new laws. But, for this warrior, life continued—not without its pleasures, since he has now over 200 descendants, including sixty-six daughters; he may have been boasting, of course. Wives? He had lost count; a good many were dead by now and he was over eighty, and not bothered by women any more. Ambition had not deserted him, however; he hoped to gain election to the Oba's council, and left the palace in a bath-chair pushed by a posse of grandsons, waving cheerfully and chattering like a starling through empty gums.

I found it curiously exciting to hear an account of the Benin massacre of 1897 and its sequel from one who had taken part.[1] It is a story that still has power to amaze and horrify, as well as to remind us that the British had motives for pushing into Africa other than the intention to exploit the natives and glorify themselves. Here, for instance, are some extracts from the diary of a surgeon who took part in the expedition.[2]

As we neared Benin City we passed several human sacrifices, live women slaves gagged and pegged on their backs to the

[1] For the full story, see *The Benin Massacre* by Captain Alan Boisragon, 1898.
[2] From *Great Benin* by H. Ling Roth. The surgeon was Dr. Roth's brother.

ground, the abdominal wall being cut in the form of a cross, and the uninjured gut hanging out. These poor women were allowed to die like this in the sun. Men slaves, with their hands tied at the back and feet lashed together, also gagged, were lying about. As we neared the city, sacrificed human beings were lying in the path and bush—even in the king's compound the sight and stench of them was awful. Dead and mutilated bodies were everywhere—by God! May I never see such sights again! ...

In the king's compound, on a raised platform or altar, beautiful idols were found. All of them were caked over with human blood. Lying about were big bronze heads, dozens in a row, with holes at the top, in which immense carved ivory tusks were fixed. One can form no idea of the impression it made on us. The whole place reeked of blood. Fresh blood was dripping off the figures and altars. Most of our men are in good health, but these awful sights rather shattered their nerves. ...

In front of the king's compound is an immense wall fully twenty feet high, two to four feet thick, formed of sun-dried red clay, and at each end are two big ju-ju trees. In front, stakes have been driven into the ground, and cross-pieces of wood lashed to them. On this frame-work live human beings are tied to die of thirst or heat. ... At the base of them the whole ground was strewn with human bones and decomposing bodies with their heads off. The bush, too, was filled with dead bodies, the hands being tied to the ankles, so as to keep them in a sitting posture. It was a gruesome sight to see these headless bodies sitting about, the smell being awful. All along the road, too, more decapitated bodies were found, blown out by the heat of the sun; the sight was sickening. Today was occupied in blowing down these ju-ju trees. Passing through the centre door of the big wall we came upon a large tree; at its foot was a deep pit, which we noticed contained dead bodies. The natives, after sacrificing their victims, threw the bodies down there. On the first afternoon of our arrival our black troops heard faint cries coming from some of these pits, and, letting themselves down, came upon some live captives amongst the dead ones, in a very emaciated condition. They had been down there many days without food and water, intermingling with the dead and rotting bodies.

Perhaps the fire that swept and destroyed most of the city was a blessing in disguise, although it burnt all the stores; for next day "fire, smoke and charcoal seemed to have removed all the smell, and the city became sweet and pure again".

And that was the end of old Benin. In due course the fugitive King surrendered. Dressed in his finery—ropes and ropes of coral, bracelets of coral, a head-dress "in the shape of a Leghorn straw hat" of coral also—he made his submission; later (with only two wives out of eighty) he was exiled to Calabar until his death in 1913. His son was restored as Oba, and rebuilt the palace. During his reign he was twice accused of sacrificing a wife, but acquitted. In 1933 the present Oba succeeded him.

A strange feature of this cruel Benin religion was the crucifixion *motif*, quite foreign to Africa. One would naturally look for an infiltration of Christianity; and one would find it. In 1486, the King of Benin sent to the King of Portugal an ambassador, who returned with a priest or priests, and so Christian teaching began in the city. A letter written in 1516 describes how the King ordered one of his sons and two leading chiefs to become Christians, and had a church built. The prosperity, might and culture of Benin were then probably at their peak, and the Catholic faith showed signs of displacing obedience to fetish. But climate proved inimical. So many missionaries died that in 1650 or thereabouts the Portuguese were recalled and the Mission directed to carry on with native priests trained in Portugal. At first, with the aid of ten-year inspections, all went well. But gradually inspections dwindled (the last was held in 1688), and ju-ju practices crept back. The Church degenerated into a perverted travesty of the original, and human sacrifice was resumed on an even bigger scale, until, by the time the city fell, all that recalled Christianity was a brass image of Jesus, several small crosses and the custom of crucifying slaves on trees.

It was a relief to get into the sunlight from the shades of this gloomy palace. Out in the street, lorries rumble by, children with satchels loiter home from school and plump young women saunter by in bright cloths. No crucifixion trees, no pits, no

School on stilts in a creek village near Lagos

Street of tinsmiths in Ibadan

Ibadan: a market stall

The herbalists' and magicians' department

Benin: the bronze
workers' street

Yoruba
market-woman

Bida: the homestead of a well-to-do guildsman

Glass bangle-making in progress

The Wamba head, belonging to the prehistoric Nok culture, found in Northern Nigeria in 1944

Photo: Mr. Bernard Fagg

An Ife bronze head, probably a past Oni

Photo: British Museum

Bronze plaque, representing an Oba with attendants, from Benin

Photo: British Museum

Kano:
street scenes

slaves, no blood-soaked images—though Africans from other regions will tell you with conviction that human sacrifices are still made in Benin, and Europeans who live there, though they have no proof, do not scoff at the assertion. Still, if they happen, they are rare and secret, and the small vices of officialdom, the stupidities, muddles and red-herring-chases that quite often occur, seem, after the lurid episodes of history, very small beer.

∾ 13 ∾

Not that Benin is always peaceful. A few weeks before my visit, a feud between the Ogboni Society and the Oba's faction had led to riots, arson and bloodshed. The Ogboni Society is a sort of league of barons which in the past possessed great influence. Frobenius, writing of Ibadan, called it a "decapitation company, limited—a union of unscrupulous persons who, without the least qualms of conscience, get rid of all inconvenient elements". By confiscating the property of their victims and exacting a large initiation fee, its members, mostly the heads of leading families, became very rich men. A league of Medicis, Sforzas and Guelphs, with fewer scruples even than those noble Florentines, would perhaps suggest a European equivalent.

In recent years the Ogboni was "reformed". Initiation ceremonies were purged of their cruder rites, and the idea was propagated that the society had become an African equivalent of Masonry. Several Europeans, including some senior officials, joined. Its leader in Benin was the Iyase, the energetic and intelligent Prime Minister. In local politics the Ogboni kept the upper hand by its control of the Native Authority—the city council—through which the Oba had to rule. Since the Oba is a strong personality he found himself more and more in opposition to an Ogboni group headed by his Prime Minister. And, since the commons considered the Ogboni tyrannical, they supported the King.

Until a year ago, all the members of the Native Authority council were nominated by the Government according to tradition. Then came reform, on the usual complicated plan. Elections were organized to bring into existence twenty-one local councils, which between them, by means of further elections,

H

chose fifty members of a central council in Benin. Elections in Benin City (whose population is about 30,000) pick out a further twenty-four members. A sop is thrown to tradition by arrangements for each of the five Palace Societies to elect two representatives. Over this council of eighty-four elected members, the Iyase presides as chairman, with the Oba as formal president.

The elections in Benin City routed the Ogboni candidates, and the excited citizens followed up their success by demolishing or burning the houses of several members. The Oba's prestige rode high on this wave of hatred for a society which had gone too far. Police drafted in from other towns quelled the riots in a few days, but the Beni are a tough, quarrelsome people, and those who know the city believe explosive emotions to lie beneath the restored surface calm. Meanwhile, the city is hotly divided into Palace and Ogboni factions, as our own (though with less fervour) into Socialists and Tories, or New York into Giants' and Dodgers' fans. Most Europeans deplore this; but, in providing an outlet for Benin's natural exuberance and craftiness, this tussle for power adds savour to a life which law and order so often reduce to a distasteful monotony. There is, of course, a danger of violence, but the loss of a few lives now and again seems unlikely greatly to shock or distress the citizens of even a reformed City of Blood.

Not far beyond the crumbled walls lies a place as new and Western as Benin is old and African: the Oil Palm Research Institute, a centre of investigation for all West Africa into ways and means of bettering the growth of West Africa's most important crop. The Oil Palm Marketing Board gave over £500,000 to start it, and 4,000 acres have been acquired on which to experiment with new varieties and methods. The oil palm is a most difficult plant to propagate artificially, but already scientists working here have so improved their technique as to be able to distribute large quantities of most promising seedlings. Research is only at the start; the riches that it offers to the Nigerian peasant are incalculable. In fact, only if scientists push ahead with this research and if—that is the big "if"— Nigerians follow their lead, will the peasants of West Africa be able, in the long run, to hold their own with the more efficient plantations of the Belgian Congo and elsewhere.

≪ 14 ≫

The saddest sight in all Benin is the brass-workers' quarter: a long street flanked by veranda'd houses, each with a smithy attached where bronze and brass articles are cast, and a ju-ju shrine where the family still worships its particular *orisha*. The brass-workers form a guild whose membership is hereditary. The *ciré-perdue* process is still used. Impressed by the thought that works of art had been made in this identical spot without a break in the tradition for at least 500 years, I entered the quarter with the excitement one feels on approaching any city where the Middle Ages live on; but the smithies were empty and cold, and what little modern work there was to see crude, perfunctory and altogether undistinguished.

The Native Authority is doing what it can to save the remnants of the craft from extinction. It has set up workshops in the town for metal casting and for woodwork. The woodcarvers seemed to me to be doing much better work, and to have an altogether brighter future, than the metal-workers. Some were carving heads in ebony. The heads themselves were copies, but at least a carving skill was being handed on, so that if fate should bring to birth an artist, he would know how to handle his tools. But the metal-workers—one can see no future for them. Their very street looked dispirited and half deserted, with some of its houses falling down. A member of the City Council took me round, a sort of alderman, wearing the long white robe and small white cap which seem to be the dress of old Benin.

"The men have gone to the farms," he said. "It pays them better to grow cocoa than to make ornaments. For who is to buy?"

That is indeed the crux. Benin work was a royal art, done for the glorification of the Oba and his barons. All that has gone. The cost of brass has soared upwards, and these metal-workers must now charge high prices—to whom? Chiefs are no longer interested, wealthy men wish to buy European goods, and there are no tourists in Benin. Some of the work is sent to Lagos and finds a small sale—hence the deterioration of the art, devoted now to making trinkets for tourists instead of idols for worship or masks for kings. All I could see were some crude bangles and ornamental bells and a few very bad copies of old heads. The last heirs of this dying art are right to go farming and cocoa-growing; they are better employed. It is tragic, but there seems to be no remedy.

The North

◇ I ◇

We left Ibadan in the dark and drove at furious speed through a tunnel of forest, our headlights knifing through deep thickets studded with villages. Small lamps and fires burnt by roadside market stands. Had they been there all night, or just lit, to catch the dawn trade? People were astir already; women walked in stately files towards the watering-places, each with an empty calabash on her head; Hausa cattle-herds, their long white robes tucked up at the waist, drove their beasts down to drink. Night withdrew, and the morning's light was scarfed by mist through whose folds houses, people, cows, trees, all appeared portentous, yet fresh and gentle as pearls. The air was rested, and full of the pungency of wood smoke.

Soon forest gave way to orchard bush with brown grass and the pear-like shea-nut trees. A cyclist in a pink robe that billowed round him like a sail hurled himself head-first into the bush. With a skirl of horns we sped by lorries packed with long-horned cattle, or with passengers atop cigar-shaped, wicker packages of kola nuts. We paused at Ilorin, in the most northerly of the Yoruba states, only long enough for the driver to greet his relative, the station-master, and buy some breakfast in a market already in full swing. It had a spent look, Ilorin; the feet of generations, and the action of storms, had so worn down its roads that twisted tree-roots were partly exposed; the spareness of the landscape proclaimed that we had left behind the rainy forest and reached the fringe of those wide, baking, open steppes of the interior.

On again: and while the day was still young we were at Jebba, where road and railway share a bridge across the Niger. There lay the great river, running strongly under rocky banks to the eastwards, white in the sun. Below the bridge, lines of canoes were loading up with kola baskets; others were being punted over to the far bank. For so great a river, the Niger is very shallow at this time of year; in the rains, its waters rise and flood much of the surrounding country.

Less than a hundred miles up-stream lies Bussa, where Mungo Park perished in the rapids. Not until 1826 was Bussa reached again—by the dashing naval officer Hugh Clapperton, who died soon afterwards at Sokoto; and it was left to his Cornish valet and companion, Richard Lander—surely one of the most remarkable gentleman's gentlemen in history, and certainly one of the best African writers—to be the first man to trace this mighty river down to its mangrove-shrouded meeting with the Gulf of Guinea. In 1830 he and his brother John paddled past these rocks towards the sea. The journey took them seventeen months, they suffered almost continuously from fever and were handsomely rewarded by the British Government (which also defrayed their expenses) with the sum of £100. Two years later, Richard Lander returned in a paddle-steamer sent by Messrs. McGregor Laird and Oldfield of Liverpool to explore the possibilities of trade. He penetrated up-stream almost as far as Jebba, but, later on, was set upon by natives in the delta, and died of wounds at Fernando Po. Out of the forty-eight Europeans who left the coast in McGregor Laird's two vessels, only nine returned.

∽ 2 ∽

Bida is the capital of Nupeland: an ancient and alluring walled city of round clay houses with pargeted walls, sometimes painted in bold red or black designs, and arranged in quarters according to their owners' crafts. For Bida is a nest of craftsmen, still organized into hereditary guilds. The houses stand in clusters, their small farms round them; although the soil looks light and sandy, everything grows: groundnuts, guinea corn, rice, cotton, beans, tomatoes, maize. The guildsmen, however, do not cultivate; they are too busy. Every day except Friday—for

Bida is a Muslim city—they start at dawn and ply their craft with speed and skill until about four o'clock. No Trade Unions here, no regulated hours, no shop-stewards, no five-day weeks; and those who work for wages draw about twopence a day. And yet they manage, and do not seem in the least oppressed or exploited. On the contrary, these glass-workers, bead-makers, weavers, brass- and silver-smiths are honoured citizens of Bida, burghers as it were, ranking only below the Fulani aristocracy.

The glass-workers are perhaps the most spectacular. In the hut's centre is a sunken furnace, its clay walls built up about a foot above the ground. A boy feeds it continually with logs; it is a Moloch of timber. Another, or an apprentice, works a leather bellows by means of two sticks. He pumps these two sticks up and down with a rhythm fast and regular, and seems to continue for hours without a break. This work must be very exhausting, but the boy or youth never falters, for the red-hot furnace must not for an instant cease to roar and glow. Some of the raw material derives from melted-down bottles, of which the dark-blue and amber medicine bottles are the most popular. There is also a kind of black, opaque, home-made glass, still fused in the traditional manner from earth rich in silica and from soda which comes (once by camel, now by lorry) all the way from Lake Chad.

Four men sit round the furnace, each with a long iron rod in his hand. One has a lump of molten glass on the end of his rod. Each of the other three pokes off a bit of the glowing stuff and, with the aid of a pair of tongs, holding it over the flames, shapes it roughly into a bangle or ring. Then, with marvellous dexterity, each man twirls his bangle round on his rod and taps it into shape as it cools, finally sliding it off on to the ground beside him. All day long he keeps this up in the heat of the fire, the pile of bangles growing by his side. The workers in each hut belong, as a rule, to one family, whose head is the guild-master. He arranges the supply of material, the work and the sales, and pays the men a fixed share of the profits.

In another quarter are the brass-smiths, who make spoons widely used as market measures, and the silver-smiths, who have fallen on evil days because they cannot get the raw material. I saw one smith breaking up an old torch-case to make ear-rings, another transforming an abandoned aluminium kettle into bracelets. The results, as could only be expected, were ugly and crude. The soaring cost of metal has hit the smiths all over West Africa so severely that, in the next generation, their craft can scarcely survive.

The glass-workers have a tradition that they came from Egypt, bringing their craft with them.[1] The whole declining art of the bead-workers is to re-grind, polish and refine beads—some perhaps derived from the graves of ancient Libyan or Egyptian kings—brought across the desert by Hausa and Arab merchants. When the head of the guild showed Frobenius the raw material, he poured from jars "a perfectly mad medley of old glass beads from Yoruba graves, Asben agates, Egyptian beads, and cornelians from Tibesti and Adrar",[2] and Tuaregs showed him wares taken from Libyan cemeteries obliterated by the desert sands.[3]

Frobenius was the first European to study the crafts of Bida, and his finds so much excited him that he abandoned all his German pedantry and grew rhapsodic, indeed almost hysterical. In Nupe, with its ancient ways, its arts and industries, its polished manners, the still unclouded splendour of its Court and King, he saw an outpost in time of the Middle Ages and, beyond that, hints of an even older history. A dynasty of Negro kings before the Islamic penetration could be traced back, he reckoned, to A.D. 1275, when a Yoruba invasion overthrew a previous régime. As to that, Frobenius unearthed a misty legend recounting how Nupe had belonged to a great empire and sent tribute to a king whose city lay beyond a wide water with no crocodiles or hippopotamuses, and whose ships had wings. The walls of the houses were of red stone and the roofs of bronze, chased, like the Nupe brasswork, in elaborate patterns; the King was carried in a litter under a canopy with lions by his side, attended by horsemen in padded armour; his first wife rode on a white horse; so distant was his capital that Nupe envoys carrying tribute took a year to make the journey.

Byzantium, said Frobenius, deeply stirred; and thereafter

[1] See *A Black Byzantium* by S. F. Nadel. International African Institute, 1942.
[2] Frobenius, *The Voice of Africa*, 1913.
[3] Nadel states: "European beads, cheaper and much more attractive in shape and colouring, have crushed the native industry. . . . The result is a complete disintegration of the guild system" (p. 284).

hunted for the truffles of Byzantine influence under the roots of Nupe custom, legend and art. He found them in the beautiful, elaborate patterns chased on brass and carved on beams; in the crosses on the high pommels of Nupe saddles and the cruciform hilts of many Nupe daggers; in various legends and customs, such as that of the festival of Gani at the spring equinox, which he equates with Easter, when the boys and girls of the nobility were given new names, their heads were shaved and a white bull was sacrificed; in the lost insignia of the ancient kings of Nupe—a crown, orb and sceptre; and in such old Nupe institutions, quenched by the Fulani invasion, as that of maintaining a Court jester.

Later ethnologists have not confirmed, or indeed taken seriously, Frobenius' flights of imagination. But if we cannot accept the Western Sudan as an outpost of Byzantium, nor can we deny the probability that, through Nubia and Ethiopia, Christian and Byzantine influences, however attenuated, may have reached across the desert by the ancient caravan routes. Nor need the legend of Nupe's membership of a great empire be false. Where Frobenius imagined the domes of Constantinople, later scholars might see the humbler but still potent palaces of Ghana, west of Timbuktu, or of Kukia, pre-Islamic capital of Songhai.

During the fifteenth century the Nupe were paying tribute to a foreign ruler, the King of Idah, in slaves. By means of a magic charm, this King recognized one of a coffle of slaves, a young man called Tsoede, to be his own son. One day the King fell sick and only Tsoede could reach a therapeutic fruit from a very high oil palm; and so the King gave his son the royal insignia— a bronze canoe, bronze trumpets, drums hung with brass bells and heavy iron fetters—and told him to flee northwards from his jealous brothers and rule over his native land.

Tsoede's flight was full of exciting and magical episodes. At last he established himself in his own land and conquered many others; his residence contained 5,555 horses; he introduced the craft of metal-working and the practice of human sacrifice, starting with his own mother's brother. The people, seeing that he was not afraid to kill even his maternal uncle, greatly respected and feared him, and from that day his conquests and his power grew. In his reign of sixty years Tsoede founded the Nupe empire, which reached its zenith in the lifetime of the nineteenth Etsu, or King, who died in 1818.[1]

Towards the end of his reign, in 1810, there appeared a crafty Fulani, Mallam Dendo, an itinerant seller of charms. The Fulani people are Semitic, and said by some to trace part of their confused ancestry back to a migration of Jews into Senegal after a rising against the Romans in Cyrenaica in A.D. 115;[2] by others to be descendants of the Hyskos Shepherd Kings. In looks the pure, nomadic type, now seldom seen, was copper-skinned and closely resembled the ancient Egyptians. From time to time there arises amongst them, as among so many Muslim people, a fanatical reformer, who stirs the hitherto peaceable tribesmen into revolt. Early in the nineteenth century one such, Uthman dan Fodio, raised a Fulani army, swore a *jihad* against the seven Hausa states on account of their religious laxity and in a very short while subdued them all and put Fulani Emirs in place of their old kings. Nupe at first escaped, but Mallam Dendo was the parasite's egg laid in the living tissues of the host. The Etsu died and his two sons disputed the succession. Dendo played one off against the other and, after much intrigue and warfare, his own son, Usman Zaki, seized the throne.

Today, succession in Nupe passes in turn to a scion of one of three houses, each descended from a son of Mallam Dendo's; and Bida is divided into three quarters, each containing the palace of a royal clan. Needless to say, it is divided also into three intriguing factions. During each Etsu's reign he must feather the nest of his own family, which must (so to say) sit out the next two reigns; yet he must not bear too hardly on the people, or they may call in his heir. This achieves a balance of sorts, but a precarious one. So long as there is a strong central authority the system will no doubt continue to work; but, should it weaken, civil war might well reappear.

~ 3 ~

The Etsu Nupe starts the day by riding in state round his domains, attended by courtiers. Back in his palace, he receives

[1] For a full account see *A Black Byzantium* by S. F. Nadel.
[2] See *Caravan Routes of the Old Sahara* by E. W. Bovill.

H*

officials and supplicants. It was here that I paid him my respects. He is an elderly man with a white fringe of beard, a dark skin and strongly Semitic features, wearing a full white robe and trousers and a purple turban with folds of it brought under the chin. He sat on a raised couch covered with an Indian rug, a red carpet in front of him and a green one on the floor of the small council chamber, where five of his councillors sat in a row on upright chairs.

The Etsu is a keen historian, and is writing a book. With many stirring gestures he described various past events, especially the railway's advent to Nupeland. First came Lugard; at that time the Etsu was seventeen.

"Lugard came," said the Etsu, "and gathered the people together, and said: There will be a railway made; it is something that will be able to take a banana to Kano and bring back a piece of meat. Everyone was astounded. For in those days a journey to Kano took twenty to thirty days.

"Lugard called for men to build the railway. My father was put in charge of them. I helped him; I received one shilling per head per month for every man I gathered in, and soon I was getting £50 per month. Everyone grew rich. Then Lugard came with two brass hoes to turn the first sod. He had one, and my father had the other. I thought: What can I do to make this great day different from all others? I decided to grow a beard. And from that day I have never cut it.

"At first, people thought that when the British had built a railway they would leave, and we should be able to continue our raids for slaves.[1] We used to get slaves in many directions south of the Niger, but mainly in Kabba. Every man of position had slaves, and they used sometimes to be sold in the market. But when it appeared that the British would not go, the richer men sent their slaves to cultivate their farms, and more food was grown, and Bida grew richer. There has been peace ever since. But now—the Nupe people do not want the Yoruba and Ibo interfering in their government. If, under self-government, they try to govern the north, there will be civil war again."

[1] It was the Etsu's habit of slave-raiding that brought him into conflict with the Royal Niger Company, and led to the Company's capture of Bida in 1897, after a short siege, with the loss of one officer and seven men.

The Etsu's words were translated by Aliyu Makama, his chief councillor, the Northern Regional Minister for Social Services. He is in fact the moving spirit of the native administration. He and his colleague Mallam Muhammadu Lapai, a member of the House of Assembly and headmaster of the Bida Middle School, were fellow guests of mine that night at the house of the District Officer, Mr. Ian Gunn. Both are Muslims, wear the robe and turban, and refuse alcohol. Both have the courteous manners of the north, the outward gentleness, the inner severity. Both are balanced, intelligent and cool-headed, though none the less patriots for that. You cannot blame some British officials for preferring men like these to crafty, demagogic, sometimes vain southerners. "Dirt and dignity" is how such officers describe the North, half-mocking their own affection for it ("Sweat and swank" describes the South). Often there is a bond between the British and these Mallams or Emirs, based as much on mutual respect as on mutual interest, and felt and resented by Southerners. Perhaps it is unwise, but it is one of those human reactions that cannot be helped.

People see in such men as these two Mallams the hope of the North. They are educated, yet neither despise nor adulate tradition; perhaps because of Islam, the West has not thrown them off balance. They wish to construct, not to pull down. While wanting ultimate independence—they come of a proud and ruling race—they have a sense of history and do not wish to rush headlong into half-baked experiments. Democracy is to them no fetish, but a system that cannot be set up overnight in a country where slavery has existed for thousands of years and been suppressed for fifty, and where education touches only the very few. They join character to intelligence, and sometimes add wit. Paragons, in fact; no doubt they have their failings; their chief disability lies in the smallness of their numbers.

Europeans hope for great things not merely from the educated, Muslim *intelligentsia* of the North but especially from those members of it who come from Nupe and the allied Emirates of what they call the Middle Belt. For these people are a blend of the southern Negro and the many races who have come down from beyond the desert. In these arts, crafts and industries they are amongst the most advanced of all Nigerian peoples. Soil and climate, too, lie half-way between the extremes of northern aridity and southern lushness, with all its fevers and fears. The earth is fertile and get-at-able, and offers high rewards. Perhaps, then, in this Middle Belt will arise new leaders of a Middle Way between xenophobic nationalism and defeatist apathy, between upstart demagogue and feudal overlord, between too little discipline and too much.

∿ 4 ∿

I visited next morning a house of clocks. Four ticked loudly in the round entrance-hut through which you must pass to reach the inner apartments. All suggested different hours, but they were not there for the purpose of time-keeping, rather for ornament and noise. Inside, every room had its clock, as well as decorated plates and vegetable-dish-covers embedded in the clay walls. My host, the chief clerk to the *alkali* (the judge in Muslim law) for one of the eight districts into which the Bida emirate is divided, was a much-respected, learned Mallam whose industry had evidently been well rewarded.

Inside his compound you pass from room to room across many small open courtyards. Most of the outside clay walls are decorated either with bold, abstract designs in bas-relief coloured red and black, or, in this case (the only one I saw like it), in blue and white chequer-board squares. The Mallam likes colour; the beams of his small bedroom are gaily painted and hung with electric-light bulbs—unattached, of course, to wires, since Bida has not achieved a power-station.

With a swish of his long white robes—amplifiers of dignity—the Mallam took me to see his four wives, busy with household tasks in a high-walled yard. They crowded round and shook hands, for a visitor must have been a big event in their secluded lives. Men of position throughout the North keep their wives in rigid purdah. This is a most un-African custom and, among these life-loving people, a cruel one. I do not think it is a piece of Western arrogance to pity the narrow, caged lives of these African Muslim spouses, who must yearn for the warm chatter of the market-place as a prisoner for the green fields. It is true that sometimes senior wives attain to positions of respect and influence, but for the most part women are kept merely for pleasure and for breeding. Frobenius mentions that once, in conversation with the Etsu Nupe, he described how the good German Empress helped her people by founding orphanages; and a chill descended on the party. Afterwards, he was told that he had offended against good taste by mentioning the Emperor's women. They should be unseen and unheard.

About eighty miles from Bida, at a place called Mokwa, the Nigerian Government is carrying out an interesting, but costly, experiment in food production in partnership with the Colonial Development Corporation. Between them they are investing £450,000 in equal shares. They have taken a block of 65,000 acres which is sparsely peopled because of tsetse-fly, and started to clear the bush for farms which they will give to settlers from overcrowded areas on a crop-sharing basis, the settler to take one-third of the crop and the Niger Agricultural Project, Ltd., as it is called, two-thirds. For his rent in kind, each settler will get hundreds of pounds' worth of development in the form of village amenities, roads, machinery and implements, fertilizers and so on, and forty-eight acres of cleared land, of which half must be cropped with the aid of tractors and machinery. Originally, ten settlements averaging eighty families each were planned, but I was told that both the number of settlements and the acreage of each holding will have to be reduced. So far, only about 8,000 acres have been cleared—it is a slow, hard and sometimes heart-breaking task—some 3,240 acres planted to guinea corn, millet, maize, groundnuts and bambarra nuts, and 135 families settled.

Another Kongwa? [1] That is everyone's first thought, and the authorities are as sensitive as a hedgehog about the scheme. I was interested to hear that mechanized clearing with bull-dozers and the like had been abandoned as too expensive, and men with the old-fashioned cutlass were felling the bush. Even so, its quick regeneration and tough roots are causing trouble. Mokwa is proving as hard on implements as Kongwa was; any dry part of Africa erodes and abrazes them, twists and tears

---

[1] Kongwa was the first and most expensive area of the Overseas Food Corporation's Groundnut Scheme in Tanganyika, which wasted £36,000,000 of British taxpayers' money.

them, chokes and tires and shakes them to bits. The cost of renewals is tremendous, and expensive white mechanics have to be employed. And, as at Kongwa, crop yields have proved in the first two years (the scheme only started in 1950) disappointingly low, amounting in value to less than £3 an acre. These big, expensive schemes to batter Africa about with machinery instead of scratching at it with hoes, desirable and feasible as they may seem, are proving, one after the other, to be economically unsound. Mokwa seems to be a great deal more sensibly managed than Kongwa, and as an experiment will have value, but even here the aims with which its hopeful planners started are not likely to be realized.[1] And yet—food will surely be needed more and more. It pays, apparently, to build railways over frozen bogs and through deep forests, to fly heavy equipment at fantastic cost into the Arctic Circle, in order to mine the raw material for arms. Perhaps it will one day seem as important to the human race to fill its belly as to destroy its cities, and then such schemes as Mokwa will appear as very small beginnings on a very big task.

I could not but reflect, on leaving Nupe, how fortunate Nigeria is to have these reserves of land that could, with energetic and costly treatment, produce a great deal more food. The trouble is that her people, like ours, prefer living in towns and villages, if possible by trade, to working in the heat of the sun. Cultivation has been slaves' work for centuries; now that slaves are forbidden, everyone hopes that mechanized, wheeled slaves will appear. Even then, there are scarcely any Africans who, as individuals, see beyond the need to grow enough for their families with a bit over for trade. A mental revolution must come before these regions will produce the big crop surpluses of which they are capable—that, or the hard-headed control of operations from outside.

---

[1] The Colonial Development Corporation's report for 1952 summarized the position thus: "Revenue per acre would have to be quadrupled or more to make the project pay; no higher value crop yet in sight; many of the settlers unsatisfactory; 70 per cent of authorized capital invested and only 20 per cent of original programme achieved; discussions initiated with Nigerian Government as to future."

❧ 5 ❧

Great, flat-faced, black rocks loom up all round Abuja, which stands on a bumpy knoll with a view of bush, rocks and more bumpy hills. There is a waterfall close by. You follow a path through dry scrub and come unexpectedly on a dark, deep, sinister gorge. Foaming water thunders into a black pool between crags which fall steeply under a curtain of undergrowth and creepers. Overhanging the pool is the execution rock whence offenders were hurled after their right hands had been cut off to show the Emir that justice had been done.

Abuja is a strange, magical country. Near the road another great rock rears out of the plain, smooth, black and formidable. This is the home of a powerful fetish guarded by a village at its foot whose inhabitants are invisible. No one who tried to reach it ever returned, but the other day three bold Mallams ventured along the shunned path and found the inhabitants to be visible and quite normal, though rather poor and inbred. Not only did the Mallams return safely, but within the year all three received promotion. Nevertheless the people of Abuja still think the village invisible and magical, and no one has ever climbed to the rock's crest, but fires are sometimes seen there, lit by spirits.

Abuja's hills and rocks enabled it, alone in all these regions, to resist the Fulani. It was never conquered. And the present Emir is the only one, apart from the great Shehu of Bornu, who is not of Fulani origin but of the original Hausa stock. Attached to his small palace (for Abuja is a very small emirate, not now above 5,000 souls) is a museum where the Emir showed me a fragment of chain mail, three sacred drums, a high-pommelled, heavy northern saddle and the skulls of three horses. These were brought from Zaria when his grandfather fled before the Fulani. Also preserved, though not on view—only the Emir himself may see it—is one of the seven sacred swords of the seven Hausa states, of which only two survive.

The Emir himself, a shy ex-schoolmaster of charm, intelligence and drive, is working hard to bring the country's government up to date, helped by a young District Officer. Seven commoners have just been elected for the first time to a reformed Native

Authority. So democracy comes with shy, halting steps to the Abujan hills.

These crumpled hills conceal a little tin, which is won not by large companies but by individual miners, most of whom seemed to be elderly, quiet and sober country gentlemen and ladies. Mr. and Mrs. Donaldson, for instance, have lived in Nigeria without a break for eighteen years. No short tours and long leaves for them, no wilting nerves and yellow faces; quite the contrary. They run their tin-mine, cultivate roses, raise hens and live a healthy, regular and, it seems, contented life in a cosy, whitewashed house with tidy thatch that might be in Sussex. Here they have brought up two daughters, both of whom are now settled in the country, and Mrs. Donaldson's cook has been with her for twenty-two years. A neighbouring couple who came in were, I think, well over seventy, and equally serene.

◇ 6 ◇

The stage northwards to Kaduna was a sombre one. All was black. Fires had reduced the grass to coarse black stubble and the trees to charred trunks from which depended dead brown leaves. Big black rocks arose with hideous bareness from this inclement scene. Over all hung a slate-grey haze and heavy grey plumes of smoke. Even the birds were black or grey: bald-headed vultures, white-collared crows and the lumbering hornbill, hopping among the ruined vegetation in search of the few insects or reptiles that had escaped the blaze. A scene of desolation, such as an artist might draw to suggest the environs of hell. Here and there, with an effect altogether startling, the brilliant scarlet flowers clustering on naked *erithryna* trees daubed the landscape with sudden colour and the promise of life.

We came to native homesteads—entirely different, these, from the settled towns and villages of the plain. For we were now among the pagans—a word applied, in Nigeria, to an aggregate of peoples dwelling on the central Plateau in a relatively primitive state. These tribes never came under the influence of the native kingdoms of Nigeria, neither Hausa states of the North nor Yoruba nations of the West, but were regarded by both as a reservoir of slaves. The women go naked with a little bunch of leaves fore and aft; people live in scattered homesteads rather than in towns or villages; faith is animistic, and less cruel than that of southerners—human sacrifice has no part in it; government is not by kings and princes but by councils of elders; families scratch a living with crude tools from poor soil and have no easy crops, like cocoa and palm oil, on which to grow rich with little effort. Some (though not all) are of Bantu stock, and you see women carrying loads on their backs, instead of on their heads. Some of the tribes resisted European government until quite late in this century, retreating into hilly strongholds and fighting back with stones and poisoned arrows. In short, these pagans are simple, primitive, shy people, greatly despised by the so-called superior races round them, loosely organized on a basis of kinship and unused to a strong central authority, who were first chivvied by their neighbours and then neglected by the Europeans. Lately, rather more attention has been paid to them; the Missions are at work and the "educated man" has begun to appear, although as yet only in very small numbers.

The pagans on the road to Kaduna live in villages plaited out of long grass. We passed several parties at work on this task. They had cut long bundles of grass before the fire came, and were now twisting it into screens, and tying the screens together into simple little houses, subsequently thatched. Swarms of naked children rushed down to the "road" (a dry-weather track) to shout and wave; cars were evidently a rarity. Women were carrying big bundles of guinea corn home on their backs. One felt a long way from Lagos or Ibadan here, and sensed something about these people more innocent and likeable than the subtle, intelligent and complex qualities of the forest nations.

Kaduna was packed with notables, for both Northern Houses were meeting in Lugard Hall, the new, domed white mansion specially built for the North's first parliament. Having decided to take the plunge into this kind of democracy, the North has gone head-first into the deepest end of the pool and adopted a system even more complicated than the West's, having an extra rung in the long electoral ladder. The aspirant to politics must first secure election (by acclamation, as a rule) to his village unit; from his village unit he must be elected to his district; from his district to his division; and from his division to the provincial "electoral college". (At this stage, the Native Authorities may "inject" nominees up to ten per cent of the total number; this is to prevent both "traditional" and more educated candidates from being altogether excluded.) The provincial "electoral college" finally elects ninety of its members to sit in the Northern House of Assembly. There is also a House of Chiefs with fifty members. These two Houses send forty members each to the Joint Council, which in turn chooses sixty-eight members to go to the House of Representatives in Lagos. Clearly, Northern elections are not to be taken lightly. In fact, nearly 20,000 primaries were held in 1951, under a general supervision by European District Officers but, as a rule, presided over by African clerks.

For as long as history and tradition reach, the Northern peoples have lived under a feudal system more pure and rigid than Europe's in the Middle Ages. Order, caste, heredity were immutable; the power of rulers was absolute, their persons sacred; and there has been no gradual transition, no apprenticeship through local government, to lead into the alien system. The number of literates is tiny, and most of the clerical work is done by southerners. It is rather as if our modern British parliamentary order had been introduced full-fledged, at a stroke of an alien pen, into the England of the Plantagenets. It is a system imposed by the foreigner, not evolved in response to the people's own demand; and, for this and other reasons, likely to prove ephemeral.

With prodigious effort, and to the people's bewilderment, it has been done, and here in Kaduna are all the turbaned, white-robed, proud-faced victors of the electoral stakes learning how to run a parliament. Here also are the Emirs and their advisers, some of whom have been made Ministers, and find themselves in charge of complex departments with sharp-nosed Europeans incessantly prodding at their elbows. There are eight African Ministers in the North, and four Northern Ministers in Lagos, of whom the majority have gained experience in charge of local departments of health, education, finance, agriculture and other subjects in their emirates, some of which are considerable states in their own right. These Mallams will do well, and everyone has confidence in them—they are civil servants rather than politicians; but there are scarcely enough of them to fill the posts in Lagos and in Kaduna, and these two centres are draining the North dry of almost every African of proved administrative ability, leaving the emirates to manage with untried understudies.

∿ 7 ∿

As for the Emirs, these changes are like an axe laid to their roof-trees. They know this; and the British officials who act as their advisers know it also, and are at pains to make the process of reform gradual, constructive and smooth. To break a system down, they think, even a system with bad faults, unless and until people have been trained to operate a new one, will make not for progress but for chaos. Modify, do not destroy: that is their creed.

This could be done, for Northerners are not impatient, were Northern Nigeria a country on its own, as most of its leaders would like it to be. But it is not. It is a part of greater Nigeria, linked with the Ibo and the Yoruba, who are racing on, with cries of anger at the least delay, towards complete self-government. This they wish to achieve by 1956 at the latest. But the North would take fifty years to reach anything like a comparable stage of development and political alertness. The task of the schools is only at the start. The task of replacing Southern clerks, teachers and artisans has barely begun. Northerners are haunted by the prospect—and at times it seems a very near one —of domination by the once-despised, non-Muslim Negroes. They want time to catch up; while the Negroes, like the Red Queen, dash forward crying "Faster! faster!" To find a pace acceptable to both is Nigeria's great problem.

It is a bad habit, this talking (as everyone does) of human or political "problems", for the word implies that, as in chess or mathematics, every problem has a theoretical solution. In human affairs, some problems do not; and this, I think, is one. It is impossible to compromise between the speed of a runaway lorry and that of a camel which may not even wish to travel in the same direction. One of two outcomes seems likely. "Nigeria" (a mere expression for a heterogeneous collection of peoples until recently almost perpetually at war) will get self-government; and, eventually, either the North will put up with a mixture of exploitation and neglect by the dominant Southerners, or (like Pakistan) it will break away to form a land-locked, economically unbalanced state.

There is a third possibility much canvassed by the more fiery of the Northern nationalists, who can match the Ibo and the Yoruba for pride of race. One of the ablest of them, Mallam Abubakar, a former headmaster of Bauchi School, created a stir in the old Legislative Council by threatening that Northern peoples would "continue their interrupted march to the sea". He was being more rhetorical than historical; still, it shows a spirit that must be reckoned with, even though the threat is, I think, a hollow one.

One cannot be long in Northern Nigeria without feeling that this is the great issue, politically—the future of the camel yoked to the runaway lorry. Fear of the South looks out at you round many corners, springs into the midst of conversation. It brings with it a terrible dilemma. The North is Muslim; and the Muslim faith rests on Koranic teaching in the schools. Koranic teaching in Arabic by Mallams—not secular teaching of the three R's by English-speaking, nominally Christian teachers. For this reason the Emirs have sometimes resisted, sometimes supported half-heartedly, the spread of education as British and Southerners understand the term—an education whose products, all too often, are brash young trousered spivs, locally known by a Hausa word meaning "sons of the wind".

The North's dilemma is whether to push on with Western education, and all that it implies in the undermining of Islam, in the hope of producing a new ruling class of its own, or whether to keep faith with the ways of Islam and risk a new kind of enslavement by the South. It is a hard choice. By and large, the North is choosing the first alternative, but not without misgivings. Already "the sons of the wind" are too many. Already the Western solvent eats into the joints of an Islamic North.

I took tea in Kaduna with three Emirs and the Lieutenant-Governor, Sir Bryan Sharwood-Smith, who, like so many whose working lives have been spent in the North, is in thrall to the people's rugged charm, their tinge of Araby, their courtesy and strength. Generations of kingship have given the Emirs an immense, monolithic dignity. The Emir of Kano wore a white embroidered silk robe and a freshly starched white muslin turban that set off his dark, imperious features. The Sultan of Sokoto, religious head of all these Northern Muslims and now a Regional Minister, wore a starched linen robe of pale blue. Zaria—Sarkin Zazzau—also a Regional Minister, was in a blue-and-white sprigged robe and blue turban; all had heavy gold rings. The eldest son of the Emir of Kano, the Chiroma, was there also, and Ahmadu, the Sardauna of Sokoto, one of the outstanding men of the North: formerly the moving spirit of his own Emirate's native administration, now the Regional Minister for Local Government and the North's principal spokesman in the House of Representatives.

They spoke of the North's future. Dr. Arnold Toynbee has defined two modes of response by societies to the impact of more dynamic cultures: the way of the Zealots, and the way of the Herodians. The Zealots wish to resist change and to preserve (or return to) the customs and faith of their ancestors; the more subtle Herodians wish to learn all they can from the aggressors and then apply this technique first to the reform of their own society, then to meeting the alien one on equal terms. These Emirs revealed themselves to be on the side of the Herodians. Progress, they said—meaning Westernism—must come; we cannot oppose it. We are not doing so. Take the freedom of women. One third of the children now in Northern schools are girls. As to purdah, only perhaps one woman in ten now keeps the veil. (That ten per cent is, however, to be found in the houses of all the rich and noble.)

Said the Sardauna of Sokoto: "There is a woman in my own household now: when the time comes, she looks at her wrist-watch and jumps on to her bicycle and rides down the street to teach in school. My father would not have allowed it. I do."

"What you give with one hand, you take away with the other," said one of the Emirs. "You bring teachers and schools. But you take away the powers we had to control our own children. The schools do not teach respect for God and for parents, which is taught in the Koran. When boys cease to obey their fathers, they listen only to their own inclinations. And these are not wise. And so the boys grow up without discipline and run wild. This is the fault of the Europeans. And it is the biggest obstacle to progress in the North."

I would have given much to have known the inner feelings of these three powerful Emirs as they sat incongruously in stiff, upholstered chairs, sipping tea and eating bread-and-butter and talking, of all things, to a woman; talking with courtesy and restraint and, it seemed, conviction—these potent, dusky Fulani princes, sons of a conquering warrior race, remote indeed in spirit from the welfare planners of London. I doubt if they will ever find their hearts moved by the attractions of women's education, trade unions or electoral colleges. Are they members of a doomed species, or rocks that the swirl of time and fashion cannot move? There were kings and priests in Egypt; will there be kings and priests in Africa in 4,000 years' time? Or Ministers and bureaucrats? Africa is full of enigmas that time alone can solve.

∽ 8 ∽

The harmattan silvers over the flat, dry, monotonous land-scape with powdery dust, reducing visibility to perhaps a hundred yards. Through it loom men on donkeys, foot-plodders, and the tall, handsome shapes of locust-bean trees. The road to Kano runs through flat, park-like country with, here and there, plots of guinea corn or cotton. The groundnut harvest is coming in on the laden backs of donkeys, to be dumped in big stockades built of sacks of groundnuts, the hollow middle piled as high as it will go with loose nuts.

We passed two or three of these collecting centres in the ninety miles between Zaria and Kano. What fantastic quantities of nuts are here! Too many to be cleared before the rains, which will damage them. The railway is the bottle-neck. It is a single line 700 miles long with insufficient locomotives, and will not bear a greatly increased traffic. This year has seen a bumper crop of 340,000 tons. So here the groundnuts stay in jeopardy, while the world goes short and fortunes have been wasted trying to grow them elsewhere.

The atmosphere is so dry that books and papers curl up, the

skin cracks, and at night it is cold enough for blankets. Now you can see the practical use of the big Northern turban with its folds under the chin. You draw these folds over your mouth and nose to filter the air and protect the skin, leaving a slit for the eyes. These, and the hands, are the only parts of the body showing.

After three days a lull occurred and the sun shone again and I could see a little more of Kano. I had an expert guide in Mr. K. P. Maddocks, the alert-minded Resident, who knows and loves Kano—it is a place that grows on the affections—and took me among its narrow, winding streets crowded with urchins and with men sitting on the rumps of donkeys, under its jutting water-spouts, its battlements tipped at each corner with a protuberance just like a rabbit's ear. (They are called dogs' ears in Hausa.) Sometimes I had the illusion that I was walking along between ranks of crouching red rabbits. The red clay walls are pargeted all over with geometric designs, but some of the new houses are built of concrete blocks in imitation of the old style, or of clay cemented over and painted to look like brickwork.

Here are the dye-pits, sour with the horrid stench of indigo, where dyers slowly lift their arms to dip and drain the cloth, and tall youths in loin-cloths empty calabashes into the pits, the water sparkling in a stream of silver as it falls. The needful potash is brought down from Lake Chad and offered in the famous Kano market, which keeps its character, even now, as one of the great marts of the Western Sudan. I saw strings of camels coming down with groundnuts from French territory beyond Sokoto, to return with kola nuts and cotton cloth; they brought also blankets made of camels' hair from Timbuktu and leather from Morocco, which Kano craftsmen fashion into sandals and the high-pommelled saddles that nobles still use. Bridles and bits are made in Kano also—heavy, cruel-looking things; this is still a country of horsemen. And here are the famed Fulani girls from the camps of the nomad cattle-herds: slim, high-breasted, Egyptian-featured, provocative and irresistible, I understand, to some Europeans. They offer milk and butter from the white Fulani cows with a self-assurance and sensuous poise strongly contrasted with the enforced modesty of the swathed and veiled wives of the town.

The market is well laid out in booths with a different quarter for each commodity, and beneath an apparent chaos of chattering, jostling, drifting crowds, order prevails. One big change has come over Kano market in the last hundred years, and that is the disappearance of the section which Captain Clapperton, who saw it in 1826, so graphically describes:

> The slave market is held in the long sheds, one for males, the other for females, where they are seated in rows, and carefully decked out for the exhibition. Young or old, plump or withered, beautiful or ugly, are sold without distinction; but, in other respects, the buyer inspects them with the utmost attention, and somewhat in the same manner as a volunteer seaman is examined by a surgeon on entering the Navy; he looks at the tongue, eyes, teeth and limbs, and endeavours to detect rupture by a forced cough. . . . Slavery here is so common, or the mind of slaves is so constituted, that they always appear much happier than their masters; the women, especially, singing with the greatest glee all the time they are at work.

Change continues: the latest, perhaps, the rout of horses by bicycles. I was startled to see a bevy of young men, sportively attired, whirling through the streets with the metal frames of their machines swathed in brown paper, as if the cycles had just arrived from the factory. This is a current fashion, and a skilled trade in wrapping frames has sprung up.

Another aspect of change is that, last year, 256 pilgrims went to Mecca by air.

~ 9 ~

The wall of Kano was once thirteen miles round and thirty feet high, with fifteen wooden gates covered in sheet-iron opened at sunrise and shut at dusk. Inside, you might come at any time upon a noble attended by horsemen covered from head to foot in quilted cotton, immensely hot and cumbrous; some wore red quilted helmets like a fire-bucket, with a hole for the face; the horses, too, wore quilted armour. Now it is only on feast-days, and especially the *Salla*, which marks the end of

Ramadan, that the famous chain mail is worn by the Emir's bodyguard. It is true that the first suits of this armour came across the desert from the Holy Land and had been worn by the Crusaders, but in later centuries an industry throve in Omdurman and Birmingham for supplying orders from the Western Sudan.

Near the edge of the city, but inside its walls, is a bare, high rock from whose summit you may see the streets and jigsaw compounds of Kano spread out beneath you like a great house of cards. By this rock once lived the founder of Kano, a mighty hunter who carried an elephant on his head and put it down on the site of the town. He was a priest and sorcerer, and alone had entry to a sacred grove before which the people sacrificed to a goddess. One day, emerging from the grove, he prophesied that a conqueror would destroy the sacred trees and rule the tribesmen. "What can we do?" the people asked. "There is no cure but resignation," he replied. Historians have identified him as the protagonist in a tenth-century invasion of the Western Sudan by Berber or Zaghawa peoples, who brought horses and the art of sinking wells, and founded the Hausa states.[1] There is some suggestion that one branch of these people came from Egypt and that the form of worship in the sacred grove of Kano was derived from the cult of Astarte.

Quite soon, the prophecy was fulfilled. A man called Bagoda conquered the district and became the first king of Kano, the first of a line of forty-eight rulers whose reigns, from A.D. 999 to 1892, are recorded in the *Kano Chronicle*, almost the only historical document to survive the Fulani conquest. Today's city is, therefore, in its origins, a thousand years old. In the fourteenth century travellers from the land of Melle (perhaps Mandingos) brought the Muslim faith and converted the King. He built a mosque, but the pagans constantly defiled it. A night of prayer was organized, with such good results that next day all those who had helped to defile the mosque were struck blind, and Kano became a Muslim state.[2]

The *Kano Chronicle* is for the most part a tale of wars with

[1] E. W. Bovill, *Caravan Routes of the Old Sahara*.
[2] See H. R. Palmer's translation of the *Kano Chronicle* published as *Sudanese Memoirs* by the Government Printer, Lagos, in 1928.

neighbouring states—Zaria, Katsina, Songhai, above all Bornu —until in 1805 an army of 10,000 spearmen clad in mail and quilted armour were routed by Fulani bowmen, and the city fell. This was in the reign of the forty-third King. The forty-fourth, and those who came after him, were Fulani, and subject to the Sultan of Sokoto.

Slavery, of course, had existed since time immemorial, but the Fulani made a business of it on a scale hitherto unknown. Parts of the road to Tripoli were almost truly white with human bones. Major Denham, in 1822, counted a hundred rotting skeletons round a well, and when he expressed horror the Arabs laughed, prodded the bones with their musket-butts and remarked that they were only blacks; and all the way along the route from Tripoli to Bornu he found this grim trail of human agony.[1] Dr. Barth, who accompanied a Bornu slave-raiding party in 1851, records that in a single raid a thousand slaves were probably taken. The women and children were kept; most of the men massacred. "To our utmost horror not less than 170 full-grown men were mercilessly slaughtered in cold blood, the greater part of them being allowed to bleed to death, a leg having been severed from the body." As the raiders passed they burnt villages and trampled crops, leaving those who had escaped into the bush to die, more slowly, from starvation. "Between 1851 and the year of the introduction of British authority into Northern Nigeria," says Lady Lugard, "the practice of slave-raiding as described by Dr. Barth had become general throughout the Protectorate."[2]

It was precisely to halt this dreadful slaughter that the British came to Northern Nigeria. In 1884 the young Scots explorer Joseph Thomson negotiated the first treaty with the Sultan of Sokoto on behalf of a concern which was merged two years later into the Royal Niger Company. This Company fell foul of the French, who were spreading over Dahomey, and a scramble for treaties with native potentates took place. Captain Lugard beat a French Captain Decoeur to a place called Nikki by five days; international tension grew; finally the short-lived Company sur-

[1] Described in *Travels and Discoveries in Northern and Central Africa* by Denham, Clapperton and Ondney. John Murray.
[2] *A Tropical Dependency* by Lady Lugard. Nisbet, 1906.

rendered its powers to the Government, and on January 1st, 1900, a British Protectorate was proclaimed over Northern Nigeria, with Lugard as the first High Commissioner.

The Protectorate was at first a word, a piece of paper. The extraordinary story of how Lugard, with a handful of British troops and native levies, took these princely emirates one after another and secured their allegiance has often been told. As for Kano, it fell in 1903 without a battle to a small column of troops, which then continued to Sokoto. The main Sokoto army attacked a detachment of the British force numbering forty-five men and two officers. The British formed a square, which was charged ten times by 1,000 horsemen and 2,000 foot. The invaders beat off all attacks and killed the Sokoto commander, and that was the end of the resistance; Sokoto surrendered on March 15th, 1903, and all the Northern emirates acknowledged British rule.

That was fifty years ago: a very short time in Kano's history. There have been individuals who ruled for a longer period. Who will be lord of Kano in fifty years' time? "A snake must have a head," an African once said to me. "But the British have buried *their* head in the sand." Fulani, Hausa, Negro—there will be many to contend for the seat so soon to be vacated by the latest conqueror; and perhaps, as Kano's founder said, "there is no cure but resignation".

◆ 10 ◆

Kano's wall has crumbled, but most of the gates are still kept up and you may drive out, past the warehouses of Syrian merchants, into a thickly populated country-side where you may see in operation a system of farming that has changed very little for a thousand years.

I travelled north, along the road to Sokoto, with two Agricultural Officers, one English and one an English-speaking Kano man. The average farm, they told me, was only about three acres, and fragmentation is far advanced into fractions of an acre; in spite of this, the light, sandy soil has not lost its fertility. There are two reasons; and we saw both, as it were, in action. Emerging from Kano was a stream of men driving donkeys loaded with refuse from the compounds—vegetable waste, mostly—to be dug into the land. This maintains humus. The other reason was at first less obvious. We drove some distance along a sandy track, stopped the car beside a field of newly harvested guinea corn and walked across the hard stubble to a cluster of stooks of guinea-corn straw. The stalks are six or eight feet high and as thick as a child's arm, so that each stook was like a small wigwam. Out of one stepped a Fulani woman carrying a baby. We had come upon an encampment of Fulani who have no more solid homes than the interior of these corn-stooks, and shift their few possessions—clay cooking-pots and calabashes, strings of beads, a few skins and a bundle of clothing—from place to place in the wake of their white cows.

This is the season when Fulani cattle move south, grazing the farmers' stubble, for which their owners pay rent in the dung of the cows. They exchange milk for grain. Thus fertility is maintained, and diet balanced. No money changes hands.

These are the "cow Fulani", nomads of the North. When they settle and become "town Fulani" they inter-marry with Hausa or Negro stocks and grow darker in colour; and their cattle also, if they still keep any, lose the pure whiteness prized by the true Fulani, and become speckled. The nomad men wear a sort of full-skirted cloak and do their hair in many stiff plaits; some will stand on one leg, pressing the other foot against the inside of the knee, like the Masai in East Africa, whom they so closely resemble that the two tribes must surely have sprung from a common stock. There are believed to be about 2,000,000 Fulani in the north, with at least 6,000,000 cattle. Without them, the soil's fertility could scarcely be maintained.

For reasons political, the Government wants to settle the Fulani. As it is, their children cannot go to school, they evade taxes, they acknowledge no authority and it is practically impossible to get them to vote. But (again like the Masai) they neglect agriculture and, so far, have resisted pretty well the pressure to turn them into voters and taxpayers. But only romantics approve of them, and they will have a hard task to survive.

The guinea-corn stalks in which they shelter fetch as much as twopence each in Kano, where fuel is desperately short. All the trees for miles round have gone, save locust-beans, which, because of their soil-regenerating properties, are protected by law. Illicit felling is rife; one tree for each twenty acres is reckoned to disappear every year. Unless a serious tree-planting programme can be launched soon—and unless the plantations can be kept inviolate—there will be no wood for the cooking-fires of Kano in a very short while. And whereas in the past you could burn camel-dung, you cannot do much with old tyres.

We came to an experimental farm where old, worn-out land is being coaxed back to fertility and new, greatly improved kinds of groundnut tested. With better seed and a very small dressing of superphosphate, groundnut yields can easily be doubled. There is a widespread deficiency of phosphates all over northern Nigeria, and the production of export crops like groundnuts is aggravating it. At Samaru, the Government's experimental station near Zaria, Dr. Greenwood and his colleagues have produced a phosphate capsule, which the groundnut grower pushes into the soil with his big toe as he plants the nut. Thus very little of the fertilizer goes to waste and, if all goes well, the resulting plant yields two or three times as many nuts as the average.

The District Head came to meet us, his yellow turban so wound as to show two peaks on top, which proclaimed his royal blood. He is a member of one of four ruling families which, between them, share the spoils of Kano emirate, and a relative of the Emir's. Practically all District Heads are, I gathered, relatives of the Emir's.

He took us to his town, Dambarta, a miniature Kano, to show us a contraption from India for shelling groundnuts which, if it catches on, will save the women millions of hours' work laboriously breaking every individual nut by hand. No consideration for the women, however, prompted this experiment. In breaking the husk, they damage also the inner skin, and from this a product called ardil, a kind of artificial wool, can now be made. The women, as a matter of fact, will suffer from a loss of income hard to make up in other ways. For picking the nuts from the haulms, which takes two days' hard work, they are paid tenpence a bag. The elders shook their turbaned heads at this; it was too much money. The average cash income of the local peasant is about £12 a year.

This royal District Head, a most courteous, spectacled elder, governs 90,000 taxpayers—probably about half a million souls in all—for a nominal salary of £150 a year. He and his fellows are autocrats to an extent undreamed of in Negro-land. There are village and district councils—reformed ones, now, elected by commoners—and in theory the chiefs are bound by their advice, but in practice few of their members would normally dare to question the word of the Emir's cousin. No such tradition as the parrots' eggs of Yoruba exists in Northern Nigeria.

·◦· II ·◦·

There is, however, a small group of anti-traditionalists in Kano who rally to the Northern Elements Progressive Union. This is affiliated to Dr. Azikiwe's N.C.N.C., which runs here a daily paper (of a sort): the *Comet*.

The Secretary of N.E.P.U. is Mallam Aminu Kano: a Cassius of a man, slight and fiery, fluent in English, his heart a scorpion and his tongue a whip. The *Comet* offices are not imposing. Through a home-made door in a mud wall I entered a small, dirty court guarded by a vulture who blinked stonily and did not budge. A desk, three chairs and piles of newsprint filled the tiny editorial cubby-hole.

For about forty-five minutes Aminu Kano spoke in English without a pause, compellingly, ardently, lashingly. First he attacked indirect rule. It had re-placed upon their thrones the arch slave-traders, giving them greater powers than ever before. The Emirs, he said, are autocratic, corrupt and tyrannous. Let a village man support N.E.P.U., and the District Head will load him with taxes or call him out for communal labour at seed-time and harvest; as a result, complaints against the régime are few, but silence does not mean contentment; it means fear. The people are dissatisfied about three things: the rule of the Emirs, the system of corruption, British overlordship. Of these, the last is the least, for the British are much more fair, honest and approachable than the Fulani ruling class.

But the British have failed over education. In the war (said Aminu Kano) a great campaign was organized to recruit men and to grow groundnuts. Word of these things was carried into the remotest villages. Why has not this been done for mass education? Because the Emirs fear education and the British back them up. It was the Emirs who kept out the Christian Missions with their schools, and the British backed them up in this too. The result is that today in Kano there are fewer than 500 pupils in three Middle Schools, drawn from a population of over 2,000,000.

Aminu Kano is a demagogue—ready-tongued, fanatical—and the *Comet* a carefree sheet which prints Communist propaganda, but there is force in some of his charges. It is true that the British have backed Fulani Emirs who were ruthless slave-raiders and often corrupt; but it is also true that the North follows Islam, that Islam follows tradition and that the British had neither the will nor the men to overturn the whole existing order, drive out the Emirs and rule directly until a Westernized generation had thrown up a handful of rulers probably no more disinterested and efficient than the Emirs. The British chose Indirect Rule; and here is its last outpost. Even here, it cannot endure, and Aminu Kano's day will come, or that of his successors.

British hopes are centred not on the extremists of N.E.P.U., but on a group of moderate, balanced and yet progressive Northerners who have founded a centre party, as it were, called the Northern People's Congress, with headquarters in Zaria. One of their leaders is Abubakar Imam, a devout Muslim who values tradition, but fears to see an unreformed North at the mercy of thrusting Southerners. Abubakar Imam was at that time the editor of the Hausa newspaper *Gaskiya*, which is produced in a large white palace in Zaria built by the Nigerian Government with the help of British funds. *Gaskiya* is an experiment in sane journalism, intended to print news without either misleading or boring its readers. A British director and a mixed Board give a free hand to Abubakar, who has become one of the best liked and trusted men in the North. *Gaskiya* is well produced and has a circulation of about 23,000, which does not seem much among a Hausa-speaking population of 8,000,000 or 9,000,000, but is considered good in this land of illiteracy and great distances. Each of the 23,000 copies is handed on many times, so that virtually the whole of the North's cadre of educated men has access to it. The experiment can so far be accounted a success. Whether Abubakar and his friends can guide the North along the Middle Way—whether the philosophy of Aminu Kano and his friends will prove a speck of chaff or a grain of mustard seed—all that remains to be seen. One feels that hitherto the position of the Emirs has scarcely been shaken; but it is early days.

∾ 12 ∾

No steep escarpment leads up to the central Plateau of Nigeria, at least on the western side, but you rise gradually through rolling parkland until suddenly the country becomes full of rocks. Rocks and gulleys and short bare grass; no trees; the wind-swept, bleak look of upland places; hovels for houses, pebbles on the road; erosion everywhere; cool air on your face, and you are in the country of fresh milk, tin mines, cold nights and naked pagans, and herds of cattle nosing for sustenance over stony pastures.

It is typical of Africa that down below, in the great heavy heat of the plains, people go muffled in a plethora of cloth and wool; but here on the heights, where the wind whistles and cold can be bitter, they wear nothing but a loin-cloth or a bunch of leaves. Some affect a handy little garment, woven from grass-stalks, called a penis-sheath, which protects that organ from scratches when its owner walks through long grass. So many outsiders have laughed at this protection that its wearers, I was told, have grown self-conscious and now use it only in the remoter regions.

We passed a horseman in a skin cloak, a dagger tied to his arm and in his hand a home-made, ineffectual spear. He had a wild, uncouth look, without the plainsman's dignity. The physique of these so-called pagans seems ungainly: stocky people, with rather long arms. Most of their forebears were driven up into the hills in order to escape the constant slave-raids of the Hausa people. They live in country that is healthy, but poor; the crops look sparse and the soil, in places, as thin as a sheet of paper. It is fortunate for the Plateau that a different form of wealth has suddenly assumed importance: tin. It has been mined for years, but a leap in prices has made the process very lucrative. Not long ago, tin fetched about £200 a ton. It rose to £1,500, and

An Emir of Northern Nigeria

A District Head on his rounds north of Kano

A Fulani woman in her home of corn-stalks north of Kano

A Birom girl outside her home near Jos

Transport in the Eastern Provinces: goods go by cycle

Palm oil puncheons float down to the sea

A "second burial" party among the Ibos: guests firing off Dane guns

"Community development" near Enugu: building a road

A fertility image on land ready for new yams in Iboland

Roadside memorial of a clerk from Calabar: juju shrine on the left

An Ibibio
masquerade
Photo: A. Aloba

Dr. Azikiwe (left,
in cap and spec-
tacles) talks to
Mr. Mbadiwe
(in cap, centre) in
the House of
Assembly
*Photo: Public
Relations Dept.*

has now steadied near the £900 mark, a price which still pays handsomely.

On the road to Jos we passed several mines, if that is the word, for they are simply large open pits from which clay is extracted by huge machines called drag-lines, and washed in shallow tanks. Generally these holes are in the bed of a river. The unwanted clay is spewed out in forlorn yellow heaps and the landscape thereby marred. Drag-lines somewhat resemble freakish, prehistoric beasts with long, tapering necks, an illusion upheld by their capacity to walk across country on a self-propelling platform.

Jos has the air of a boom town, with many new buildings, costly cars and prosperous Syrians. It is an ugly little place in an attractive setting; the plains and rocks, wide skies and bracing air reminded me of parts of the American north-west, Wyoming for example, or of Kenya. Gardens are gay with flowers and you enjoy fresh vegetables; the Government runs a comfortable but expensive Hill Station for jaded officials. I was fortunate enough to stay with one who is far from jaded, in fact a by-word for efficiency and possessed of a tart, sardonic humour which sometimes wins him respect rather than affection; a granary of information about the North and its peoples: Mr. Rex Niven, now President of the House of Assembly. All round Jos are the clustered huts, the unthrifty-looking fields of the pagans, who belong to so many different tribes that no official can master their languages. To reach their villages, you take a narrow, winding path between high cactus hedges, with tiny hedged fields on either side.

We visited a headman in his compound: a skinny, amiable and wealthy man with ten wives and a family of forty or fifty. We found him in his reception room, so to say, with his cronies, addressing himself to a forty-five-gallon drum of beer. Every day, he said, his wives brew a full drum from millet or guinea corn, which is first sprouted on skins; and every day forty-five gallons goes down the throats of himself and his relatives.

"And then we talk about improving the lot of the African!" exclaimed a District Officer. "If you come to think of it, this old boy has reached the stage every Englishman dreams of but never attains, unless he wins on the pools—perpetual leisure, unlimited

I

beer and plenty of women. Women, what's more, who work for him like slaves instead of always demanding attention. How could *we* improve his lot?"

Such worries as this headman has are mainly caused by the District Officer. The headman's predecessor was defrocked for holding unofficial courts and pocketing the fines, and the headman before that removed to jail for some other financial offence. So the present incumbent must walk warily.

Although the area actually disturbed by tin-mining is very small, land is so scarce in these parts that the loss of even a few acres here and there is resented, and some of the younger men have formed the Birom Progressive Union, mainly to oppose the tin interests. Two members of this Union have been elected to the Northern House of Assembly. But mining brings too much wealth to Nigeria to be restricted. The miners pay compensation to families whose land is ripped up and the Government will provide good land elsewhere, but the Birom are most reluctant to take it. Some of them remain resentful and suspicious. And no wonder. What good can come of a great monster like a drag-line tearing up their river-beds? Of course, we answer, good has come, and more will come to them—schools, for instance, and they want schools; and the winning of new land from the bush on which, if they choose to work, they can wax fatter than they have ever waxed before. But they remain unconvinced.

❧ 13 ❧

On the Plateau outside Jos, at Vom, some light is breaking over Nigeria's greatest agricultural puzzle and handicap—the tsetse-fly. Practically the whole country is infested except for a belt in the far north, and the Plateau. This means not merely no milk or meat for the people but—in the long run even more disastrous—no renewal of fertility for the soil.

So there has come into being, mainly with British funds, the West African Institute of Trypanosomiasis Research, known more succinctly as Waiter. This has two branches in Nigeria: one at Vom, under Lt.-Col. Mulligan, and one at Kaduna, under

Dr. Nash. Broadly speaking, Kaduna studies the life-history of the tsetse and Vom the behaviour of the parasite.

Here at Vom I saw at close quarters those little humpless, fawn-coloured *ndama* cattle, much like Jerseys and full of charm, which come from French Senegal and, almost alone among African breeds, show a high degree of immunity to the blood parasite or "tryps" carried by tsetse-flies. The vital question is whether this resistance, or immunity, can be passed on when the *ndama* (which are small and few in number) are crossed with cattle of other breeds. Here they are mated with the big white Fulani, and the resulting offspring tested for immunity. Of ten so far infected with tryps, half proved immune and half did not. The scale of this experiment is too small yet for proof, but such results could indicate that immunity is, indeed, a genetic factor. If this proves to be so, tremendous prospects open up: a new breed of cattle almost immune to Africa's most deadly bovine disease. Both at Kaduna and at Vom, patient research into the behaviour of tsetse-flies is revealing facts new to science of great interest and promise. For six years, for instance, flies have been caught every week by a stream near Kaduna, coloured according to the section they were trapped in and then released, only to be re-caught again.

Partial clearing of the bush is the standard method of driving back the fly, especially the two species (*Glossina palpalis* and *Glossina tachinoides*) which favour riverine thickets. A good deal of success has come from this method, but plant-growth is so quick and exuberant here that "slashing" of cleared bush has to be carried out at frequent intervals. This falls on the local people, under their chiefs, and after the first enthusiasm has worn off they sometimes need a good deal of persuasion to keep up the work, which is often classed as unpaid communal labour. Yet, if they relax, the bush creeps back and tsetses follow. By and large, control measures are not doing more than hold the line and prevent further encroachments. The kind of tsetse which infests more open bush country away from streams— *Glossina morsitans*—is even harder to master.

The use of drugs against the tiny, snake-like parasite in the blood is another line of attack. Antrycide is the best-known drug, but while it will protect cattle for about four months against infection carried by *tachinoides* or *palpalis*, it is useless for longer periods and against the type of parasite carried by *morsitans*. Chemists are working assiduously to improve this and other drugs, and with some optimism. But it would seem as if the best hope of all lies in these neat, thrifty little fawn *ndama* cattle and their mysterious immunity.

Side by side with the research labs at Vom is a school for training veterinary assistants. It is very hard to get recruits of the right quality, for vets cannot make as much money as doctors and barristers. While Ibos and other Southerners are the brightest students, they have no skill with animals, whereas Northerners are born cattle-men, but often stupid and lazy at their books. There is, however, one Fulani in training as a vet in Liverpool. Only about twenty of these future veterinary assistants (not all of whom make the grade) can be enticed each year from the whole of Nigeria, a very inadequate number in a country whose major agricultural problem is to develop animal husbandry in order to save the soil's over-taxed fertility.

It is a pity that the better-educated Africans so rarely feel themselves concerned in these vast needs of, and dangers to, the land by which their country lives. They think mainly of politics, of law, of constitutions, of money. There is no greater term of abuse than to say a man is "bush". It is the insult unforgivable. Farming is "bush", cattle are "bush", peasants are "bush", and so the less said about them the better. Although politicians pay lip-service to the needs of agriculture, and some indeed really understand them, African self-government will bring the rule of barristers, journalists, teachers and civil servants—urban through and through—over a nation of peasants, with the needs of the land running a poor second to the satisfaction of the cities.

◦ 14 ◦

One day in 1944 an African told Mr. Bernard Fagg, a District Officer turned antiquarian, that he had seen a kind of head stuck up on a stick to scare birds. Mr. Fagg found it to be a terra-cotta head of a type hitherto unknown, and of a much greater antiquity than anything he had seen before, which had been dug up in some tin workings near a place called Nok in

Zaria province, about twenty-five feet down. Digging brought to light other fragments, and more finds are still being made. Mr. Fagg has estimated them to be rather more than 2,000 years old.

And then, last year, came another find. At a place called Katsina Ala, 130 miles south-east of Nok, some schoolboys digging out the stump of a tree unearthed a head of a similar kind, but with a somewhat Chinese-looking moustache. Nearby a monkey came to light, and more fragments followed, about thirty of which have since been fitted together to make an almost complete figure, seated on a stool, about three feet high. Since then, about twenty pieces of importance in the Nok style have been recovered from an area some 200 miles broad by 100 miles deep, on the flanks of the Plateau. The majority are human heads, but there are also some animal figures, for instance an elephant's head from Odegi, and several monkeys.

The significance of these finds is that they are at least 1,000 years older than any previous known example of West African art. This suggests that a culture existed in Nigeria that antedated even the ancient empires of the desert; a culture contemporaneous with the Greek and Roman and Egyptian. Was it indigenous or immigrant? Evanescent or tenacious? Were its creators destroyed, or did they merge with the aboriginals? Why did it vanish, and when? So many fascinating speculations cluster round this group of heads and figures, which display the purity, the strength, the freshness of the best primitives. They are far more naturalistic than comparatively modern African sculptures, but show certain faint affinities with modern Yoruba art, especially in the elongated treatment of the eyes. While they do not resemble the Ife heads, Mr. Fagg postulates a link, probably tenuous, between the Nok and the far more recent Ife cultures. Do these fragile terra-cotta heads and fragments, excellently displayed in a fascinating small museum in Jos arranged by Mr. Fagg, hold the key to the mystery of the origin of that strange naturalistic Ife style? The distorted later art of West Africa, often admired by Europeans for its primitive vigour, appears by comparison at its best baroque, at less than best, decadent. These Nok finds might constitute the source of its origin—2,000 years old. But where it arose, who fashioned it and what became of them, no one can say. Meanwhile, digging proceeds, and further finds of equal importance are by no means improbable.

❧ 15 ❧

From Jos I had reluctantly to turn south, although the road beckoned temptingly: northwards through Bauchi to the dry plains of Bornu, so long an independent empire stretching to the swampy shores of Lake Chad, where a breed of cattle lives with horns that, though they look enormously heavy—at the base they are as thick as a man's thigh—are honeycombed with air passages which confer on them a buoyancy advantageous to their owners, who browse on the swampy vegetation that saturates the margins of the lake; northwards to Maiduguri, Bornu's dusty, baking capital, and its dark-skinned, independent Kanuri people, and the great deserts beyond; and eastwards to the hills of Adamawa, the bridle-paths and lofty crags and naked pagan people with their round, thatched houses, their priest-kings and rain-makers, and the high Cameroon Mountains beyond. This is the wildest part of Nigeria, the least accessible, where life has changed very little in the last fifty years, and self-government is still of less importance than the correct ritual at harvest, the bride-price and the sacrifices that will bring rain or avert disease. How fortunate those older travellers who set out unfettered by time-tables, beyond the reach of posts and telephones! Dr. Barth, who came from Tripoli and Timbuktu to Bornu and Kano, was away for five years. But then, a great many of those older travellers never got home at all.

And so I headed south, at first across the bare Plateau heaped with queer piles of granite, one stone balanced on another as if on the verge of toppling over. Herds of Fulani cattle were going south too, in search of grazing; and droves of ponies, some as thin as hurdles, plodding wearily on.

"That's how almost every horse in Northern Nigeria meets its end," I was told. "Beaten to death by the progressive Ibo in one of their revolting ceremonies."

Later, I made enquiries and found that my informant had not exaggerated. Old horses fetch large prices from Ibos who "take a title", as the saying is. This means, in effect, joining a society which has a large initiation fee. Once in, each member is assured of a regular income from his share of the initiation fees of subsequent entrants. The initiation ceremony involves the sacrifice of a horse.

The principal horse market is at Ibagwa Nkwor, near Nsukka in Onitsha province, where 200 to 300 horses are offered on every market day in the dry season. They are bought for the "second burial" of important men, and also for the "horse titles", especially that of *Otigbu anyinya*, which means literally "the man who kills the horse by beating". The emblem is a horse's tail. Generally, the horse is roped and thrown and dragged into the ju-ju house, where its throat is partially cut so that blood may drip on to the altar. Then it is dragged outside, its tail cut off, and it may be beaten to death with clubs, or the participants may break its legs and drag it on to a fire. Sometimes, while still living, it is hung up by a rope to a tree. At least 500 or 600 horses, and probably more, are dealt with in this way every year.

Action to stop these practices has been pressed on the Government ever since 1920, especially by vets, and on each occasion the buck has been passed between the Northern and the Eastern Regions. Northern officials suggest banning the sale of horses in Eastern markets; Easterners propose stopping the export of horses from the North. Neither side acts, for fear of offending the Ibos. High officials point out that the horse custom has replaced human sacrifice, and so marks an advance; further education, they say, is the remedy. Now there is talk of encouraging the use of humane killers. But no one is instructed to make their use compulsory. In fact, it is questionable whether education, as we understand the term, will alter matters. "Horse titles" are generally taken not by rude savages but by wealthy Ibo professional men: traders, lawyers, transport owners and even, it is said, eminent politicians. Only rich men can afford the entrance fee, and the richest men are to be found among the relatively educated. This is no relic of barbarism; it is a recognized social custom of the new middle class.

Without being sentimental about horses, it is distressing to see these ageing animals, who have been the pride of their Fulani or

Hausa owners, driven down the thirsty road to such a shocking end. Can nothing be done? Will the Ibo not relinquish such practices? They do not seem inclined to do so, and the powers which Englishmen once had, and never used, have now passed to Africans—and especially, in the Eastern Region, to the Ibo peoples. We have never faced the fact that a great many people, including a lot of Africans, enjoy inflicting cruelty and find bloodshed stimulating, not appalling.

∿ 16 ∿

The road south from Jos winds down an escarpment which drops from 4,300 to 300 feet. It crosses many streams, some now dry, and below almost every bridge lies the corpse of a lorry. The mortality among motor vehicles—as indeed among passengers—must be enormous. One such wreck had occurred only just in front of us. The lorry was strewn about in small pieces and six men had perished, including the driver, a Hausa trader. His current profits had been found stuffed in the bottom of an old sack: £1,500 in one-pound notes.

On our way down we looked in at two re-settlement schemes. These are the fashion just now—miniature Mokwas.

Two things, above all others, are needed: supervision, and money. For these schemes are based on no popular movement; there is no wish to re-settle. The people themselves would evidently prefer to continue eroding their ancestral lands on a very low standard of living. Therefore, without supervision, they are soon discouraged, and retreat. And such schemes are always costly, since so much has to be done to bribe the settlers to come and, once there, to stay. The cost of settling each family is so high that nothing can make these schemes economic. There are three such ventures in the North, financed from groundnut profits by the Regional Production Development Board.

The Jemaa project is designed to re-settle members of the Birom tribe displaced by tin-mining. Each settler receives twenty acres, two round his house and eighteen behind it; in addition, he gets the free range of forty acres on which to cut firewood. A house is built for him—a good one, much above the average, costing £40. Six acres of bush are cleared for each man, free of charge to him, although it costs the Government £5 an acre.

The village we saw is, by African standards, a model one; the compounds clean and tidy, a square in the middle for dances and parades, a dispensary, a school, a church, a clean water supply from concreted wells. The only thing wrong with it, from a Birom point of view, is that it is a long way off in the bush. In spite of its attractions, and the prospects it offers of growing rich, in spite of the many people dispossessed (according to the Birom Progressive Union) by tin-mines, and in spite of much official propaganda, in the first year only twenty-one men volunteered to come, with their families; in the second year, seventeen; and last year, three. Even the chiefs refuse to pay a visit to Jemaa. The Birom are to have one more chance. If they still boycott the scheme, it is to be opened to men of other tribes, many of whom are watching it with envy.

The Scottish Development Officer in charge, Mr. Bickett, lives with his wife and small baby in a thatched hut, fifty or sixty miles from Jos. Does he not feel isolated, I asked? Or lonely? He looked surprised.

"I play football every Saturday," he said, "and I often get a game of deck-tennis in the evening with Mr. Kabu, the agricultural assistant. Oh no, it's not lonely."

He works with the men, clearing bush against sleeping sickness, which is rife in the district. Might he not contract the disease?

"Well, it doesn't matter if I do," he said. "There's a dispensary here, and the medical assistant takes a blood slide now and then. If any of us gets it, he gives us a shot, and that puts things right again."

At the escarpment's base lies the broad, hot valley of the Benue, another Niger in size. The cool air of the Plateau is now far behind: all is once again steamy and oppressive. At Makurdi the river lies as wide and silent as a great lake, and at night the warm darkness, the beating pulse of drums, tell you that you are back on the borders of Negro-land.

The Resident kindly invited me to dinner. Mr. MacBride is a man of the old school: a bachelor who understands comfort, with perfect servants, perfect manners, a good table, a French beard, a love of tradition; he would be most at home, you feel, in a university common room, or in the now extinct kind of parsonage with useful daughters and cricketing sons. We dined at ten o'clock, according to the West Coast custom, after sipping drinks for two hours on the lawn under the stars: a custom pleasant enough if you are used to it and congenial to hot climates, but hard on the traveller bumped about amid new impressions all day.

Next morning I drove through the country of the Tiv, a sturdy, formerly war-like tribe of semi-Bantu origin only just beginning to take to education. Now that they have started, they are evidently determined to go the whole hog; written on a blackboard in a round, thatched little village school I found the formidable word "disestablishmentarianism". We called on a patriarch with seventeen wives whose clan occupied a whole village: an old, white-bearded, lean-shanked man in a blue homespun cloth leaning on a staff in a most biblical manner. Seeing the lens of my camera exposed, he gently but firmly covered it over and shut the case, wanting no trouble here with stolen souls. A grandson translated for us: he was an agricultural instructor, trying to teach the virtues of contour ridging to his relatives.

Tiv country is closely settled and quite treeless; every bit of timber has been cut down, and firewood is a problem to all. The Tiv have no natural chiefs, but the Government has appointed artificial ones; the head chief is an ex-sergeant-major, and one can see his hand in the tidiness and orderly lay-out of the capital, Gboko. Now a complicated network of councils has been set up and the Tiv send their representatives to the Northern House of Assembly.

Leprosy is common here, and among a nearby tribe called the Eggon the rate of infection is said to be the highest in the world, reaching eight per cent of the population. The South African branch of the Sudan United Mission has for twenty years alleviated the sufferings of thousands of lepers, both by treatment at its hospital near Gboko and by the management of a large leper colony—one of several successful leper settlements started by Christian Missions in the North.

An elderly Afrikaner couple, Mr. and Mrs. Loedolff, showed

me round. They came, they told me, twenty years ago to the Mission, which concentrated then on evangelical work. Mr. Loedolff was an engineer. He and his wife, although not medically qualified, became interested in leprosy and started the first crude hospital with, as he put it, two syringes and one hut. Now the Mission has a well-equipped hospital, nine clinics throughout the province and a colony of over 1,250 lepers. There are nearly 4,000 people under treatment, Mr. Loedolff said.

And now has come the new drug—diaminodiphenylsulphone: one of the great discoveries of modern medicine, which offers the first certain cure. In the early stages of its use it sent some lepers mad, and in other cases peeled off their entire skin. It was then discovered that patients must first be "de-sensitized" by injections of iron, to build up the hæmoglobin content of the blood on which the drug acts. The treatment is now safe, and leprosy can be cured in six months. The shade of Father Damien must indeed be satisfied.

The Southern Cameroons

◦ 1 ◦

A Dove put me down at Tiko, the airport of the Cameroons, a clearing amid millions of banana trees. The road winds uphill all the way to Buea, the capital, which stands on the slopes of the Cameroon Mountain at an altitude of 2,800 feet. For West Africa, this is a health resort, and the view is lovely over hills and forests and, in the early morning, up to the bare pink heights of the mountain, 13,350 feet high, which gathers round it a cloak of cloud when the sun rises. That is in the dry weather. In the long rainy season Buea is so thickly drenched in Scotch mist that cars may need their headlights at mid-day.

Buea's glory is the Schloss. This noble pile was built in the Gothic and baronial style in 1899 by Herr von Puttkamer, third German Governor of Kamerun; its massive walls are two feet thick and it is liberally provided with turrets and balconies. Von Puttkamer seems to have combined all the qualities generally believed to be most Germanic; he was harsh, stiff, sometimes cruel, ruthless and realistic, but on the other hand efficient, just, and full of drive. There is a legend that the Schloss was built out of a road fund for his mistress, a Berlin opera-singer, but when all was ready to receive her, she refused to come; and that her lover thereafter filled the house with photographs and flowers, and ordered an extra place always to be laid at table. Her name was Pauline. Below the Schloss stands a wrought-iron gate with two P's entwined—Pauline and Puttkamer.

I cannot speak for the truth of the legend, but it adds interest to the Schloss, as indeed does a tale recounted by its present incumbent, a keen-witted, caustic-tongued, cigar-smoking Brigadier, John Gibbons, Commissioner for the Southern Cameroons. A wide stairway leads from the hall to a first-floor lobby, where a grand piano stands. One afternoon the Brigadier, working downstairs, heard the piano and recognized an air from Liszt; he was surprised, because his wife had not played for some years, but did not disturb her. At the same time his wife, resting in her room, heard the piano and recognized an air from Liszt; she, too, was surprised, as her husband had not played for some years, but left him alone. Later, comparing notes, they discovered that neither had touched the piano and both had recognized, at the same moment, the same tune. And there were no guests in the house.

The garden is the pride of the Schloss. Green lawns fall in a series of terraces, and a profusion of flowers fills in the beds: roses perennially blooming, salvias blue and red, the misty plumbago, the golden-cupped bignonia; snapdragons and dianthus, dahlias and lilies, violets and primulas, asters (which flower when they are one inch high, so fertile is the soil) and blaring scarlet cannas.

The British-administered section of the Cameroons (a Trusteeship Territory under the United Nations) is a long, thin strip of country, nowhere more than 100 miles wide, stretching over 600 miles northwards almost to Lake Chad, and sandwiched between Nigeria and the French-administered section of the Cameroons. It is divided into two by a corridor of Northern Nigerian territory; the southern part, by far the most developed, is administered from Buea, but the northern strip falls directly under three Nigerian provinces: Benue, Adamawa and Bornu. To make matters more difficult, the country is very mountainous, and badly served by roads. Beyond Kumba, one-way traffic comes into force: you go north on Mondays, Wednesdays and Fridays, and south on Tuesdays, Thursdays and Saturdays.

Every few years a Commission from the Trusteeship Council visits these formerly German countries to report on the stewardship of the two Powers. The Visiting Mission (composed of an Iraqui, a Belgian, a Mexican and an American) which came at the end of 1949 gave a favourable account of British management, and investigated the matrimonial activities of the Fon of Bikom. This gentleman enjoyed, it was said, eighty to a hundred wives, a fact which aroused great indignation among many delegates to the United Nations on the grounds that it was immoral and un-Christian, and imposed conditions near to slavery on the wives. Soon the Fon's marriages became imperialist crimes. Only a wicked and reactionary Government controlled by capitalist exploiters, it was implied, would allow one individual to corner so many wives.

So the Visiting Mission climbed a very steep hill one hot morning to call upon the Fon, a man of over eighty who, according to the Mission's report, "remained calm and polite throughout a discussion which, by the standards of his culture, must have appeared an unwarranted interference"; whilst some of the wives—though not all, for others later left him to return home— presented a manifesto expressing satisfaction with their lot. The Mission withdrew, perhaps considering the Fon was too old to change his habits, and pointed out that he was not the only man in Africa to practise polygamy. Calling one Sunday morning on a neighbouring chief with an equal plenitude of wives, and seeing very few of them about, the visitors asked where they had gone. "Most of them are at Mass," their husband said.

◆ 2 ◆

Bananas are the economic mainspring of the Southern Cameroons. They were inherited from the Germans—not only bananas but rubber and palm-oil plantations as well. All these were started before 1914, captured by the British in the First World War and auctioned in London in 1923, when no one put in a bid. A year later, they were sold back to their original German owners, who developed them further, only to lose them again in the Second World War. In 1946, the Nigerian Government bought the plantations from the Custodian of Enemy Property for £850,000 and set up an independent body called the Cameroons Development Corporation to run them "for the use and common benefit of the inhabitants of the territory". The Corporation's directorate consists of a chairman and eight members, three of them Cameroonians, who control four blocks of plantations totalling some 290,000 acres. Ultimately, it is hoped that Cameroonians will direct and staff the whole concern themselves. The concept is idealistic, the management so far efficient. This is due largely to the hard work and business acumen of a Canadian, Mr. F. E. V. Smith, who took over a moribund, disorganized concern with derelict buildings and obsolete or spoiled plant and left, on his recent retirement, a going concern which turned over to the Governor of Nigeria, for the benefit of the Cameroonians, a net profit of over £50,000.

The best way to see the bananas is from a little narrow-gauge railway which runs in and out of the plantations, over gorges, past rubber factories and down to the wharf. Bananas seem endless: untidy trees with (it appears) ragged skirts of brown paper. Cutting goes on continuously. A banana boat is filled and away roughly every five days all the year round. Tornadoes are the worst enemy: two years ago they knocked down 2,500,000 trees in a few hours. The soil here is marvellously fertile and will grow anything that likes a lot of rain. It must, however, like that; on one of the plantations, the annual rainfall is over 400 inches, and twenty-two inches once fell in a single day. Yet, for four or five months, no rain falls at all, and everyone gets short of water. I saw a train hauling water on the miniature railway to an inland estate where the annual rainfall is over 200 inches.

The C.D.C.'s labour force at present consists of about 140 Europeans and 19,000 Africans, mostly Cameroonians from over eighty different tribes. Work starts at seven, and most of the men finish their tasks by eleven o'clock or, at latest, noon, but extra pay very seldom tempts them to extra labour. "Bonus incentives", I was told, "simply do not work." The working of (roughly) a twenty-four-hour week involves the Corporation in a big housing problem, for by law the labour must be housed free of charge; and it is a formidable task to accommodate 19,000 people, many of whom bring their families.

Houses built of "carraboard"—thin, roughly-cut planks which for some strange reason do not seem to get eaten by termites—are giving way, in the new estates, to semi-detached cottages built of concrete blocks, with kitchens and verandas, and little gardens round. (Some of the verandas had already turned into general stores.) Houses for the better-paid workers have baths and lavatories, gay curtains and decent furniture. One of the new housing estates I saw would satisfy any European worker; the big school, with airy, gaily painted classrooms, is a much better building than most of its English fellows; the village green and clock-tower, the scattered trees, the sports ground and pavilion give the whole place a settled, civilized air. Distributed over the various estates are seven hospitals, each in charge of European sisters, providing a bed for every 150 workers, surely one of the most generous ratios in the world. Maternity wards and ante-natal clinics are all the rage; at night adult education classes draw over 4,000 people to sheds converted into community halls. A film unit provides material for six mobile cinemas which tour the smaller labour camps; the football league has over fifty teams. This welfare side, under the direction of Sir Ralph Stoneham, is altogether most impressive, and its officers, never stinted for money, full of enthusiasm.

No doubt there are weak spots hidden from the fleeting visitor, and it could be argued that life is almost too much embellished for these fortunate people who, with very little effort on their part, are presented with amenities for which most have to toil and sacrifice. But here is a community of at least 50,000 men, women and children sucked from their tribal background, most of the men employed for roughly four hours a day; it is only common prudence to provide some occupation for their ample leisure, to feed and stimulate minds already stirred by change. The C.D.C. is carrying out a great experiment with the imagination and boldness made possible by faith and funds; beyond doubt, it is living up to its charge to use its profits for the good of the people of the Cameroons.

One evening, I watched the finals of an inter-tribal dancing competition. Each of the nine successful teams had to give a floodlit performance which must have seemed woefully short—fifteen minutes instead of the usual eight or ten hours. The winning team, daubed with white spots and stars, had horns and tails and undulated wildly to the beating of drums; they represented antelopes of some kind. Others wore masks of crocodiles and buffaloes, or snouts like porcupines. One team had roughly contrived wings on their shoulders and shook all over in brilliant imitation of an insect's quiver; these wore an alarming aspect; they were savage, angry insects, not in the least resembling moths or butterflies. One team danced cleverly on stilts, covered from top to bottom in a long raffia robe. Several of the ballets had battles for their theme. In every dance there lies the aim to threaten and to terrify; *sylphides* have no place in African choreography. But great virtuosity is there, a rough, cruel humour, and above all vigour: and, of course, never far away, a pulsing sexuality. Sooner or later almost every African dance presents an enthusiastic and prolonged representation of the sexual act, often to the embarrassment of European organizers who have paraded notables and their ladies to give the prizes away.

∽ 3 ∽

The coast between Victoria and the mouth of the Cameroon River is deeply indented and full of sparkling, rocky bays with forest running down almost to the water-line. A smartly manned C.D.C. launch took us about four miles along this coast into a small bay within a large bay, enfolded by hills to make a place of calm and shelter. We landed on a jutting spit of rock and climbed to a camp hidden among the trees. This is Man o' War Bay, where British frigates once laid in wait for slavers. One of the most enigmatic experiments in West Africa is now in progress here.

Mr. Alec Dickson, who started it, served with East African troops during the war and afterwards launched the mass-education campaign in the Gold Coast. Both in the army and out of it he saw much of African young men, and brooded upon one deficiency which seemed common to them all—the spirit of adventure. All young men, he argued, instal in their mind's eye heroes, patterns of perfection. In Europe, the hero is nearly always a person of courage, achievement and a certain recklessness: his own life and comfort are to him of less moment than the cause he serves. From Richard Cœur-de-Lion to Captain Scott, from Drake and Nelson to Vian and Hillary, from crusaders to jet-aircraft pilots, it is all the same. But the young African—his happy warrior seems to be the civil servant with a pensionable job, a smart suit and a bicycle, or (more ambitious) the lawyer-politician with a shiny American car, unlimited gin and plenty of women. Probably he would not even wish to repel single-handed an invasion of Treens, to climb Mount Everest or to dive through the sound barrier. Tales of adventure play no part in African children's mythology.

Does this matter? *Chacun à son goût.* But Mr. Dickson thinks it does matter, if these new African nations are to make their mark in the world. He quotes Trevelyan: "Without the instinct for adventure in young men, any civilization, however enlightened, and any state, however well ordered, must wilt and wither". (Or, in this case, never burgeon and bloom?) And then again William Penn: "We are in pain to make them scholars—but not men".

And so he has set himself the formidable task of trying to strike sparks of high-principled adventure from the hearts of African young men. He has to work on a small, a very small, cross-section of Nigerians and he has to make his mark in a month. It may be impossible; but at least he is having a good try.

About sixty young men from all parts of Nigeria and the Cameroons are gathered here. Their average age is twenty-six. They have been selected from each region for qualities of leadership, actual or potential. Among them are schoolmasters, police-men, clerks, sanitary inspectors, traders, blacksmiths, dispensers—men of all kinds; the common denominator is that they are literate and up-and-coming. They are samples of the young nationalists who will soon be ruling and running Nigeria. Their characters and outlooks are therefore momentous to the future, for each individual will, in his own corner, help to shape the mind of his generation.

In pursuit of the spirit of adventure, these young men go out to sea in small boats, they learn to swim, they help to load banana boats, they clamber up the Cameroon Mountain. (It has been climbed—there and back—from Buea in under seven-and-a-half hours by Mr. Mick Walters.) These feats at first seem to many of the young men pointless and unpleasant. Members of the first course were most reluctant to scale the mountain, having been assured by local Bakweri students that the top was white with human bones.[1] Sickness was often invoked, or invented, to escape these outdoor excursions; many arrived with a full supply of patent medicines and strengthening foods; the phrase "I suffer" was, it seems, constantly on the lips of the students and could alternatively be rendered as "I have had to work". In spite of all this, a few seeds did fall on fertile ground. A schoolmaster who had been delighted and amazed to find that it really did get colder the higher you went, added that he had discovered something even more surprising: that will can triumph over bodily weakness, "for I made up my mind that, small as I was, I would be the first to reach the top—and first I was".

An equally important aim is to teach these young men the virtues and methods of community development. That is the official name for self-help. If a village wants a clinic, a road, a school, a bridge, a water scheme, the answer is—community development. Build it with voluntary labour and with materials found by the District Officer. But someone has to organize the voluntary labour and make it feel a pride in the job; and this is the object of the Man o' War Bay training. In camp, the students are taught how to make simple, useful things like incinerators, how to render first aid, even how to telephone clearly. Their camp uniform is a pair of shorts and plimsolls, and nothing else. Sometimes the dressier clerks object to abandoning their collars and ties, but to do so is compulsory. (Muslims are allowed to put their robes on to pray.) Sweat and blisters are the badges of this course, and although the students may learn to tolerate them, it is unlikely that they come to feel for them any enthusiasm. Next day I saw them driving in a fleet of lorries to a district near Enugu in Nigeria where they will be welcomed as bridge-builders and road-makers, the local Cameroonians having re-

[1] Unfortunately, since my visit two students have died on the mountain during the climb.

sisted stubbornly all further designs to have their lot improved by voluntary effort.

I left Man o' War Bay with a great respect for the effort being made, using few tools beyond faith and energy, to change the leopard's spots. If faith can move mountains, perhaps it can change characters; it is at least heroic to try. But in four weeks! Yet the students cannot be spared for longer, since they all hold jobs.

"We'd make ourselves ridiculous if we claimed to train character in a month," Alec Dickson said. "But what I think we can do is to create a greater awareness in a man's mind—awareness of himself, of his country and of his chances to help it forward. We regard this brief, intensive treatment as a kind of shock therapy that can jerk people out of their complacent rut and give them a new outlook which, perhaps, they may never altogether lose. But the course must be *practical*." And it must, he could have added, find the right instructors. Several District Officers and others have given up their local leave for this purpose, and young men have been lent from the Outward Bound course in Britain; but to get the staff is not easy.

A regatta was in progress when I departed, and victory in the swimming race had just gone to a village head from Katsina who had never seen the sea until a fortnight before. It is refreshing to spend a day with idealists who know what they work for and love what they know. And if one day a young Nigerian sets out to climb Mount Everest or paddle up the Amazon, it will perhaps be Mr. Dickson who has set him on the path.

I think it is a big "if", however.

Next day I flew to Calabar from Tiko, back over the bananas and ravines, over the maze of creeks and dark green mangrove swamps of the estuary of the Rio del Rey, and finally over the wide streak of the curling River Calabar. Among my fellow-passengers was Dr. Emmanuel Endeley, leader of the Cameroon contingent in the Eastern House of Assembly and also a Minister without Portfolio in the Central Government in Lagos. A tall, lanky, spectacled, gentle-mannered man, still only thirty-five years of age, whose hobby is book-binding, he holds a diploma in medicine from Yaba Higher College (a forerunner of Ibadan) in Nigeria, and is descended from the chiefs of the Bakweri tribe, whose grievances over land—the C.D.C.'s bananas grow on some of it—first brought him into politics. He helped to organize a trade union among the C.D.C.'s workers and is now one of the Corporation's directors. He and his twelve followers in the Eastern House of Assembly are affiliated to N.C.N.C., a partnership that must at times grow irksome, for the Ibos, as their numbers increase, are regarded with less and less enthusiasm in the Cameroons.

The Dove came down at Calabar, and I stepped out into the queerest and (I think) most fascinating part of Nigeria, a country that is half water and half land, of all regions the most modern and the most ancient, the most altered and the most unchanged.

The East

∞ I ∞

The great days of Calabar were in the last half of the nineteenth century, when it was a centre of the palm-oil trade, and native "kings" in fancy dress (footman's gold-laced cockaded hats and dancers' pink tights included) did business with "palm-oil ruffians" quartered in their hulks on the river. Between 1884, when these "kings" asked to be taken under the Queen's protection, and 1906, Calabar was the headquarters of the Oil Rivers Protectorate. (The first Commissioner took up his residence here in 1891.) Now it is a mere provincial capital, and Port Harcourt, at the end of a railway, is the growing-point of trade and progress.

Calabar town is strung out along the left bank of the Calabar River, just before it enters the estuary of the greater Cross. The oldest part is Duke Town, and the school, opened in 1846, was the first in Nigeria. It was started by Presbyterian missionaries, and today has 1,500 pupils in buildings that now look very antiquated. The Presbyterians here in Calabar, and the Church Missionary Society in Abeokuta, were the pioneers of missionary endeavour in Nigeria.

Duke Town looks sleepy, steamy and squalid. We are back among the Negroes' mud and palm-thatch houses huddled along unpaved streets. The inhabitants are mainly Efiks, who retreated here from wars with fiercer neighbours farther north and founded settlements at Creek Town and Duke Town. (As is so often the case in Africa, they arrived in their present country after the Europeans, who were trading here in the sixteenth century.) They became the great slave-dealers of the region and grew rich and proud, but their power waned with the end of slavery.

I called one afternoon upon the Obong, the Efik chief. Local self-government has come to Calabar as to other places, and the Obong decided to have a coronation as a counter-blast. He ordered an exact copy of the King of England's coronation robe, which came out by air, and a resplendent ceremony was held. He wore the purple when I met him: a lush velvet robe, set off by a fan made from the wing of a vulture. A very old man, old and decrepit. He responded to every conversation-opening gambit in the best civil service manner: "I will consult my elders and give you a reply later on". Round him sat a mumble of equally decrepit old men, listless and bleary-eyed as worn-out cab-horses, belonging so clearly to a past age. There will be no place for the Obong in the new machinery of local government, with elections from wards to an Urban District Council, and finally a County Council at the top. Nor does it appear that there is widespread enthusiasm among the citizens. Of (roughly) 16,000 qualified to vote, 200 have registered, and these only because they came to see the District Officer on other business and were obliged to do so on the way out.

Efik society is divided into a number of "houses", as it were like Montagus and Capulets. In the days of slavery, each "house" was headed by a powerful slave-dealer, and its members were the men who manned his war-canoe. Later, the "houses" took to trade, and each head wore a large brass plate on his chest. The "houses" grew into close-knit groups whose dwellings clustered together, and their heads, who were chosen by the members, ruled the river. Even the British consul, in those days a man of great prestige (Sir Roger Casement was one), needed their permission before he could travel up the river. The names of these old "houses"—Pepple, Yellow, Duke —are famous in the district, and "houses" are still the basis of society. There are some pleasing names, in the old records, of house chiefs—for example, John West India, Quaker Bob and Reuben Standfast Jack.

On a hill above the town, overlooking the silver-misted river, stands one of the best-known schools in Nigeria, the Hope Waddell College of the Church of Scotland Mission, where boys are put through a rigorous course designed to train character and make good citizens, not merely clever ones—a much more difficult feat. Some of the best-known citizens of Nigeria learnt their early lessons at this austere but well-equipped academy: among them Sir Francis Ibiam, a most successful doctor, politician, Governor of the school and Elder of the Church of Scotland; Mr. Njoku, a lecturer in botany and now Central Minister for Mines and Power; and Professor Eyo Ita, perhaps the most highly respected of any participant in Eastern public life.

An Efik, just fifty years of age, the Professor, as he is known to all—though his Chair is complimentary—attended Tuskegee and Hampton Colleges in the United States, and Columbia and London Universities, and is a Master of Science. He founded a secondary school in Calabar, the West African People's Institute, where he tries to build character as well as brains and to teach skill as well as theory. Professor Ita was not in Calabar at the time of my visit, and I was sorry to miss a man whose outlook appears to contrast so sharply with that of his political colleagues. For he seems quite free from personal ambition and from avarice, and to follow Gandhi's teachings of non-violence and simple living. (He is a Christian, and an adherent of Moral Rearmament.) I asked a European friend of his how a man so idealistic and undemagogic could have won such popular esteem.

"I've asked that question of a number of Nigerians," he replied, "and they can't explain it. Partly it may be that most of the nationalists are young men, and Ita has the standing of an elder—the sage counsellor—without being out-of-date, for he's one of the very few among his generation with a university degree. And then, he's very much a man of the people—a man of simple habits and simple faith, a dreamer of dreams. He's never bothered about material things like smart clothes and cars and houses, and this is so unusual—I think unique—that it commands an awed respect.

"He's never set out to be a 'leader', and the Ibo (unlike the Efik) distrust 'big men'. He never talks down to the people, as some politicians do. He's certainly no orator, but when he speaks it is always from deep conviction. He never tries—or very rarely—to score debating points off his opponents. He says what is in his mind and sits down: but I noticed in the last meeting of the House (which was a noisy one) that, although he was the target for much abuse, when he got up to speak, everyone listened in rapt silence."

Professor Ita is now the Minister for Natural Resources in the Regional Government in Enugu. He dreams of introducing communal farming into the Region, and is a strong supporter of research and experiment.

The Church of Scotland Mission maintains outposts for 250 miles up the Cross River, but has great difficulty in manning them. Because of the low pay, African recruits to the Ministry are sadly few, and a Mission that, after a century of hard work, cannot staff itself with local Christians has reason for disappointment. The posts up-river are, besides, too lonely and alarming for most educated men. Mrs. Cuthbert Mayne, the Resident's wife, told me that the people of a village in the bush had crowded round her in great excitement, a year or two ago, because they had never seen a white woman before. This was within seventy miles of Calabar, where Europeans have traded and preached for five centuries. And District Officers who occasionally penetrate to remote villages on bicycles are often addressed as "Father", since Roman Catholic priests are the only white men whom the people have seen.

Some say that young girls are still captured up the Cross River and smuggled by canoe to Fernando Po, and thence to the Gold Coast, where they are in demand as prostitutes—a lucrative occupation. "When they come back", a European was told, "they have as many loads as a District Officer". So perhaps it becomes a voluntary form of slavery. There is a market near Afikpo, in Ibo-land (Uburu by name), where men have been seen to sell sticks of different lengths for large sums. There is no law against that, of course. On the assumption that Ibos would

not pay good money for common sticks, some believe each stick
to represent a girl of a different height, who lies concealed in a
hut and ready to be smuggled down-river on a dark night in the
bottom of a canoe.

❧ 2 ❧

The Residency is one of the few European buildings of character in Nigeria: spacious, solid and Victorian, it was brought
from England beam by beam. The Provincial office occupies
the ground floor, and in it some fascinating records await the
historian. Here, for instance, are the court books of Mary
Slessor, that remarkable Scotswoman whose bones lie in Calabar
cemetery. Her mission was to save the lives of twins who, until
her coming, were killed by being stuffed head-first into pots and
abandoned, while the mother was often driven into the bush to
die. Mary Slessor travelled hot-foot to any village where the
birth of twins was rumoured and managed to rescue a great
many, whom she brought up in a village called Itu, where she
lived for many years, and whose women still venerate her
memory by clearing the grass, every year, on the site of her
house. She worked in Nigeria for thirty-nine years, became an
unofficial but highly respected magistrate and died, truly loved
by thousands of Africans, in 1915.

You reach the Residency's living quarters, now occupied by
Mr. Cuthbert Mayne, by climbing up an outside wooden staircase, like a grandiose fire-escape, to enter a lofty, pillared room
full of dark wood and massive furniture. Everything has been
designed to defy the termites for eternity. A heavy oak sideboard is adorned with ornate silver candelabra and fruit dishes,
and the initials "V.R." are carved on the backs of the wide oak
chairs. Martial prints decorate the walls; in my bedroom heroes
weighed down by helmets and moustaches fought the battle of
Laing's Nek over the title "Floreat Etona". There is something
deeply touching about these relics of a vanished splendour and
self-confidence, whose price was the graves of young men which
lie so thickly in the cemetery. The captains and the kings depart
—the Sanders and the Standfast Jacks—leaving these massive

English houses, as English as plum-pudding and as untropical, to moulder and decay, as they are doing at Bonny, one of the old palm-oil ports down the creeks, and now a sort of ghost town.

The two-storey houses built there by European traders are flaking and crumbling away, and filled with the down-at-heel descendants of old house-chiefs. The last white trader left in 1921. The bones of his many forerunners lie in the neglected cemetery. Eight were buried there in one week—a yellow-fever epidemic, probably. Funerals in Calabar at one time averaged two or three weekly.

All these Oil River ports—Calabar, Bonny, Opobo, Brass— are full of ghosts and history. To this day, the language of the palm-oil trade is nautical: young men ensconced in modern offices talk of the day's heave ("I hove-to ten puncheons this morning"), reckon cloth in fathoms and time in ships' bells. To-day they are governed by Marketing Boards, yesterday by "Courts of Equity" which settled arguments and levied fines: mixed courts, for merchants could be African or European. Often the chiefs, with their "houses" and big war canoes behind them, were very high-handed. In 1885 a Mr. Townsend complained that unruly crowds were invading his beach at all hours, and the Court fined him two puncheons of palm oil "for being proud". (He got them back later, however.)

In those days the traders' painted hulks were moored to now rotting jetties, and the "palm-oil ruffians"—stout, disreputable and short-lived—spent their gin-soaked lives heaving-to puncheons of oil brought down the creeks in canoes by native traders. On Sundays, they were rowed in gigs from Bonny to Opobo town for a meal with McPepple Jaja, son of the famous King Jaja who, starting as a slave-boy bought in an Ibo market, established himself at Opobo as a rich and powerful chief, was awarded a sword of honour by Queen Victoria for sending fifty warriors to fight in the Ashanti Wars, and fell from grace when he raided a tribe up the creeks in war canoes flying the blue ensign and butchered over a hundred prisoners on his return. Growing ever prouder, he tried to prevent British merchants from trading with people up-river, started to ship palm oil to England himself and even seized the mails of English merchants; until at last, growing weary of his tactics, the Consul inveigled him on board a naval vessel and took him to Accra for trial, whence he was deported to the West Indies.

Sunday dinner with his son McPepple was a protracted business. It started with two or three chilli-flavoured soups, each hotter than the last, went on to curried fish full of bite and continued with huge platters of curried chicken; meanwhile trade gin was served as liberally from jugs as if it had been water. At the end of the day, McPepple Jaja presented to each of his guests a fathom of cloth and they were rowed back, comatose, to their hulks. No wonder the life of palm-oil ruffians was short. If they lived they made quick fortunes, but spent them even more quickly.

One of the last of the breed was a German called Hartze, who came to Calabar in the 'fifties. He would trade there for two years and then buy a return ticket to London, engage an entire private hotel in Lancaster Gate, with a full staff and bar, and entertain all his friends on champagne and the best food money could buy. After three months or so he would one day announce: "The money's finished; the party's over; we must go." Back he would sail to Calabar, and there he would rebuild his fortune. He survived this life year after year until the age of palm-oil ruffians faded and the age of big combines came. The United Africa Company took him on as a manager. When he reached the age of seventy-eight, the Company told him that he must retire. He refused, but they insisted, and, on the day his ship was due to sail, he was found with his throat cut from ear to ear. He survived even that. As he was stitched up, he told the doctors that they were wasting their time. The Company's manager took him out to catch the next liner, and on the way he jumped into the river and was drowned.

Some of the best and some of the worst men that England could breed lived and died up these fever-soaked creeks: missionaries who worked selflessly and in face of constant sickness all their lives to alleviate suffering, and men who with equal fervour enjoyed inflicting it, like the captain of a brig who whitewashed his men from head to foot while they were ill with fever, so blinding his cook. No wonder that many local chiefs coveted the white men's goods but despised their purveyors, and used their own powers no less tyrannically. When two Liverpool seamen, rolling a cask of water from the beach, accidentally killed a monitor lizard—a reptile sacred to the Bonny people—the "king" sentenced them to death, but accepted a bribe from their captain to commute the penalty to a heavy fine, in whose default the men would be sold into slavery. As the captain could not raise so large a sum, he sailed without the men, who presumably died as slaves, perhaps as victims of sacrifice. Monitor lizards continued to be held in great esteem until the missionaries, in 1884, persuaded their converts in Bonny to celebrate Easter by a massacre of the sacred reptiles.

❧ 3 ❧

Ever since the start of the British connection, Nigeria has been strictly preserved for peasants and all concessions, leases and plantations excluded.[1] This has enabled the British political end —the quick realization of African self-government—to be pursued, but at the expense of economic growth, peasants being greatly inferior, as producers, to plantation owners. Since the war, a new idea has been injected—hitherto in very small doses —into this somewhat stagnant situation. This is to have plantations run not by private enterprise but by the Government, acting through the Eastern Regional Production Board, and drawing capital from profits made by the Palm Oil Marketing Board.

The first of these new plantations has been started about thirty miles from Calabar. To reach it, we proceeded slowly across several ferries and observed with respect the enormous loads borne by English bicycles: one man had a case of beer and two full-sized wooden doors on his carrier, and a lamp-glass slung over his shoulder. Villages scooped from forest lined the road. A house in one of them was all be-flagged; outside its veranda stood a large kitchen chair canopied with cloths, shirts and underwear. All alone on the cushioned seat reposed a white topee. A man had died, some English-speaking children said: a big man who had come from Calabar, and his relatives would mourn him

---

[1] Or very nearly all: the United Africa Company leases a 6,500-acre plantation near Calabar where it produces palm oil by up-to-date methods. The Government allowed this mainly as an object-lesson in how production can be greatly increased by plantation methods.

—but gaily, it appeared—for a week. Almost every house has a large white headstone or two just outside the front door; underneath lie dead relations; even in death, families are not divided.

We came to the plantation on a spur of some low hills near the Cameroons border, and found the manager presiding over a handmill that squeezed orange-coloured oil from the reddish fruit. Throughout Nigeria, the peasant harvests his oil either by treading the fruit under his feet, which extracts only 55 per cent of it, or by using these wooden hand-presses, which raise the extraction rate to 65 per cent. The Government's Pioneer Mills extract about 85 per cent of the oil. Thus merely by expressing the oil more efficiently, production could be almost doubled without harvesting a single extra nut. It seems astonishing that, in over a century, nothing effective has been done, until the last two or three years, to reduce this great wastage of rich and valuable merchandise. Now the Eastern Regional Production Board has set up fifty Pioneer Mills, but, even so, this is only a beginning.

Drums of oil were bubbling away outside the shed over open fires. This is another easy way in which the oil's value can be enhanced: merely boiling it removes much of the free fatty acid, which, it seems, is deleterious to the quality. Yet very few peasant producers trouble to perform this simple act, perhaps because money can be made so easily. A four-gallon kerosene tin of palm oil used to fetch fourpence; it is now worth eighteen shillings or more. Everywhere you see cyclists with four, six, or even eight of these four-gallon containers roped to the carrier. Each must weigh at least fifty pounds. Nigerian bicycles have hard lives.

About 3,000 acres of thick bush and forest are being cleared by hand (hard, expensive work) on this plantation, and palms, taken from a nursery of 30,000 seedlings, planted out in rows at properly spaced intervals. These seedlings have been scientifically bred to yield four or five times as much oil per tree as the wild plant. Were all the wild trees to be replaced by these improved ones, think what it would mean to West Africa! But all peasants are conservative. Although at various centres pedigree seedlings are pressed upon them free of charge, very few bother to plant them. There are plenty of oil palms in the bush.

The "bush" here is forest which looks quite impenetrable, but is in fact full of secret paths and hidden villages. Somewhere in its recesses, engineers making a new highway to link Calabar with the rest of the Eastern Region (at present it can be reached only by ferry) came upon traces of an old road whose existence no one had suspected: a ghost road, quite overgrown, but recognizable by broken culverts, the rotted piles of bridges and buried milestones. Obviously it had been made by Europeans, but where it led, when it was built and by whom, was all a mystery.

A search through the records in Calabar at last revealed a solution. This was part of a military road built in 1901–2 during a campaign to suppress the so-called "Long Ju-Ju" of Aro-Chuku, which was terrorizing much of southern Nigeria and claiming thousands of human victims.

The Aro people were, and are, members of the Ibo-speaking group, but in other ways a race apart, having, it is commonly said, more intelligence and powers of organization than the majority of Ibo and being lighter in colour. Their "Long Ju-Ju" was an oracle with its temple and "priests", hidden deep in the forest. All disputes in the district were referred to it for judgment. Both parties were compelled to propitiate it with gifts, especially of slaves; the loser not only forfeited all his property but was generally seized by the "priests" and himself sold into slavery. Most of the slaves were sold to relatives of dead chiefs, for sacrifice at funerals. The "priests" formed a caste apart, grew exceedingly rich and dominated the surrounding Ibo.

A military expedition sent up the Cross River from Calabar at the end of 1901 found and destroyed the "Long Ju-Ju" temple and some of its insignia. The Aro continued for many years to set up smaller fetish-temples in the bush, some of which were subsequently hunted out and destroyed,[1] but they were never able to re-establish their reign of terror. In Calabar there are rumours that a small-scale successor to the "Long Ju-Ju" has been started up again near Aro-Chuku. This seems less incredible than it may sound after one has seen the dense forest, the

---

[1] A racy account of one such episode is contained in the entertaining sketch-book of an early District Officer's life, *Ju-ju and Justice in Nigeria*, by Frank Hives.

gorges, the narrow winding paths that lead to villages invisible ten yards away, the isolation and secretiveness of this creek-incised country.

Adjoining the Eastern Regional Production Board's plantation is a project whose future seems less bright. This is the Bamenda–Cameroons–Cross River scheme, financed by the Colonial Development and Welfare Fund and intended to re-settle a few of the Ibo from Owerri, west of Calabar, where overcrowding on exhausted land is so acute that in places the population rises to over 1,200 to the square mile. The intention was to give each settler thirty acres, of which ten would be planted for him in improved oil palms, and a free £60 grant, and to provide him with all the trappings of a miniature welfare state. At first very few settlers could be attracted, and those who came quickly took to trading instead of farming. They did so well that a town of several thousand people has sprawled into existence, with its life in the market rather than in the social centre. The model plantations are so neglected that the management has had to take them over, and has at present less than sixty settlers on the land.

•◇• 4 •◇•

From Calabar, a ferry steamer traverses the wide estuary of the Cross River to a small town on the opposite bank called Oron. The mangroves, their roots half out of water, display small huts for fishermen in their branches, and canoes are drawn up alongside in the mud.

The boat was crowded with well-dressed passengers. Tea and buns were served from a kiosk on deck. There was a parson setting out on his parochial rounds—the jolly, beaming type; a policeman going home on leave; several clerks; all fluent in English, all friendly. What did I think of Calabar? Whom did I represent? (Practically no one comes to Nigeria just to look at it; you are credited with some official intent.) Had I met their cousin Mr. So-and-so in London? They are for the most part agreeable and good-mannered, these men of the new middle class. They sat and sipped their tea, reading newspapers that spluttered with polemics, and at their destination rode off on bicycles.

On the road to Ikot Ekpene we passed many shrines, the richest having a coloured statue of the deceased on a pedestal. One had an old patchwork cover erected behind it like a screen, on which was hung the oddest collection of fetishes: a skull, some jawbones and other human fragments, strips of hide, calabashes, buckles, bits of old sacking. A tablet recorded the dignity of the deceased—a head clerk in Calabar. Farther on, at a village near Ikot Ekpene, a man led us along a forest path to a screen of matting, about eight feet high, to which clung many feathers. In front stretched a row of little matting shelters, or miniature igloos, open at one end and hung with a collection of charms which included the battered chain-guard off an old cycle. This, said our guide, was a shrine of the Egbo, one of those secret societies to which the Ibibio tribe, into whose country we had now entered, are especially partial.

Why, then, I wondered, did the guide bring a stranger, a European, to this forest shrine? The Egbo Society had been banned, he said, so no one came here any more to feast and sacrifice. Yet the shrine did not look deserted; offerings had been freshly brought to the igloos, the path and floor of the clearing were well pounded. Perhaps this was merely an outer gate to a shrine that lay deeper in the forest.

Perhaps it is imagination that invests these dark, silent forests with an eerie, sinister quality—that, and the knowledge that the Ibibio people who inhabit it were, at least until a few years ago, followers of the leopard cult. Early in 1945 the District Officer at Abak, some twenty miles south, grew suspicious about the number of people in his district being killed by leopards. And not only at the number: all the bodies were mutilated in much the same way. Nearly all the victims were women or children killed between five and seven in the evening as they returned from the farms. Leopards, of course, lived in the forest, and sometimes attacked humans; but leopard societies existed too,[1]

[1] A. G. Leonard, writing in 1906, states that leopard men have a system of calls by which they can communicate with each other (*The Lower Niger and its Tribes*); P. Amaury Talbot illustrates a chief's shrine into which he retired when about to change himself into a leopard; should anything happen to the beast temporarily occupied by his spirit, he himself would suffer or die (*Tribes of the Niger Delta*, 1930). During the recent outbreak, a man who brought an injured hand to a dispensary for treatment identified himself with a leopard which had torn its way out of a trap, leaving behind part of its paw.

together with a widespread general belief in lycanthropy, the power of men to become leopards at will.

By the end of 1945, 150 deaths were under investigation. In many cases—not all—leopards' pad-marks were found near the bodies and claw-marks on the flesh. Were these real or false? Some of the pad-marks were clumsy and ill-spaced, and the police discovered bamboo canes concealing sharp steel spikes which they believed were used to smite the victim in the top vertebræ of the neck.

Proof is a hard thing to get from people who draw no line between the actual and the probable, between objective and subjective truth. It is known that men change themselves into leopards; it is known that the headman Odisi has bought medicine to do so; it is known that just outside Odisi's village a woman was killed. People coming back at nightfall saw a dark shape moving in the undergrowth. Was she killed by a leopard? Yes, it was a leopard that we saw. Or was she killed by a man? Yes, by Odisi, who had got medicine from the witch-doctor, and had a padlock and key to lock up the victim's voice. She was killed by Odisi and by a leopard; they were one. Jesting Pilate would have had to wait a long time for his answer in the forests of Abak.

The most suspicious fact of all was that flesh was nearly always scraped from the arm—generally the left arm—and head of the victim, and it was the evidence of pathologists to the effect that these scrapings were done by knives and not by teeth or claws that did more than anything to hang some of the suspected murderers. In one case the head was found some way from the body, wrapped in a cloth; a hard feat, that, for any real leopard.

By the end of 1946, 157 probable murders had been investigated, thirty-nine people had been convicted—mostly on their own confessions—and eighteen had been hanged.

By now, the police had traced the instigation of these murders to a secret society called the Idiong. This, like many similar societies, while mainly magical, had also become a league of local barons who used it to terrorize the community and enrich themselves. The "Long Ju-Ju" of Aro-Chuku had been the mouthpiece of the Idiong society among the Aro tribe.

Idiong shrines existed in many villages, and in the past they had been fed at intervals with human blood. With the white man's coming these rites had lapsed; but they had been revived, in the words of an official report, "when it was found that justice could be obtained neither in the Native Courts, which were corrupt, nor in the white man's court, which often acquitted on technical points of law persons who were generally known to be guilty". People went for redress, therefore, to the Idiong society, which, regaining many of its old powers, revived the practice of feeding its ju-ju with blood, and probably the practice, also, of eating parts of the victims. Members of the Idiong society, it was thought, did not actually carry out the murders. They were diviners, who named the time and place and "called" the victim to the spot.

And so, early in 1947, a greatly enlarged "leopard force" of police raided over 1,000 Idiong shrines. The regalia was carried away and publicly burnt. According to the police, there was much rejoicing among the people, who lived in terror of the society; but, disappointingly, the murders continued much as before.

Then the Ibibio Union entered the scene. This was a society of mainly educated men, clerks and the like; and its secretary, Mr. Usen, the district clerk at Abak, bravely came out into the open against the leopard men. A delegation from the Union toured the district, swearing the people on a powerful but beneficent ju-ju that they would take no part in any future leopard crimes. When a suspected leopard man who took the oath died almost immediately afterwards, the campaign gathered such prestige that no murders occurred for four months. But then, early in 1948, they broke out again.

By now the district was thickly policed, and many arrests followed. At the same time, a determined effort to trap real leopards led to the destruction of about twenty beasts. The Idiong society was in abeyance, and informers against suspected leopard men were taking heart. Whether because of one or all of these factors, or for some other reason, the leopard murders petered out. The final count was: 196 proved or strongly suspected leopard murders; ninety-six persons convicted, of whom seventy-seven were hanged; 106 acquitted; died in custody,

K

two. In addition, there were many other deaths which genuine leopards could have caused.

There have been no more leopard murders since 1948. That old customs die hard, however, is proved by the recent outbreak of trials by ordeal with the poisonous *esere* bean, one of the oldest and most widely practised ordeals in Southern Nigeria. In 1951, eight men were tried in Calabar for administering an *esere* bean ordeal to a number of people who were suspected of murdering an enemy by sorcery. (The enemy was a member of the Apostolic Church at Okesi, and died of pneumonia.) It is believed that innocent men who swallow the *esere* concoction vomit but that the guilty perish in agony.[1] In this case, five people perished. In another, a man dying of smallpox accused several people of killing him by sorcery, and they were put to the test. One, who did not vomit but managed to survive the poison, had his eyes put out with red-hot irons.

◇ 5 ◇

The year 1951 saw not only an outbreak of *esere* bean ordeals, however, but also the setting up of the Ikot Ekpene County Council—the first in Nigeria. (Elected County Councils are to replace Native Authorities, which have been the rule since 1933.) To prepare the way, District Officers toured the region extolling the virtues of local government and democracy. The people's first reactions were naturally cautious. "A man would be afraid to vote openly for a rogue, but he could be bribed to do so in secret." "When a man is alone in a room, he will forget what he has to do." "Is this because the people want it, or because the Government wants it?" "The people may talk about spending money, but the District Officer must keep the key of the safe." And—"Does this mean that we can treat our prisoners as we used to?" (A favourite method, when they were not needed for funeral sacrifices, was to smear them with honey and peg them to an ant-heap.) "Perhaps the utter lack of financial

[1] *Esere* beans (seeds of a leguminous creeper *Physostigma venenosum*) contain several poisonous alkaloids of which one, *physostigmine*, is used pharmaceutically in drugs affecting the eye. When swallowed, it reacts violently upon the muscles and causes acute vomiting followed by death due to dilation of the heart and suffocation.

honesty and responsibility is the most dangerous rock ahead,"
observed an outspoken official report. "Among the mass of the
people, there is an innate apathy to progress, a selfish indivi-
dualism, a complete lack of decent public opinion and an acquiescence in an age-old system of corruption. Among the
leaders the weaknesses are inexperience, self-interest, dishonesty,
an absence of public spirit, no sense of responsibility and a fear of
accepting it in case it should cause unpopularity. With material
such as this, local government can at best be an experiment with
many years of trial and error ahead."

A gloomy view! Was the writer, perhaps, due for leave? Depressed by the dank forest? A natural pessimist? After the
County Council got into its stride, observers grew much more
hopeful. A budget totalling £42,000 was drawn up with a real
sense of responsibility, committees were set up (and met) and
the District Officer asked to attend them and the Councillors
seemed genuinely anxious to do their job conscientiously and
well. Authorities in Calabar take a robust view of the future of
the Ikot Ekpene County Council in the land of ex-leopard men
and *esere* bean administrators, and everyone wishes it well.

∾ 6 ∾

Few places in the world can offer greater contrasts than Port
Harcourt, the terminus of a railway that leads via the Enugu
coalfields to Kano and beyond, almost to the borders of the
French Sudan. It is a European creation; a busy, expanding
commercial town, visited by the smaller ships of many nations,
full of traders making and spending money.

I was taken for a drive along Millionaire's Row. (Its proper
name is Bernard Carr Street.) One of its richest householders is
Mrs. Mary Nzimero, the United Africa Company's biggest cus-
tomer. Starting as an ordinary market mammy, through buying
palm oil and selling merchandise she has become one of the
wealthiest people in West Africa and, on her occasional visits to
London, is dined and wined at the Savoy by the directors of the
Company. One of her neighbours is a relative, Mr. Chukudifu
Nwapa, a graduate of Fourah Bay College in Sierra Leone and
Selwyn College, Cambridge; a young barrister whose family

owns a big palm-oil business, and who is now the Minister for Commerce and Industries in the central Government.

The houses of Millionaire's Row are three or four storeys high, flat-roofed, and built of concrete blocks in modern style. Balconies with rounded corners give the buildings a look of big white battleships, anchored so close together that the crew could almost shake hands from bridge to bridge. Each house is full of servants, and the scene of many banquets on family occasions; however rich a man is, his family remains his axis; there is not much entertaining for the world at large. There are no gardens. I was sorry that Mrs. Nzimero was away trading, so that I had no chance to meet her; the house was let to a Syrian. What she makes, she is allowed to keep, for women in Eastern Nigeria are fortunate enough to be exempted from direct taxation.

"Port Harcourt has the biggest graft in the world," claimed a young District Officer, taking from his pocket a letter he had just received. The writer wanted to be interviewed for the police and offered him £20 plus ten shillings to arrange it—the ten shillings being a premium, he pointed out, over the standard rate. This was for an interview only, with no place guaranteed. Once in, a constable would very soon recoup his expenses. At the city boundary, for instance, all lorries are stopped to see whether they are carrying more than the permitted number of passengers. All lorries are, and the passengers pay so much a head to the police in pass-money. Last month over £1,000 worth of goods were stolen from a warehouse—by the police. An easy-going Town Council refuses to prosecute any of the numerous people who defraud and swindle it. After some pressure from the Resident, the Council reluctantly imposed a fine of ten shillings on a man proved guilty of making off with the materials ordered for the roof of a new school.

◇ 7 ◇

Most of the administration of the delta is done by launch and canoe. There must be almost more water here than dry land, and the fishermen seem amphibious, living all day in canoes and sleeping in little huts in the foliage of mangroves. There are strips of dry land between creeks, however, where permanent villages are built.

There are two local tribes which maintain an ancient enmity: the Okrika and the Kalabari. Their feud has the nature of an epic, so long has it flourished; and the latest outbreak occurred only in 1950. The Kalabaris were established here before the Okrikans, and claim rent for huts built by Okrikan fishermen in the mangroves. This the Okrikans, not for the first time, refused to pay; so, gathering together their war canoes fitted with cannon, the Kalabaris descended on the fishing fleet of the Okrikans. The engagement was sharp and deadly; when the count was taken, 120 Okrikans were missing. Most of the bodies were never found, because the Kalabaris slashed their stomachs open to prevent them rising; but in markets up the creeks the meat-vendors, it was said, did a big trade for several days afterwards. (There is a local law in these parts obliging butchers to sell meat with the hide still on, the better to identify its origin.)

How can British law deal with a case of this kind? A whole Kalabari town was guilty of the massacre; it was impracticable to hang all its males. British law fell back on the expedient of collective punishment, and fixed a fine of £20,000, a sum intended to crush the tribesmen utterly; many people, in fact, thought it impossibly heavy. The Kalabaris called for subscriptions, mainly from rich traders and from "sons abroad", and in a very short while collected £38,000. The Government then distributed £12,000 of it among the Okrikans in cash compensation at the rate of £85 per lost relative. Seldom had Okrika known such a flush of prosperity.

The pride of Okrika is a huge stone church, a really splendid edifice, designed by an architect brought out specially from England and built at a cost of £20,000, every penny locally raised. Nearly all Okrikans are by now nominally Christian, and on Sunday morning present a very gay appearance, with everyone dressed to kill, and, on special occasions, upwards of a thousand people crowding into the church. The heads of houses bring out their frock coats and dress shirts, whose tails are worn outside the trousers, with two tabs in front, fastening on to the waistband, made to prevent the starched front popping out. In the church-yard is a statue of one of Okrika's notables, Chief Daniel Kalio, wearing just such a costume, complete with tabs. The morals of the Okrikans lag somewhat behind their outward manifestations of Christian fervour. Polygamy is rife, the local bride-price fixed at £40 and young girls are said to have been purchased up-river for £5 each. The Bishop has threatened to close the church altogether if morals do not improve.

Somewhere near the church was the site of a great Okrikan ju-ju with the odd name Fene-Be-So. Once a year, at the time of the yam harvest, a youth without blemish, and light in colour, was caught and impaled in the bush, and Fene-Be-So came in the shape of a leopard to devour the sacrifice; after that, a feast was held and the new yams could be eaten. A great many sacrifices were offered up to this spirit and their bodies consumed by the Okrikans. In fact the ju-ju house seems to have been run almost as a restaurant. The pastor of Opobo observed: "In this house there was always a supply of human flesh. At almost any time, when passing by, you could look in and see old men pounding the meat. All prisoners taken in war were eaten there, bones and all." [1]

In 1915 a bonfire was made of all the ju-ju objects in the town. Only one escaped, a carved wooden figure of the Fene-Be-So, which floated down the creek, was rescued, and ended up in the British Museum. So now Fene-Be-So has vanished from Okrika; but perhaps, in these crowded, narrow streets, his spirit lingers on, with that of his colleagues: Chi the Creator, a female (if you come to think of it, more logical than the Græco-Semitic male), Ale the earth-goddess and her brother the thunder-god, to whom drums were beaten at the time of storms. Traces can still be seen of the two emblems of fertility—a tortoise for the female, a serpent for the male—in carvings on houses and old stools; and Talbot found a representation on a war-drum of the Cretan double-headed axe, the *labrys*, far indeed from its home in Minos.[2]

---

[1] Quoted in Talbot's *Tribes of the Niger Delta*, p. 87.

[2] "A considerable number of examples of the Old Minoan double-headed axe cult were found in other parts of West and Central Africa." *Nigerian Fertility Cults* by P. A. Talbot, 1927.

Talbot also detected traces of the worship of the ram as a personification of the Sun-god—a link perhaps with Ammon—among the Kalabari. One chief, questioned about the sacrifice of a white ram to the sea-god, replied: "I know

The grey, clayish soil won from the mangroves is only about eighteen inches deep, and below lies brackish water. It is the custom of the Okrikans to bury their dead under the floor of their houses, and a large man is more than eighteen inches thick. This creates a hygienic *impasse*, but the Okrikans do not seem to mind. The hot, flat, dusty town swarmed with children, some smeared all over with white clay and others smartly dressed in Boy Scouts' uniform. These were at the jetty when we left, in the care of a burly, smiling scoutmaster, to greet a mobile cinema unit arriving by launch from the Information Office to show improving films.

Those brighter boys who qualify for secondary education attend a boarding school on the mainland, reached by canoe. Not long ago, information trickled in to the District Officer at Degema that two boys had left school at the start of the holidays, and disappeared. A party of Ibos, it transpired, had offered them a lift in a canoe—for nothing, a highly suspicious circumstance. In time, some of the boys' possessions were found in an Ibo dwelling up the creeks and the men confessed to having eaten their passengers.

"They should have known better than to accept anything for nothing from Ibos," said the District Officer.

❧ 8 ❧

From Port Harcourt I took the road north-westwards to Ahoada, still in the land of swamps and mangroves; but, away from the creeks, one could see more cultivation. This is the season when new yam gardens are made. All along the road, in small clearings, I saw mounds of earth surrounded by clay images twelve to eighteen inches high and painted red, often with blue markings. All these images are phallic, some plain as candles, others with rounded tops crudely shaped into heads with a surprised expression, and bearing two rudimentary arms. These are fertility symbols connected with the worship of the

---

only that such was the law handed down from our forefathers; but I once heard that it was connected with the sinking of the sun into the sea every night. These are matters of far-off times and we have long ago forgotten the precise cause for which they were ordered."

earth-goddess Ale, whose main festivals are celebrated when yams are planted or dug. There is, besides, a yam spirit, believed to take up its abode in the biggest yam of the year's crop, which is set aside and kept from one season to another. During the year this "king yam" must be kept sweet with goat's or fowl's blood, and in return it protects the whole crop from theft. Near Ahoada I passed through a village called Elele, where, in former times, dwelt a yam priest who for seven years never set foot outside his compound, because if he did so, any man strong enough could kill him and fill the office in his stead. The position brought much wealth and honour, but when the seven years were up the priest, if no one had vanquished him, was expected to commit suicide.

Throughout Ibo-land, a great feast and sacrifice is held at harvest time and, until that is over, no one is allowed (in former days on pain of death) to taste the new yams. It was thought that to do so would endanger the tribe's most sacred possession, its fertility. Behind this ancient practice lies, perhaps by accident, a scientific justification: immature yams contain an acid which can cause serious illness. When the yams are fully ripe, this acid vanishes.

At Ahoada I met Miss Jo Scraggs; a middle-aged, spectacled, cheerful and warm-hearted lady in a cotton frock and topee driving a jeep, who was to take me to her Mission at Joinkrama, on one of the creeks.

We drove for thirty miles or so through dense forest, set with oil palms, along a brand-new Community Development road: a rough, home-made affair impassable in wet weather, but still (in the dry season) a road, where none had previously penetrated. We saw no village all the way, nor any human beings, yet, hidden behind a screen of tree and creeper, a teeming population thrives. The only sign of life we saw was, surprisingly, a solitary taxi, taking a trader from Joinkrama to Port Harcourt and back, a trip of about 150 miles, to buy a shot-gun.

One hears much of how Americans insulate themselves from the discomforts of the tropics by means of air conditioning, refrigerators, canned food, air-mail deliveries of tender-loin and ice cream, and similar measures. There is nothing like that at Joinkrama. You reach the Mission station by canoe. Walls are of mud, roofs of thatch, heat unmoderated; lights are hurricane lamps, water is carried from the river, food is native, sanitation primitive; these Baptists almost revive the tradition of the pioneers.

Joinkrama Mission holds four Americans: Miss Scraggs; a young woman doctor; her energetic Texan husband, Mr. Edwards, who devotes himself to building and sometimes darts into the forest on a bicycle with a blunderbuss to shoot at elephants; and a woman in her late sixties who was born in Nigeria, forced to abandon her missionary career for over forty years in order to nurse ailing relatives, and has at last returned to fulfil the hopes of a lifetime. Dr. Edwards runs a small hospital whose erection and equipment she and her husband brought about from scratch, and which is always packed, especially during the rains when the sick can travel from remote villages by canoe. The work is hard, for she has not even the help of a trained sister; the nursing is done by converts who are willing, but seldom qualified.

Miss Jo Scraggs, the evangelist, presses tirelessly into the remotest villages, by cycle and canoe, to spread the Word of God. She has under her care no less than forty-two churches, each in charge of an African pastor, and every Sunday she is off along the creeks to hold prayer meetings in as many of them as she can reach, assisted by one of a small band of devoted women. One of these, a generous-bosomed, forceful, deep-voiced lady dressed in fashionable cloths and head-ties, is delightfully named Mrs. Butterball.

Next morning we set out on bicycles to explore the long, straggling village whose inhabitants support themselves by gathering palm nuts in the forest. These Ijaw people are said to have come, a very long while ago, from Benin, and are divided into a great many sub-tribes living in mutual *apartheid* and, in the past, frequent warfare. "A very excitable, passionate and quarrelsome race," an observer called them,[1] adding that they committed suicide on the slightest provocation, even when insulted (as they thought) in jest. One is struck by the strong, muscular appearance and fine chest development of the men, who spend so much of their lives paddling canoes. They live surrounded by water

[1] *The Lower Niger and its Tribes.* A. G. Leonard. Macmillan, 1906.

spirits of all kinds, some with webbed feet springing from their knees, others with faces that glow in the dark. Sections of the tribe used to follow a cult of python-worship with women priests, mystically married to the great snake, who danced for days on end. I felt sure that, a generation ago, Mrs. Butterball would have been a head priestess. But now they are obsessed by a desire for schools, and the people of Joinkrama are building themselves a most ambitious new one, which has already cost them in cash, apart from free labour, some £1,100, raised by a levy of £1 a head on all males.

Next to the Mission is a "beach" belonging to the U.A.C., in charge of a young man fresh from England. The Baptists are his only white neighbours for many miles. After a period of aloofness—prayer and plain water are not what a young trader bargains for in West Africa—he has settled down to a phase of cordial Anglo-American banter with his neighbours, perhaps not without a last regretful wave at the spectre of Tondeleyo, who has vanished with the topee, the moored hulks and the trade gin.

Puncheons are here still, however: great barrels roped in batches of sixty into rafts which are floated down to Degema by polers who live on bamboo platforms built above the casks. Formerly a fear of enslavement, flogging and painful death kept the property of chiefs and traders intact, but a great many puncheons now arrive full of water, the oil having been extracted *en route*. Canoes paddle down-river, bearing under canopies bags of palm kernels, or more barrels of oil. All these find their way to one of the Company's wharves and thence to Europe and America—Nigeria's greatest export in value and oldest in time, the first recorded shipment in a British vessel having reached England in the same year as the Armada—and are bought for fixed prices by a Government cartel, the West African Produce Marketing Board.

◇ 9 ◇

At Owerri, the Shell D'Arcy Company is drilling for oil. A town has sprung up there, full of prefabricated bungalows for European technicians—sixty or seventy of these—and compounds for African staff. At night the place is floodlit like a greyhound racing track, for drilling goes on all round the clock. Yet oil has not been found in paying quantities, although the drill has reached down already to 12,000 feet. At 7,000 feet and below, fossils of shellfish started to appear. (The age of this continent staggers the imagination—the time it must have taken for nearly two miles of land to be added, particle by particle, to what was once the sea.)

Fossils, but as yet no oil. The Company, however, are reputed not to be worrying, for oil will be found somewhere in the end; meanwhile, even if they spend a couple of million pounds on unsuccessful drills, no harm will come.[1]

A few miles from Owerri, a fusillade of shots sounded from a compound in which a large, happy Ibo crowd was dancing and capering. Shouts, bursts of song and a renewed volley welcomed us in. Excited men were firing Dane-guns—long, barrel-loading muskets—in all directions, luckily without shot; an orchestra of drums, native guitars and rattles was playing fit to burst; women were cavorting round with jerky motions like marionettes; palm wine was flowing and nearly everyone was drunk. Overhead, slung on a rope between two trees, hung the body of a goat which was to be eaten at the end of the day. It was a lovely party: a "second burial", we were told.

This is a ceremony even more important than the actual interment of the corpse, which takes place under the floor of the house, accompanied by the sacrifice of goats, fowls and dogs (and formerly of humans) in each room that the dead person was in the habit of using.[2] It was believed that the dead man's spirit

[1] No oil *was* found at Owerri; this drill was abandoned and new ones sunk in the Opobo division of Calabar Province.

[2] "Human sacrifice was an indispensable part of this ceremony, the number sacrificed varying from one up to a hundred or more according to the locality and rank or wealth of the deceased, twelve being considered the ordinary number for a chief of some standing or a king. . . . After the usual human and animal sacrifices have taken place the final 'okuku' or ceremony in memory of the departed is performed in the house in which the late chief has been buried, its most important feature being the sacrifice and eating of a male or female slave. This unfortunate creature is generally bought after the chief's death and is fattened and well treated." *The Lower Niger and Its Tribes* by A. G. Leonard, 1906.

"Among the slave wives of most prominent chiefs was one always addressed by her husband by the name of Aho'm, i.e. 'my skin'. This one was destined to be killed and flung into her husband's grave. The rest of the slave wives . . . had their legs and arms broken and were then laid alive at the bottom of

wandered in the shades, eating leaves like an animal, while his wives and daughters, confined to the house and dressed only in plaited grass, were obliged to mourn continuously and vociferously, wailing and sobbing without respite for weeks or even months, though never longer than a year.[1]

From this unhappy state both relatives and the deceased were released by the second burial, which enabled the latter's spirit to join its ancestors; and the position that it would subsequently hold in this Nirvana, whether of honour or of ignominy, depended upon the splendour of the ceremony. Every member of the family, however distant, was, and still is, obliged to subscribe; every store of yams must be broached and every pound of gunpowder bought that the joint resources of the family can possibly run to. All this puts a severe financial strain on the relatives, especially on "sons abroad", who are expected to contribute according to their means and often incur heavy debts in doing so.

From Owerri to Enugu we passed through the heart of Iboland, so thickly populated that very little bush remains and the compounds cluster as closely as spots on a leopard. Enugu, the capital of the Eastern Region, is a big, busy, modern town; and, on its outskirts, you can walk for two miles down a tunnel into a mountain of coal. What holds back output from these mines is not lack of the raw material, but difficulties of labour and transport. Enugu is on a single-line railway and to double it, and enlarge Port Harcourt, would cost, they say, £130,000,000.

---

the grave. It is significant that the men who broke the limbs of these unhappy sufferers prided themselves on thereby showing strength and bravery. From the front of the *Obiri* shed, where the body lay, to the end of the open square, human sacrifices might be seen hanging from posts or trees. . . . The place of burial was always within the room where the dead chief used to entertain strangers. After the burial, a great feast of human flesh, together with that of goats, fowls, yams and plantains, was given to relatives and friends. The skulls of all victims slain for the funeral rites were placed as ornaments in the *Obiri* shed. The principal posts and inner roofs of these were sometimes covered with skulls." *Tribes of the Niger Delta* by P. Amaury Talbot, 1930.

[1] Kalabari women were confined for six days in a small dark room and were compelled to sit in a fixed position on a piece of broken canoe; on no account were they to relieve nature between sunrise and sunset. To do so was taken as a sign of unfaithfulness, and they were sold as slaves. After six days they were taken to a stretch of "ju-ju" water and dived seven times under their husband's canoe; if they touched it, this was also taken as proof of unfaithfulness.

It is too much. So output remains considerably lower than it could be, especially as each man hews roughly one-sixth the quantity produced by an English or Welsh miner.

Meanwhile, Enugu thrives. I was told that it has the highest birth-rate in Africa. (In Britain, the figure is seventeen per thousand; here, fifty-five.) A proposal to start a birth-control clinic has been put before the Town Council, but indignantly rejected. Yet a number of African women have asked the wife of its European sponsor for contraceptive advice, because of the high cost of education. And I met an African doctor, in private practice here, who strongly supports the proposal. But no men (he says) are interested, or, in his view, likely to become so. A child in Africa is still an asset, not a liability; and generations of struggle against the forces of Nature to keep the population stable, reinforced by fertility rites which lie at the core of African religion, have produced an outlook, and buttressed an instinct, which cannot be altered as quickly as the environment. This is so obviously a case where Africans are right and Europeans wrong, that Europeans feel some hesitancy in pressing their own point of view. Yet what alternative is there to starvation? The equilibrium set up by Nature between the human population and its food supply has been thrown completely out by the control of epidemic diseases and the removal of such effective checks as periodic famines, slavery and human sacrifice. Logic demands that we should either restore smallpox, yellow fever, slavery and sacrifice; introduce birth control; or discover how to make synthetic food. It may be that synthetic foods will save the situation, but until they do, birth control seems to be the only feasible way to escape the nemesis of wholesale starvation.

◆ 10 ◆

The Eastern House of Assembly is in session, and Enugu seethes with politics. I met here two of the three young Ibos who hold Cabinet posts in Lagos: Mr. Eni Njoku, in charge of Mines and Power, and Mr. Okoi Arikpo, presiding over Land, Survey and Local Development. The third, Mr. Chukufidu Nwapa of Port Harcourt, was away.

All three are under thirty-five and, until two or three years ago, had no experience of politics. Mr. Arikpo was a student of anthropology when summoned, after the briefest of periods as an Assemblyman, to be a Cabinet Minister.

"Does it make you nervous," I asked, "to stand up and speak in the House of Representatives?"

Mr. Arikpo and his fellow politicians looked puzzled by the question. "Of course not! Why should it? I enjoy speaking. We all do."

Later, I asked the Lieutenant-Governor a similar question. He replied that every time he had to address the Assembly he felt so intensely nervous that his mouth was dry and his hands shook. Here, it seems, is a real difference between the temperaments of the two peoples.

The Central Minister of Mines and Power was, until he took office, a lecturer in botany at Ibadan, having gained a first-class honours degree in that subject at Manchester University. A native of a small village near Aro-Chuku (strange to think that, a generation ago, he might have been a slave of the "Long Ju-Ju") he proved brilliant at his books from the start, and taught science at the Hope Waddell College. His ambition, he said, has always been to make a contribution to the study of Nigerian flora, and he took the most difficult decision of his life when he resolved to abandon his scientific career and represent his division in the Regional parliament.

"For myself, I would rather stay a botanist," Mr. Njoku said. "But there are so very few of us who are educated, so very many who are not; would we be right to refuse? I felt I must return to Nigeria, at least until my country is free. . . . When you are a colonial, freedom becomes an obsession, and everything else must wait. . . . The whole country must be modernized, but that must come after. Our first needs are education, and to industrialize. We must develop the country with mechanized farming, oil-palm plantations, the extension of mining, new factories. . . ." Mr. Njoku spoke with sincerity, fire and common sense. In office, these three young men from the East have shown already a quick grasp of affairs, a capacity for work and a growing maturity of judgment.

These qualities have not been much in evidence in the Eastern House of Assembly where, within a year of the constitution's birth, what has been described as a *coup d'état* very nearly succeeded, and the Regional Government was all but paralysed.

The essence of a story too long and complex to be told in detail here is the struggle for power between Dr. Azikiwe and his instrument, the NCNC, on the one hand, and, on the other, a group of "new" men, including three Central and six Eastern Ministers, led by Professor Eyo Ita: who, formerly a Vice-President and loyal member of the NCNC, broke away in face of Zik's attempt to control the actions of the Eastern Ministers from outside the Regional Government.

Dr. Azikiwe, it will be recalled—the outstanding figure in Nigerian politics and National President of the NCNC—although an Ibo, and a native of Onitsha in the Eastern Region, chose to work his way up the electoral ladder of the West into the Western House of Assembly, where, an Ibo lamb among the vulpine Yorubas, he naturally received no Ministerial office. Whether he miscalculated his chances, whether he chose deliberately to hold aloof the better to harass a constitution which fell short of his demands or whether, as some have suggested, he feared assassination or defeat had he returned to Onitsha, is a matter for speculation.

As both the Central and the Eastern Regional Governments got into their stride, a tendency appeared which evidently stung Zik's pride and sharpened his hostility: some of the hitherto loyal members of the NCNC began to pay more attention to the country's needs—or, as he averred, to their own advancement—than to the Party's policy, as laid down by Zik. And no number of digs in Zik's newspaper the *Pilot* about "knighted Uncle Toms" produced a change of Ministerial heart.

This was not to be tolerated: and, after complex manœuvres, an NCNC convention expelled the three Central Ministers (Nwapa, Njoku and Arikpo) from the Party and denounced the new constitution. Six weeks later, Zik's dialectical skill, prestige and personality compelled the nine Regional Ministers to sign a letter of resignation provided, ready typed, by the NCNC. With morning light six of them—headed by Professor Ita—recanted, to be later expelled "for life with ignominy" from the NCNC.

War between Zik and the rebels now became open, bitter and prolonged. The NCNC commanded a majority in the House of

Assembly, which passed a vote of no confidence in the Ministers and paralysed all business, but the Lieutenant-Governor had no power to dismiss the Ministers or dissolve the House.[1] By day, Zik sat in the gallery; by night, he directed strategy in private meetings with his loyal henchmen. The Lieutenant-Governor was forced to use his reserve powers to pass a long-deferred budget. Thus government in the Eastern Region went on, but only by calling on safeguards of which no nationalist (and they were all that) approved. A new party arose from the ashes of this virulent controversy: the National Independence Party, with Professor Ita at its head, and the rebel Central and Regional Ministers as members.

Soon the whole constitution is to be revised. What can scarcely be quickly remedied is the wholesale bribery and corruption which accompany elections to the Houses of Assembly. Here in the East the prices of seats are openly quoted and fabulously high—£2,000, £3,000 or even more. Without the NCNC's backing, there is little hope of election. No doubt this is a sorry state of affairs: but we must candidly recognize that it is not peculiar to Nigeria. American politics are not much more respectable, and nor were England's in the eighteenth century.

•◦• II •◦•

On non-political levels, life in Enugu goes on with an equal intensity. Almost any evening, you can hear the sound of drums, rattles and lusty singing: a party is getting under way. Joining one at random, I found a crowd gathered in a street between two rows of small, detached, breeze-block bungalows. Chairs and benches filled the dusty street and on a table improvised from planks stood bedroom jugs of palm wine, bottled beer, platters of bread and hunks of meat. Enthusiasts were dancing to the punching rhythm of drums and rattles, women waved handkerchiefs, men performed a separate jig. A large, fat woman in a loose, brilliantly-coloured blouse was eeling to and fro, her hips fluid as oil, rolling her eyes with tremendous roguery at the seated men doing justice to beer and palm wine. This was

---

[1] These powers have since been given to the Lieutenant-Governors of the three Regions.

only the beginning; the party would go on all night. A wedding, a betrothal, a funeral? No, they said, merely a get-together of the Bende Improvement Society. It is the custom for the "sons abroad" of every district to band themselves together into these clubs and hold meetings and dances, as it is the duty of members to befriend any native of the district needing help.

You can feel the pulse of a thriving city. Every day, country folk arrive to seek a fortune, and a much smaller number—those who have found one—leave on return visits, to dazzle their relatives with new suits, bright ties and smart suit-cases. Buses stream in and out of town, many bearing on their sides the sign of the Greater Tomorrow Transport Service, one of the East's most successful businesses, founded by a prominent politician and supporter of Zik's, Mr. Ozuomba Mbadiwe. In addition to building up an enterprise which has made him enviably rich, Mr. Mbadiwe, who has studied at Lincoln, Columbia and New York Universities and holds degrees both in the arts and the sciences, founded the African Academy of Arts and Research, one of whose activities has been to raise subscriptions from the public to send Nigerian students to the United States. After money had been collected for several years but few, if any, students had gained admittance to reputable American universities, a certain public uneasiness led the Government to insist on the publication of an audit, which did little to satisfy the critical. Mr. Mbadiwe was, however, elected with enthusiasm to the House of Assembly, and many of his supporters were disappointed and chagrined when he was not made a Minister.

The attraction which American universities hold for Nigerians has stimulated other schemes of a like nature, such as the American Council for African Education, which hit upon the effective plan of inviting each aspirant to a scholarship to send an entry fee of £1 with his application. I was told that 11,000 people had responded, but could not verify this. The Council claims to have sent a number of Nigerians to the United States, although whether their qualifications permitted them to enter the colleges of their choice is uncertain. The accounts did not satisfy the authorities, who caused the arrest of the Council's President, "Prince" Orizu, in the House of Assembly, and his appearance before the Supreme Court on a charge of fraud. He, too, is a leading figure in the NCNC and one of Zik's "shadow-cabinet".

·∾· 12 ·∾·

Half an hour's drive from Enugu lies the district headquarters made famous by the film *Daybreak in Udi*, which showed how the people of a village banded themselves together to build a maternity centre by their own efforts, and despite witch-doctors who tried to scare away the nurse. Virtue triumphed, and babies thrived. The instigator of this film, then District Officer at Udi—Mr. Chadwick—is now Director of Community Development for the Eastern Region. He had kindly arranged to show me some of the work, but a sharp attack of malaria prevented this. In spite of a high temperature, however, he expounded from his sick-bed the principles of the movement to which all his great faith and energy are given.

"It's a question of self-help. We've got to rouse that spirit in the people, to stop them leaving everything to the Government. To stop them thinking that the only thing worth doing is to get an 'education' and go away to Port Harcourt or Lagos. We've got to start at the village level—the vital spark is *there*." Mr. Chadwick has the enthusiasm and singleness of purpose of men who get things done. He was full of stories of villages that had buckled to and built things for themselves with unpaid, voluntary labour, of people who had worked for the community as they used to work, under duress, for the chief. Schools, maternity wards, co-operative shops, reading-rooms, hygienic markets, roads, bridges, wells, latrines. . . .

Next day I went with his successor at Udi to some of the villages which had helped themselves. (The Government, like God, helps those who do this; it has a fund of £50,000 to be drawn on at the discretion of District Officers for corrugated iron, cement, girders, tools and other things which peasants cannot find; their contribution is the labour, and the village council must suggest ideas.)

Round Enugu the country is hilly, closely cultivated and bare, save for a thick grove of trees left round each village to make the inhabitants feel at home and provide shelter for spirits. Between groves there stretches an almost continuous sheet of little patch-work farms, each with its cassava, its guinea corn, its yam crop stored in racks beside the homestead. The hillsides are scarred by gulleys due to soil erosion, as bad here, in places, as almost anywhere in Africa; and I saw few, if any, signs of remedial measures.

In the first village a small reading-room and a co-operative shop had been built. The chief showed us round: a youngish man in a topee whose brother, he said, was a barrister in Enugu, while two cousins were in Britain studying law. He lived in the only double-storeyed house in the village, made wholly of corrugated iron; outside was a larger-than-life bust of his father standing on a wooden pedestal.

"A wicked man," my driver said, indicating the statue. "He got plenty money selling people to the Government to build the railway. He caught men by night. Other men, he killed them and stole their property and threw them in the bush. He coffined his wife alive. Bad man too much!" In the end the police turned against him, so he shot himself. Several of his sons became chiefs, however.

The next village had a Community Development maternity home. These were once the height of fashion, but seem now to be yielding to co-operative shops. The trained nurse inside lacked enthusiasm; she came from another district and found it lonely here, she said, and women on the whole preferred to be confined at home. However, there were plenty of out-patients.

The most ambitious project I saw was in a village called Lokpanta. We drove over and round many short hills with fine, rolling views from their summits until we reached its shady grove of trees. In the centre arose a huge silk-cotton tree with buttresses that would have supported a cathedral. Under it stood a meat-stall offering mainly bits of dog—one could see heads and paws. A little farther on arose the stone walls of a school, roofed in corrugated iron, big enough to hold at least 200 pupils, and erected by the villagers. Last year it cost each taxpayer eleven and sixpence in levies, and the "sons abroad" have contributed lavishly. But it is not finished yet, and the teacher who showed us round observed that the Lokpantans were growing tired. They had paid enough, and would the Government find the remainder? But they wanted to be free from the influence of Missions, who quarrelled too much among themselves.

On our way home we passed a large gang of men, naked save for loin-cloths, toiling with picks in the sun to make (without pay) a branch road to their village. A foreman came up to my companion, the District Officer, all bows and smiles; he seemed to be even more than usually polite, but after a few words his shining countenance dimmed.

"Oh! So this is not the Resident's car," he observed sadly. The Resident, it seemed, was expected, and a pleasing reception prepared. It so happened that next day I drove back along the same stretch of road. Not a community labourer was to be seen.

The contrasts of Africa never cease to astonish. Near Enugu we passed a dance in progress on the main road. The spectators wore magenta shirts or puce and chocolate velvet cloths; one sparkled in a maroon and blue striped tunic with gold embroidery; the performers were wrapped from head to foot in raffia palm, their faces masked, and capered on the tarmac like dervishes. A few miles on, and we were amid limousines conveying natty Ministers and lawyers about their business, or perhaps to an official cocktail party. Back in the country, we had passed slim, shy girls with nothing but a red belt round their waists; one carried an elephant's tusk on her head; and in many of the villages we could have found a "fattening hut" where Ibo parents prepare their girls for marriage by stuffing them with yams, plantains and cassava all day long and forbidding them any exercise. In Enugu, I visited the newly completed Girls' Training College, built at a cost of £106,000 from the Development and Welfare Fund: a group of lofty two-storeyed halls and dormitories with kitchens, laundries, ironing- and sewing-rooms far more commodious and well-equipped than any I have seen in English colleges. On the staff are African women of a type new in the continent's history: women of independence, unmarried (and, stranger still, childless), resolved to choose their own husbands if they do decide to change their state. One such whom I met, a self-possessed instructor of twenty-eight, had spent three years at an English domestic training college.

"I loved Cheltenham—better than Enugu," she said. "I made many, many friends." Her face shone with recollection, and it seemed sad that those companions had passed so far out of her life.

⌒ 13 ⌒

The largest inland Ibo town is Onitsha, on the banks of the Niger. To the loyal nationalist it is almost as sacred as the home-town of Dr. Azikiwe, who still keeps a house here for his occasional visits. It is also said to harbour more lawyers and more schools than any other town in Nigeria.

Some of the meanest, most squalid hovels imaginable face on to the main streets and display on their lean-to verandas ju-ju medicines, fly-blown cakes or lamps made from old tins; and some of the most pretentious two- or three-storeyed mansions stand beside them. Such houses, built right on the street without walls or gardens, belong to rich traders or lawyers. According to report, one owns a fleet of forty lorries and is said—these figures are almost certainly exaggerated—to have made over £40,000 in a single year. Two or three families who claim ownership of the land in and around Onitsha have built housing estates which pay enormous dividends, yet the head of the wealthiest family works as a clerk at a salary of £120 a year.

I asked what they spent their money on, apart from cars and houses.

"Educating children—their own and other people's," said the District Officer. "I get at least two applications a week for youngsters to go to the U.K. to train in every imaginable subject, from electrical engineering to confectionery. Their sponsors pay all the expenses." Onitsha is education-mad, and possesses no less than sixteen secondary schools.

I called on the C.M.S. Bishop, the oldest cleric in Onitsha. We talked on his veranda, while behind us, in his living-room, several young matrons sitting in a row on a bench suckled their babies. The house was full of "piccans", mostly, I gathered, belonging to his son, a clerk from Calabar on holiday with his wife and eight children; the rest were nieces and grandchildren, all in the family. His mother, the Bishop said, had been one of the earliest Nigerian Christians; because of her faith she was turned out by her husband and sought shelter with a Christian uncle, and there raised her two children in the new faith. Life

for converts was hard then, the Bishop said; chiefs and witch-
doctors opposed and sometimes killed them and they had to plod
many miles on foot. But the Word spread everywhere, and now
the Church numbers its members in hundreds of thousands.

"The blood of the Lamb will save us," the Bishop said, "but
there was one good thing about those older times: young men
obeyed their fathers and showed respect to elders. They do so
no longer. Some do not even marry, either in church or by
native custom. They think not of God, but of Mammon. I do
not know what will become of them. . . ."

Out of Africa, very often, comes something old and familiar.

Close to the Bishop lives Mrs. Leith-Ross, the widow of an
anthropologist. She has mingled much with Ibo women,[1] and
hoped to help them by holding classes for older girls equivalent
to those provided by European finishing schools: to teach a little
of deportment, gentle manners, needlework, music and the finer
arts of life to daughters of rich Onitsha lawyers and traders, who
might marry professional men and become the wives of civil
servants and Cabinet Ministers. But the fathers asked what
qualifications their daughters would gain, and when they heard
that no degrees could be awarded their interest faded, and the
school failed.

Onitsha claims to have the largest and most resourceful market in Nigeria, a daily mart where anything can be bought, from
an elephant to an admiral's uniform. Items which I was assured
had been seen there included an airspeed indicator, and printed
silk from Jacqmar's in Grosvenor Street offered at half the London price. It goes without saying that there is no difficulty about
nylons—or about raw meat, whisky, gold ear-rings, avocado
pears, Irish turkeys, penicillin or practically anything else.

The Niger here is very wide—perhaps a mile or more—and
crossed by a crowded ferry-boat. On this bank are the progressive, pullulating Ibo; on the far shore, the people of Benin. The
river is here the boundary between the Eastern and the Western
Regions.

I crossed the Niger at four o'clock one afternoon, packed like
a yam in a rack amid a chattering crowd of well-dressed, pros-

[1] And written a book about them: *African Women* (Faber and Faber); also
some illuminating sketches of Onitsha life, *African Conversation Piece*.

perous-looking, sturdy, acquisitive and mysterious people bound on errands of trade or matrimony. The ferry-boat drew away with much clanking and hooting, and soon Onitsha became a mere protuberance upon the flat, grey horizon. The Niger, shallow and sluggish at this time of year, stretched out like a lake. Hard to believe that these waters swept past Timbuktu and will enlarge the Atlantic; that for a shilling I should cross in perfect health and safety a river whose course and origin for so many centuries baffled the world's geographers and tempted to their death so many courageous challengers. There sweated and struggled the explorers—Clapperton, Park, the Landers, Baikie, McGregor Laird—constantly exposed to sickness and attacks by warriors; and there I stand, talking to a Methodist teacher going home for the week-end and to a student at a Rural Training Centre opposite whose chief ambition is to own a tractor. It is, if you come to think of it, a remarkable achievement on everybody's part that in a country where, until so very recently, to venture a mile from your village unprotected was an act of suicide, where strangers might be killed and eaten like bush cows, a casual tourist should travel now as safely and freely as in America, and almost as comfortably.

So vast a country, traversed at so helter-skelter a speed, cannot create certainty or prescience in any traveller's mind. Older explorers went to seek the source of rivers and to map their tributaries. Today one seeks the source of human conduct and tries to map the course of history. Their search was much more uncomfortable but, if they survived it, more rewarding. Today's traveller is attacked by swarms of question marks, none of them attached to answers. There are no problems in Africa. For problems have solutions, and the enigmas of human behaviour can never be solved.

There is a set of clichés which proclaims Africa to be on the march, astir, in a ferment; that the age-old sleep of centuries is over. The continent is pictured like a turbulent river about to burst its banks and irrigate a fertile country-side.

> *Was that indeed salt wind?*
> *Came that noise from falling*
> *Wild waters on a stony shore?*

Oh what is this new troubling tide
Of eager waves that pour
Around and over, leaping, parting, recalling?

A new troubling tide—that is what we are, we Westerners, a tide that has stirred the deposit of centuries. Tides, by their nature, recede. In one sense we are already in recession; as the ruling power, Britain is everywhere disengaging her grip. The speed of this retreat is indeed phenomenal, and much greater than it needs to be if Britain's work is to endure. As it is, the time has been too short to lay secure, or even rudimentary, foundations. Yet, had it been prolonged, the ill-will engendered by sloth in abdication—once abdication had been proclaimed as the objective—would so have inflamed and poisoned the body politic that Britain's constructive task would have become impossible, since rifles do not promote racial harmony. This was Britain's dilemma, which she solved by deciding to hurry quickly and risk the results. In less than sixty years of organized government, her withdrawal may be complete.

How deeply has this brief impact penetrated? Will the values we have tried to inculcate endure? Or will Africans reject them, preferring their own less irksome and exacting standards? One can say with certainty only that the British are but the latest of a long succession of invaders who have come to Africa to trade, to escape or to adventure, from the days of ancient Egypt and Phœnicia until modern times. Wave after wave of immigrants has rolled along its ancient highways, down the Nile, across the desert, to be absorbed into that great conglomeration of races labelled "African". From all these, the jackdaw continent has picked out the bits that caught her fancy and built them into a subtle, ruthless and ancient society, cruel as Tamerlane's, which ingenuous foreigners have dismissed as childlike because its material wants are few. The rest has disintegrated, leaving little trace.

Will this happen again? The work of selection has begun already. Our material goods are welcomed eagerly—hats and trousers, basins and bicycles, patent medicines and cars—and will be sought whatever the future shape of things, for Africans will trade their eye-teeth for something they want. Our ideas are treated with more discrimination. Some please: the process of law, the intrigues of politics, the rites of bureaucracy. Others displease: monogamy, taxation, women's rights, fair shares, tolerance, hard work. Much that we are at pains to build in Africa may prove evanescent because the Roman virtues whose presence, or at least quick appearance, we postulate are lacking, and not greatly desired.

It sometimes appears that our modern colonies are forcing-houses where, under conditions of great heat and sultriness, we cultivated transplanted seedlings in soil deficient in certain ingredients needed for the healthy growth of those particular exotics. We force an omnipotent bureaucracy without honesty, a democracy without enlightenment, an economy without toil, a nation without unity, a culture without art: in short, a society without a faith to give it purpose or a code of morals to give it strength. Strange blooms may result.

Yet, in the event, things may not turn out so badly as pessimists foresee—though I am sure they will not turn out in the least as optimists expect. Africa is no *tabula rasa*; it will impose its own pattern, perhaps as different from ours as the shape of a Yoruba *orisha* from that of the Apollo Belvedere. We too readily forget, I think, that Africa, insofar as it is linked with other countries, belongs to the Orient. Its people are enthralled with Western science and wealth and cleverness, but in mind and habit they are less akin to Europeans than to Asiatics. However things turn out we shall be surprised, I think, and very likely shocked, to discover, in another sixty years, which of our offerings they have kept and which they have discarded, or twisted to an unfamiliar shape.

For our part, we came to Africa as traders and it is as traders that we shall, in the last resort, remain; for it is our trade that is wanted, and African trade that we need. In this, the inclinations of the two peoples coincide. The future of our missionary endeavour—the spread of the gospel of parliamentary democracy—is, I think, a great deal more dubious. But the parable of the sower warns us to expect only a modicum of fertile ground—as do the words of the poet that there are nine and sixty ways of constructing tribal lays, and every single one of them is right.

Our ferry-boat, under its African captain, approached the Niger's western bank. My fellow-passengers would not have been Nigerian had their conversation not turned on politics. The farm student, an Ibo, was a burning nationalist; the teacher's ardour a little tempered by caution. "We must have our freedom!" cried the student, his face aglow. "If Europeans leave now," the teacher said, "we Africans will fight one another." "And why not?" asked the student. "Europeans have fought each other for centuries, it is a stage all countries must go through. Freedom is the will of the people! Anyone who resists it should die." "But," I asked, "what people? The Northerners, the Yorubas, the Ibos? They all want different things." The student looked amazed. "*We* are the people!" "You mean the Ibos?" "Of course! The Ibos will rule Nigeria!" "You will first have to kill a lot of Yorubas," I suggested. His face gleamed. "Oh, yes! We shall!"

We reached our destination, a ramp was lowered and several lorries rumbled ashore over strips of metal mesh laid across the mud. Passengers streamed after them: women with piccans on their backs and baskets of food on their heads, the smiling student and the Methodist teacher pushing bicycles, well-dressed traders carrying fibre suit-cases, glossy-skinned matrons returning from their market stalls. The ferry-boat emptied, and the little bars and food-stalls on shore filled with customers. The sun sank quickly, light swiftly withdrew, and soon the Niger was a pool of grey and silver under a blank, unfathomed sky pricked by the first and boldest of the great company of stars.

INDEX